34/95

SO-DRD-478

MEXICAN
AND
MEXICAN AMERICAN
FARM WORKERS

MEXICAN AND MEXICAN AMERICAN FARM WORKERS

The California Agricultural Industry

Juan L. Gonzales, Jr.

PRAEGER SPECIAL STUDIES • PRAEGER SCIENTIFIC

New York • Philadelphia • Eastbourne, UK
Toronto • Hong Kong • Tokyo • Sydney

Library of Congress Cataloging in Publication Data

Gonzales, Juan L.
  Mexican and Mexican American farm workers.

  Includes index.
  1. Mexican American agricultural laborers –
Employment – California, Northern. 2. Mexican American
agricultural laborers – California, Northern – Economic
conditions. 3. Mexicans – Employment – California,
Northern. 4. Mexicans – California, Northern – Economic
conditions. 5. Alien labor, Mexican – California,
Northern. I. Title.
HD1527.C2G66 1985   331.6'2'720794   84-26401
ISBN 0-03-002763-2 (alk. paper)

Published in 1985 by Praeger Publishers
CBS Educational and Professional Publishing, a Division of CBS Inc.
521 Fifth Avenue, New York, NY 10175 USA

56789 052 987654321

Printed in the United States of America on acid-free paper

INTERNATIONAL OFFICES

Orders from outside the United States should be sent to the appropriate address listed below. Orders from areas not
listed below should be placed through CBS International Publishing, 383 Madison Ave., New York, NY 10175 USA

Australia, New Zealand
Holt Saunders. Pty. Ltd., 9 Waltham St., Artarmon, N.S.W. 2064, Sydney, Australia

Canada
Holt, Rinehart & Winston of Canada, 55 Horner Ave., Toronto, Ontario, Canada M8Z 4X6

Europe, the Middle East, & Africa
Holt Saunders, Ltd., 1 St. Anne's Road, Eastbourne, East Sussex, England BN21 3UN

Japan
Holt Saunders. Ltd., Ichibancho Central Building, 22-1 Ichibancho, 3rd Floor, Chiyodaku, Tokyo, Japan

Hong Kong, Southeast Asia
Holt Saunders Asia, Ltd., 10 Fl, Intercontinental Plaza, 94 Granville Road, Tsim Sha Tsui East, Kowloon,
Hong Kong

**Manuscript submissions should be sent to the Editorial Director, Praeger Publishers, 521 Fifth Avenue,
New York, NY 10175 USA**

For My Parents

JUAN L. GONZALES, SR. and ALICE M. GONZALES

And

For My Wife

ROSA L. GONZALES

FOREWORD

The unique merit of Juan Gonzales's important new book about Mexican and Mexican-American agricultural workers is that it is based on ethnography: participant observation and depth interviews—as well as a detailed attitude survey, and a careful analysis of government statistics and historical data most often used by researchers in agricultural economics. Dr. Gonzales spent three years in five agricultural counties of California where he extracted "the truth that lies in the hearts and minds of men and women who are confronted with the daily struggle for existence."

Gonzales's study demolishes the simplistic imagery of the typical farm laborer as either the Mexican-American migrant following the crops from state to state or the illegal alien from Mexico constantly dodging INS agents and other government authorities. What emerges instead is a complex portrait, one that emphasized the considerable diversity that exists in the circumstances and aspirations of those who produce California's agricultural harvest. The author underscores this diversity through the development of an elaborate, multi-dimensional typology of the agricultural labor force. One dimension is commitment to agricultural work as a full-time occupation, and here he distinguishes the "professionals" who have year-long and lifetime attachments from the "semiprofessionals," the "amateurs" and the "dilettantes," whose commitments, as the names imply, are increasingly more tenuous.

A second dimension is legal status. Even the "illegals" are not a homogenous category. Undocumented Mexican nationals include "Border Jumpers" who leave Mexico daily for jobs in the United States, returning home each night; "adventurers" who come for longer periods and reside on the growers' property; "innovators" who migrate as a family and follow the crops from one area to another; and "climbers" who work for the same employer for long periods of time, year after year in order to improve the status of the families they've left behind.

Legal Mexican nationals also include a variety of types: "commuters," "opportunists," and "loyalists," each with their distinctive social characteristics and motivations. In the California agricultural industry Mexican Americans—citizens by birth or by naturalization—are actually the smallest group of all. Their tenure in the fields tends to be brief, and tends to come early in their lives, before they move on to more secure and better paying jobs in other industries.

Gonzales's research concentrates on the "professionals," who in a sense form the real backbone of the agricultural industry in California today. Because they don't fit the stereotype of the typical Mexican bracero, the professionals are an overlooked, neglected group. They are not rootless migrants, but rather are stable family men who work for the same employer year after year, sometimes even becoming socially integrated into the Spanish-speaking communities in the agricultural valleys of California. Nor are they unskilled stoop laborers, but rather they are highly skilled agriculturalists who understand the nuances of crops and farming techniques and can operate and repair a variety of farm equipment. One is reminded of Carey McWilliams's point that it was the Mexicans who developed the skills and advanced techniques that underly the burgeoning agricultural economy of the Southwest.

Yet even these professionals, the mainstay of the farm labor force, are underpaid and overworked. Calculating the income of seasonal workers, particularly in such a volatile and unbureaucratized industry, is notoriously difficult. Through painstaking detective work Professor Gonzales has invented an ingenious method for arriving at his sample's average family income of $8,900 per year. Hardly an adequate compensation for those who provide a well-fed and prosperous nation with two of its most essential "food groups." And it takes an equivalent of 15 months of labor to achieve this modest stipend, since the workers are paid such low hourly wages that they work 70 hours a week during the nine and a half months of good weather before the rains and the cold weather bring on two and a half months of enforced idleness each winter. One of the author's most fascinating descriptions is the way the men spend their "spare time" during these winter months: catching up on house and car repairs, seeking odd jobs to bring in some income, visiting friends and relatives neglected during the work months, and embarking on their annual trip home to Mexico.

Few Americans, whether of Mexican descent or not, find such remuneration and working conditions attractive, especially since other alternatives are possible for English-speaking citizens with an education and other skills. The author concludes therefore that Mexican "guest workers," except for some of the Border Jumpers, in general do not take jobs away from American citizens. Rather, they are doing us an incalculable service by working skillfully and cheaply in our most basic industry. And this is only one of the myths about Mexican farm labor that is dispelled by Juan Gonzales's careful and comprehensive analysis of their lives, work, and social attitudes.

Bob Blauner
Department of Sociology
University of California, Berkeley

PREFACE

The search for a community appropriate for this study began during the spring of 1977. Initial efforts to locate a research site were limited only by my specific interest in Mexican agricultural workers and by an interest in studying their adaptation to community life. In short, my research interest centered on learning more about the daily lives and problems of Mexican and Mexican-American agricultural workers in their respective communities.

With this objective in hand preliminary field observations were made in the Northern counties of Butte, Glenn, Yolo, Sacramento, Solano, Napa, Sonoma, and Contra Costa. One or more agricultural communities were selected in each of these counties for the initial field investigations. As a result, a good deal of time was spent in each of these counties making observations, and meeting and talking with agricultural workers. For intensive study and formal interviewing, the counties of Glenn, Solano, Napa, and Contra Costa were selected, from among the others, as the most propitious for the ultimate research objectives.

As indicated, the initial field work began as an exploratory study of life in a small Mexican agricultural community in northern California. During this period the main objectives were to meet community leaders, gain their confidence, and learn more about the life and problems of the community from their individual perspectives. To this end I made contact with the staff members of a recently established community service agency. These individuals proved to be extremely helpful in providing an overall view of life in the community. At this point I began conducting informal guided interviews with each staff member in order to learn as much as I could about "Ciudad de Esperanza" (a pseudonym). At the end of each day, I would take notes on all that I had learned about life in the community. In addition, I began to keep a field journal in which notes were kept on all of my daily activities.

I also became involved with various community groups and organizations. My involvement occurred on two levels; one was by regular attendance at community and organizational meetings, and the other was by volunteering for a number of community programs. As a result, I attended three or four community meetings each week. These meetings provided an excellent opportunity to meet the people from the community, and I was sometimes asked to give a brief presentation of my research plans. After the first month, I found that I had a full calendar of meetings to attend in different communities each week, so that very soon I became an accepted participant of these meetings.

The second-most-important method by which I was able to gain community acceptance was by doing volunteer work for several community agencies. Volunteer work, I found, is very important to successfully conduct field research, since it lets members of the community know that you are truly interested in their community and their problems. In addition, volunteer work provides the researcher with an opportunity to meet and know the people of the community, at their level of existence and understanding.

After due consideration it was decided to focus on the counties of Glenn, Solano, Napa, and Contra Costa for intensive study and formal interviewing. This was in addition to my participant observations and informal interviewing in eight counties of northern California. For this purpose, the Farm Worker survey was the most important survey instrument used in this study in that its implementation allowed me to obtain the most in-depth and comprehensive information concerning the conditions found among Mexican agricultural workers.

Approximately three months, from March to May of 1978 were devoted to the preparation of the two survey instruments utilized in this study. Both the Farm Worker survey and Key Informant survey were prepared in English and Spanish. Similarly, both were precoded for computer analysis. In field application, the Farm Worker survey was administered in Spanish on all but two occasions.

The administration of the Farm Worker survey was limited to Mexican and Mexican-American agricultural workers in the selected counties who had at least ten years of work experience in the agricultural industry. In addition, I only interviewed those who were stable to the particular area. Most had lived in the area two or more years. The majority of the respondents were males, as female farm workers were more difficult to locate and were also more reluctant to participate in the survey.

From August to December 1978, I was able to complete 91 interviews, with 22 in Napa county, 24 in Solano county, 22 in Glenn county, 20 in Contra Costa county, and 3 in Sonoma county. Therefore, the information obtained in these 91 interviews forms the basis of a major portion of the data that will be presented in the following chapters.

The Key Informant survey was designed to be administered to those individuals in each of the study communities who were intimately knowledgeable about local Mexican agricultural workers and the various problems and issues in their communities. Key informants were always long-term residents of these agricultural communities; consequently, they were in a position to provide valuable information concerning the various problems facing local farm workers. They often had previous experience as agricultural workers, but not necessarily. In either case, they were very familiar with the community in which they lived and worked; hence, the rubric, "key informants." The key informants in this study were of three different types: the agency official, the educated activist, and the retired or semi-retired agricultural worker.

This survey was also prepared in English and Spanish and was administered in both languages during this research period which extended from August to December of 1978. The survey form itself was precoded and covered such items as personal data, familiarity with agricultural workers, major problems and concerns of agricultural workers, working conditions, job opportunities, opportunities for advancement, their views on the unionization of agricultural workers, their opinions concerning some of the solutions to the major problems that confront agricultural workers, the participation of women in the agricultural labor force, children in the fields, housing conditions of agricultural workers, and the general social and economic conditions among Mexican and Mexican-American agricultural workers in their communities. In effect they not only provided entrée to agencies in the community and members of the community but were also an invaluable source of information concerning community life in their respective communities. But more important, they provided an overall view of the day-to-day life of the agricultural worker in each of these communities.

The formal interviews were completed in mid-December of 1978 and data processing began in January 1979. The Farm Worker survey and the Key Informant survey were both designed with a precoded format so that this greatly facilitated the data processing. The first draft of this book was completed in the fall of 1980.

Every farm worker who is the subject of this study certainly deserves my greatest appreciation for their cooperation and guidance. For obvious reasons these gracious individuals must remain anonymous. However, I would simply like to express my personal gratitude to these anonymous individuals for giving their precious time and energy, for inviting a perfect stranger into their homes and treating me as an honored guest, for sitting for hours at a time as I proceeded to ask one question after another, and for recounting their life stories and revealing their innermost feelings.

For these and many other reasons I shall always remain indebted to the Mexican agricultural workers of California who not only put me in direct contact with my origins, but who have demonstrated that not all truth and knowledge reside in the stacks of a university library. Rather the truth lies in the hearts and minds of the men and women who are confronted with the daily struggle for existence. I only hope that I have done justice to their stories in this book.

ACKNOWLEDGMENTS

At the culmination of a long and arduous task one owes many debts of personal gratitude. My first words of gratitude should go to those individuals who offered their sagacious counsel during the three years of initial preparation of this book, Professors David Matza, Robert Blauner, Kenneth Bock, Philip E. LeVeen, and Refugio I. Rochin. Without their encouragement, confidence, and personal consultations I doubt that this book would have ever seen the light of day. In addition I would like to thank my colleagues at California State University, Hayward, for their congeniality and support during the past four years, in particular David Graeven, Department Chair, Robert Dunn, my trusted confidant, and Terry Jones, my reader and amiable critic.

In addition to the debt of gratitude that I owe to my mentors and colleagues, I would also like to thank a number of charitable organizations for their support, without whose largesse none of this would have been possible: in particular, the Graduate Minority Program at the University of California, Berkeley, the Minority Fellowship Program of the American Sociological Association, and the Affirmative Action Faculty Development Program, at California State University, Hayward.

The individual persons who are the subject matter of this study also deserve many words of thanks and appreciation. For obvious reasons these gracious collaborators must remain anonymous. I would also like to thank the members of my family who have been so understanding and considerate during this prolonged learning experience: Love and appreciation go to Fidel, Roy, Ralph, and Alice.

I have reserved a very special note of appreciation for three very important individuals in my life, my parents and my wife Rosa. It can truly be said that if it had not been for their unfailing support and encouragement, none of this would have been possible. To my parents, who just wanted me to secure a good education, and to Rosa, who saw to it that I did, I dedicate this book.

Juan L. Gonzales, Jr.
Pittsburg, California
September, 1984

CONTENTS

LIST OF TABLES, FIGURES, AND CHARTS

Table

Figure

Chart

1

The Contributions of Mexican Laborers to the Development of the Agricultural Industry of the Southwest

INTRODUCTION: THE EARLY MOVEMENT OF MEXICAN LABORERS INTO THE SOUTHWEST

In order to understand the early movement of Mexican laborers into the Southwest one must take into consideration their unique role in the industrial development of this vast portion of the United States. Consequently this will require a brief historical excursion into the nature and scope of the immigration process and the experiences of Mexicans and Mexican Americans in the Southwest.

Given the historical development of this country, it is certainly a truism to point out that this is a nation of immigrants. But in making such an obvious statement we must also observe that the immigration experience of Mexicans in the Southwest is certainly different from the experiences of European immigrants and indeed rather unique. Even a cursory examination of the European immigration experience reveals a number of key characteristics that are not found in the immigration experiences of Mexican laborers in the Southwest. For example, the European immigration experience required a long, expensive, and arduous journey across an ocean, the termination of family and kinship ties, a drastic physical separation from the homeland, and a social and psychological commitment to a new land and a new nation. However, in the Southwest, Mexican immigrants simply moved North from Mexico and did not experience a traumatic social or psychological adjustment; for in fact they simply moved across an arbitrary border.

Indeed their ancestors had founded permanent settlements throughout the Southwest long before the signing of the Declaration of Independence. Consequently the Mexican immigrants were already familiar with the semi-desert environment, the topography, and the place names of the Southwest. In addition they were able to cross and recross this arbitrary international boundary with great ease, and only suffer a slight drain on their meager economic resources. Therefore their psychological adjustment was negligible, and they only suffered a temporary loss of family and kinship ties. In fact, most only intended to remain for a short period of time in the United States, in an effort to improve their social and economic conditions in the homeland.

The position of Mexican laborers in the Southwest is also unique, when compared to the European immigration, inasmuch as many were granted American citizenship by government fiat. In signing the Treaty of Guadalupe Hidalgo that ended the war between the United States and Mexico in 1848, the U.S. government promised to grant citizenship to all Mexican nationals residing in this country one year after the ratification of the treaty. One authority has estimated that the Mexican population in the United States at that time was approximately 100,000.[1]

However, the Mexican Americans of the Southwest did not become a very significant source of cheap labor until the turn of the century. Prior to this time the major industries of the Southwest relied on Chinese labor, particularly in California between 1850 and 1880, and later the labor of Japanese immigrants, again mostly in California, beginning in 1885. In addition, during the period between 1850 and 1900 the major industries in the Southwest, such as cattle and sheep, wheat and grain, and mining interests, did not require a vast army of seasonal workers, as would be true beginning in the early 1900s.

While the available immigration figures may not be completely accurate, they nonetheless do provide a general overview of the development of the labor intensive industries of the Southwest, and their complete dependence on the toil of Mexican laborers. The data reveals that the movement of Mexican nationals into the United States was insignificant between 1850 and 1900, as their number for each decade during this time period varied from a low of 971 (that is, between 1891-1900) to a high of 5,162 (1871-1880).[2] However, the actual number of immigrants must have been higher, since most authorities agree that the official government figures invariably and pervasively suffer from undercount. Specifically, they did not take into consideration the total number of Mexican nationals who did not bother to complete the official immigration forms at the various border crossing points. Nonetheless the available data does serve to indicate that the total number of immigrants arriving from Mexico during the early period was not at all significant.[3]

THE DEVELOPMENT OF INDUSTRIES IN THE SOUTHWEST

Naturally this discussion brings us to a consideration of why and how the industries of the greater Southwest developed and, more importantly, why there was such a sudden demand for a large, mobile, tractable labor force. The question consists of two parts: one, why did the industries of the Southwest experience such a rapid expansion during the early 1900s, and two, why was there such a sudden demand for Mexican laborers in the Southwest at this time?

Sociologists, historians, and others who study the flux and flow of immigration across international boundaries often refer to the internal dynamics of these processes in terms of "push" and "pull" factors. Simply stated, the push factors are those that make conditions in the home environment uncomfortable or undesirable for the potential immigrant, while the pull factors are those that serve to attract potential immigrants to another nation. Most often these push and pull factors work in conjunction, and therefore have a general synergistic effect on each other. Social demographers generally view the pull factors in a positive light and hold the push factors in a negative light.

For example, these factors would be positive if they offered such incentives as: employment opportunities, investment opportunities, higher wages, educational opportunities, and so on. While another set of factors would be considered negative in the sense that they make it uncomfortable or undesirable for people to remain in their homeland; for example, these might include such events as a civil war, natural catastrophes, overpopulation, lack of employment opportunities, and others. But in most cases a combination of push factors will work hand in hand with a combination of pull factors, and set the dynamics of the immigration process into motion.

Consequently, in order to understand the Mexican immigration process one must take into consideration the whole host of push-pull factors that had a combined impact, and resulted in the mass movement of people across the border. By the turn of the century conditions in Mexico were ripe for social change inasmuch as the majority of the population lived in dire poverty, were harnessed to a system of virtual slavery known as peonage, lacked employment or educational opportunities, had to depend on infertile lands, and were already suffering from overpopulation and the constant threat of famine.

However, as early as 1884 the forces of social change were already at work in Mexico with the completion of a railroad line from Mexico City to Ciudad Juarez. Most of the railroad construction that took place in Mexico during the late 1800s was carried on under the supervision and economic support of American capitalists. By 1910 there were five railway connections between the interior of Mexico and the U.S. border.[4] Naturally the completion of these modern railway lines served as a very strong incentive for Mexican immigrants to travel to the United States.

Meanwhile the burgeoning agricultural industries of the Southwest were suffering from a severe labor shortage. In 1882 Chinese immigration into the United States was terminated, and while the Japanese began to arrive in 1885, they were concentrated in Northern California, and their numbers were rather insignificant. Consequently, by the late 1890s the capitalists in the Southwest were suffering from a most severe labor shortage, or rather they lacked a source of cheap and tractable labor.

The Federal Reclamation Act of 1902 served as the major catalyst in the economic development of the agricultural industry of the Southwest. This government act provided funds for the construction of vast irrigation systems throughout the Southwest that resulted in the construction of hundreds of miles of canals, dykes, reservoirs and wells. At about the same time the railroad industry was engaged in a massive expansion program. The government's support of the agricultural interests in the Southwest, and the rapid expansion of the railroad system, meant that thousands of laborers were needed for the successful completion of these projects.[5]

In addition to the construction of canals and reservoirs, thousands of laborers were required to grub and clear the land, and prepare the soil for cultivation. All of these projects required intensive hand labor. As early as 1905, cotton was being produced on a commercial basis in three major areas of the Southwest: the semi-desert regions of Texas, the Salt River Valley in Arizona, and the Imperial Valley of California.

Besides the commercial production of cotton in the Southwest, the cultivation of sugar beets on a commercial basis gained a foothold in California and a number of midwestern states. The initial cultivation of sugar beets commercially is said to have occurred in Alvarado, California in 1870. However, this was primarily an experimental operation and was only carried out on a temporary basis. But the first successful sugar beet-processing plant was constructed at Watsonville, California in 1888.[6] Nevertheless, the sugar beet industry did not attain any degree of commercial success until Congress passed the Dingley Tariff Act of 1897, which taxed all foreign sugar at 75 percent of its value.[7] Once again the agricultural interests in the greater Southwest were in need of a large, mobile, tractable labor force that they could depend upon as a source of cheap labor.

At about the same time the social, economic, and political conditions in Mexico were deteriorating rapidly. Besides suffering from the effects of hundreds of hectares of unproductive and infertile soil, the northern sections of Mexico were also suffering from the rigors of a long drought. Unlike American farmers, the Mexican agriculturalists could not take advantage of the recently constructed irrigation systems in the Southwest. In the face of an ever increasing population, combined with crop failures and drought, the agony of mass starvation loomed on the horizon for many of the peasants of central and northern Mexico. To make matters even worse, the Mexican economy was plagued with runaway inflation, mass unemployment, and incredible national debt, and political corruption at the highest levels of government. In short, the population and the government in Mexico were confronted with complete chaos, and a whole host of unresolved social, economic, and political problems.

By 1910 these festering social and economic problems came to a head, and the result was social upheaval,

and the ensuing Civil War. In a desperate effort to escape the ravages of the Civil War thousands of Mexicans
fled in droves across the border in the hope of finding a
safe place to live and work. The Civil War also meant
that thousands of peasants were released from their virtual
bonds of slavery on the large haciendas. Coincidently, by
1910 Mexico had completed the construction of five main
railway arteries leading from Mexico City to the principal
border towns in Texas, New Mexico, Arizona, and California. Naturally this safe and modern means of transportation insured that thousands of homeless peasants would
immigrate to the United States.

In retrospect, it is clear that all of these social,
economic, and political forces worked in unison and historical harmony, in order to bring about one of the most
significant movements of people into this country. As if
all of these push-pull factors were not enough to encour-
age the mass migration of Mexican nationals into the American Southwest, it is also true that the agriculture and
railroad interests, in particular, actively recruited Mexican
laborers along the border, and even from the interior of
Mexico. As early as 1905 the sugar beet cartels of Colorado and the cotton farmers of Texas were known to dis-
patch corps of labor contractors and recruiters to all of
the major border towns.[8] Of course the main attraction
and advantage for Mexican laborers were the very high
wages paid by U.S. agriculturists, that is, when compared
to the wages that were being offered in Mexico at the
time. Historians have collected the data and have documented the fact that an agricultural worker in Mexico
could expect to increase his daily wage, for the same
type of work, by as much as seven to ten times.[9]

The available immigration data certainly reveals
the overall impact of these social, economic, and political
forces. For example, in 1907 some 1,406 Mexican immigrants arrived in this country. In the following year,
6,067 arrived, and in 1909 their number increased to
16,251. By 1910, some 17,760 arrived, and the following
year their number increased slightly to 18,784. The important point to remember, however, is that these official
figures only represent a rough estimate of the actual number of Mexican immigrants that actually arrived in the
United States during this time period. In fact the numbers
were probably two or three times higher. Indeed, one
historian has documented several cases in which whole

towns and villages migrated en masse across the border, in order to escape the death and destruction of the Civil War.[10]

From the turn of the century to the early 1930s, Mexican laborers were most highly concentrated in railroad maintenance and construction, in the agricultural industries of the Southwest, and in the development of key industries of the Midwest. It should go without saying that, without the availability of cheap Mexican labor in unlimited quantities, the agricultural and industrial development of the greater Southwest would have been delayed for many years.

MEXICAN LABORERS AND THE DEVELOPMENT OF THE RAILROAD INDUSTRY

By the turn of the century labor recruiters for the railroads in the Southwest realized that many of the Mexican immigrants had previous experience in railroad construction and maintenance. Many had worked on the original construction of the Mexican railway system during the mid-1880s and 1890s. Naturally they were attracted to the United States by the higher wages offered by American companies. In 1910 an agricultural worker in Mexico could expect to earn from 20 to 25 cents a day, while the Southern Pacific was paying $1.25 to $1.50 per day.[11] Nonetheless, Mexican laborers were always paid less, as a matter of company policy, than their Anglo counterparts. In fact, the railroad companies were never able to secure a sufficient number of white laborers at the rate of pay that they were willing to offer, for few Anglos were willing to accept a "Mexican wage." Furthermore, past experience had demonstrated that Anglo workers would not tolerate the working conditions or the intense heat of the Southwestern deserts. As a result, the railroad companies showed a very strong preference for Mexican laborers.

Not surprisingly, Mexican laborers were considered indispensable for the development of the extensive railway system of the Southwest. As early as 1880 Mexican laborers made up approximately 70 percent of the section crews, and 90 percent of the extra gangs.[12] During an eight-month period in 1908, the railroad companies of the Southwest brought in 16,471 laborers from Mexico.[13] Therefore, without a cheap, mobile, and tractable labor force, com-

posed primarily of Mexican laborers, the development of
the railroad industry in the Southwest would have been
long delayed.

The railroad industry's heavy reliance upon Mexican laborers as their chief source of manpower continued
into the 1960s. One result of their extensive participation in the construction and maintenance of the railroad
systems of the Southwest was that many Mexican–American
communities were founded along the right of way of the
various railroad lines running throughout Texas, New
Mexico, Arizona, and California.

MEXICAN LABORERS IN THE NORTHERN INDUSTRIES

Given their concentration in the railroad industry,
many Mexican laborers had an opportunity to visit and
become acquainted with new and often distant areas of the
United States. Beginning in the early 1920s they were
used extensively in many of the northern and central
states, particularly during the spring and summer months
when these additional work crews attended to the major
maintenance and construction projects.

However, during this same period of time many of
the northern industries, such as the steel mills, automobile
factories, meat–packing plants, cement manufacturers, and
so on were suffering from an acute labor shortage, primarily as a result of the disrupted flow of immigrants
from Europe. Faced with this very serious situation the
captains of industry did not hesitate to take full advantage of the opportunity to exploit a new source of cheap
labor. To this end they immediately dispatched a platoon
of labor recruiters to distribute pamphlets written in Spanish to Mexican railroad workers in an effort to entice them
into signing employment contracts with their respective
industries. In reality factory work offered many advantages over employment in the railroad industry, such as
higher wages, housing facilities, greater job security, and
partial relief from the perpetual search for sources of
employment.[14]

By the mid–1920s it became common practice for these
Mexican laborers to go to their homes in Texas or Mexico
during the winter, and return in the spring. However,
they soon established their own communities in cities such

as Bethlehem, Chicago, East Chicago, Flint, Saginaw, and others. Before long, a number of Mexican Colonias germinated and sprang forth into full bloom.

THE TENACITY OF MEXICAN IMMIGRATION

By the late 1920s it was clear that many of the Mexican immigrants in this country had decided to make their stay permanent. This was true in spite of the prevailing public image, promulgated by local growers and others, that Mexican migrants returned to Mexico at the completion of the agricultural season. As part of their propaganda campaign, it was in the growers' interest to make these laborers appear as "birds of passage," that is, as sojourners, in an effort to avoid the disreputable accusation that they would become public charges in the local communities to which they generally moved at the end of the harvest season.

However, the historical data indicates that a large proportion of these Mexican laborers decided, early on, to remain in this country. According to the census of 1930 there were 1,422,533 Chicanos living in this country. Certainly this figure must have been closer to 2 million, particularly in view of the historical undercount of minority groups in the United States.

But while they were certainly attracted by the plethora of job opportunities available in this country, in addition to the higher wages, their population increase can also be attributed to the fact that their services were actively sought out by those who were in a position to realize a substantial profit from their continued presence. Naturally, they were actively recruited because they represented an inexhaustible source of cheap labor and would work under conditions that no other laborers were willing to accept.

However, the most important contribution made by Mexican laborers to the economic development of this country was in the development of the agricultural industry of the Southwest. In every aspect of agriculture, the labor of Mexican immigrants has been the key and indispensable ingredient for the economic success of American agriculturalists. Their role in the development of the American agricultural industry was particularly important in the

states of Texas, California, and Colorado--specifically in
the development of winter gardens in Texas and California
and the development of the sugar beet industries of the
midwestern states and in California.

MEXICAN LABORERS IN TEXAS COTTON

Cotton was grown on a commercial basis in East
Texas since before the Civil War, when it was cultivated
and harvested by slave labor.   In fact, cotton was first
introduced into Texas by Stephen F. Austin and his group
of settlers in 1822.[15]   By the late 1880s and the early
1890s the economic pressures of "king cotton" began to
dominate other parts of Texas, and this resulted in the
exodus of cattle and sheep from their traditional territories
within the state.   By the mid-1890s the central and western
sections of Texas were budding forth with cotton and this,
naturally enough, resulted in the sudden need for additional harvest laborers.   Once again the agriculturalists
turned to the ever present Mexican, as a source of cheap
and tractable labor.

In order to plant cotton in Texas the semi-desert
lands had to be cleared of chaparral brush, cacti, and
other indigenous desert vegetation.   Once again this arduous, and sometimes dangerous task, fell upon the backs of
Mexican laborers.   The clearing process was commonly referred to as grubbing, as it generally required the use of
a "grubbing hoe."   This toilsome labor was contracted out
on the basis of a flat rate per acre, depending on the
density of the brush and cacti.   In a very short time this
type of work was considered "Mexican work," because
there were so few white or black workers who would consider doing such strenuous work.

Understandably the cotton industry of Texas grew at
a phenomenal rate.   In the 11-year period between 1917
and 1928 the cotton production in Texas jumped from just
over a quarter million bales to almost 900,000 bales, an
overall increase of more than 330 percent.[16]   Concomitant
with this rapid growth and development was the urgent
need for a tremendously large, yet docile and highly mobile, labor force.   For this hapless task Mexican laborers
were sought out and enticed to enter the vicious cycle of
migratory labor.

From the early 1900s it was generally known that Mexican agricultural laborers traveled in family groups and followed the cotton harvest throughout Texas. This situation was much to the liking of the planters, for they maintained that the children, as a rule, could pick almost as much cotton as the grown-ups. These migratory groups usually consisted of a man and his wife, their children, grandparents and other relatives, and sometimes certain close friends. In effect, the family operated as a very efficient social and economic unit, with each member, even the children, making a contribution to their overall survival. Indeed children were required to work in view of the urgent need for the meager income that they were able to contribute.

Before long the Mexican laborer and his family became the mainstay of the cotton industry of Texas. In fact, the planters of Texas developed their own "reserve army of labor," inasmuch as they did not have to compete with city labor. In addition, the large proportion of women and children in the labor force meant that their labor went unpaid, for the family unit was considered the center of production in the fields. It is estimated that at the peak of the season in 1940 there were more than 800,000 men, women, and children picking cotton in Texas, the majority of whom were Mexican agricultural workers.[17]

Is it any wonder that Mexican laborers came to be viewed as the chattel of the Texas cotton industry? This observation certainly has some very significant sociological ramifications in view of the fact that the back-breaking work of the agricultural industry came to be viewed as work that was somehow "suitable" for all Chicanos. For the most part the Mexican migratory worker in Texas was viewed as a necessary evil, that is, as just another appendage or extension of the agricultural cycle, with no past, no future, and only an anonymous present.

MEXICAN LABORERS IN THE WINTER GARDEN OF TEXAS

The transition from a cattle empire to a cotton and vegetable monopoly was made possible by the symbiotic interplay of two factors: the development of large-scale irrigation systems in the semi-desert regions of Texas and, more important, the availability of cheap labor from Mexico.

Just as Texas ranchers had learned the essentials of sheep
and cattle husbandry from the Mexican vaqueros, so they
were also given their first lessons in the various methods
and techniques of irrigation by the ever-present Mexican.

The Mexican's knowledge of irrigation techniques
resulted from the confluence of the experiences of the
Pueblo Indians, and the Spanish explorers. The Pueblo
Indians of New Mexico had thousands of acres of land
under irrigation when the Spanish conquistadores appeared
in their villages. However, the Spanish had also developed
a very elaborate irrigation system in their homeland and
were irrigating the semi-desert lands around Las Cruces
when the Mayflower arrived at Plymouth.[18]

It was not until the passage of the Federal Reclamation Act in 1902 that the irrigation systems of the greater
Southwest were developed on a large-scale basis. Naturally, the construction of hundreds of miles of canals,
dykes, reservoirs, and wells depended upon the blood and
sweat of Mexican laborers. It was the construction of
these extensive irrigation systems that served to revolution-
ize the agricultural economy of Texas, and, furthermore,
put Texas at the forefront of the U.S. agricultural industry.

Within a matter of years the construction of these
irrigation systems in the semi-desert regions of Texas resulted in a virtual year-round green house, in the Southwestern part of the state, commonly referred to as the
"Winter Garden." By the 1940s the Winter Garden consisted
of a strip of irrigated agricultural land approximately 40
miles long and eight miles wide situated principally in
Zavalla and Dimit counties. The Winter Garden was best
known for its annual production, in carloads, of vegetables
such as spinach, cabbage, beans, and tomatoes. Most of
the Mexican agricultural laborers and their families lived
in hovels near the communities of Harlingen, Edinburg,
Laredo, Eagle Pass, and Crystal City; while others were
routinely trucked in from such areas as Robstown, Corpus
Christi, and San Antonio.[19]

The majority of agricultural workers in this region
worked under the direct supervision and control of labor contractors, who in turn were paid by the growers to cultivate
and harvest their crops. In reality this age-old system of
labor exploitation that is inherent in the farmworker-labor
contractor system is allowed to flourish, to the detriment of
the agricultural workers, and is the most efficient and
cheapest method yet devised to harvest the crops. It will
probably remain in effect for another millennium.

MEXICAN LABORERS IN THE SUGAR BEETS OF COLORADO

In the United States there are three geographical
areas that are topographically and climatically suitable for
the commercial production of sugar beets, namely the midwestern states of Michigan, Ohio, and Wisconsin; the moun-
tain states of Colorado, Utah, and Idaho; and California.
While the first successful sugar beet processing
plant was constructed in Watsonville, California in 1888, it
was 12 years later before the first successful commercial
sugar beet processing plant was constructed at Loveland,
Colorado. In the next two years a series of plants were
constructed in Eaton, Greeley, Windsor, Fort Collins, and
Longmont. Once these plants were in operation it was the
task of the sugar beet industrialists to convince the farmers in each of these areas to convert from their traditional
table and cattle grains to the full production of sugar
beets. They even went so far as to send their field representatives out to help farmers plant their seeds and cultivate and harvest their first crop of sugar beets. In addition they leased thousands of acres of land and planted
them with row upon row of sugar beets. They also purchased
their own land and converted it to the mass production of
sugar beets.
Once the sugar cartels convinced local farmers to
convert to sugar beet production, they used the additional
incentive of paying them for their harvest at the beginning
of the season. However, they were confronted with a very
serious labor shortage, which was particularly acute since
the entire sugar beet season lasted for approximately nine
months, while, as a result of lags in the growing season,
the agricultural workers were only needed in the fields for
a total of five months.
In the beginning the sugar cartels relied most
heavily on the availability of German-Russian immigrants.
However, their usefulness to the growers was sharply cur-
tailed by the immigration restrictions of 1917. Furthermore, their numbers were not sufficient to satisfy the incredible labor needs of the sugar beet industry in Colorado.
As early as 1903 the first contingent of Mexican laborers
appeared in the beet fields of Colorado, but their numbers
were small and, for the most part, they simply served as
a good source of competition against the German-Russians.
Even as late as 1909 there were only about a thousand
Mexicans working in the sugar beet fields of Colorado.[20]

By 1916 the Colorado growers were actively recruiting Mexican laborers from the southern parts of the state, and from the neighboring state of New Mexico. However, the supply of Mexican laborers in these parts was quickly used up. In a desperate effort to tap additional sources of cheap labor the sugar cartels of Colorado sent professional labor recruiters deep into Texas, and even into Mexico. These recruiters frequently arrived with railway tickets and bonus checks in their hands for those Mexican laborers who decided to sign a work contract.

Before long the sugar cartels found themselves in a competitive struggle with the growers of Texas for the much needed labor of Mexican immigrants. But the Colorado growers were very determined and soon opened and maintained offices in such strategic locations as El Paso, Fort Worth, and San Antonio. These growers were known to deal directly with coyotes, that is, professional labor smugglers, who in turn were involved in the transportation of laborers from across the border.

Once again it was not long before Mexican agricultural laborers became the key to the successful production of sugar beets throughout the Midwest. In 1927 the federal government conducted a survey and found that from 75 to 90 percent of the sugar beet workers in the states of Ohio, Michigan, Minnesota, and North Dakota were Mexican laborers.[21] In fact, the reliance on Mexican labor became so great that it was customary for the Colorado WPA to lay off men with Spanish surnames each spring so that they could work out in the fields.[22]

MEXICAN LABORERS IN THE WINTER GARDEN OF CALIFORNIA

While it is a historical fact that the Mexican has always been a part of the California scene, it is often assumed that they have always been a numerically significant proportion of the population of this state. However, in 1850 there were only 6,454 Mexicans domiciled in this state, and from 1860 to 1900 their population fluctuated between a low of 7,164 and a high of 9,339. On a percentage basis they only represented a mere one-half of 1 percent of the population of California in 1900.[23]

However, between 1900 and 1910 a very dramatic change took place in the population distribution in California, when their numbers jumped from only 8,086 to 48,391, that is, the Mexican population in this state experienced a six-fold increase during this ten-year period. For the most part this population boom can be attributed to California's growing need for a new source of cheap, tractable labor, particularly in the agricultural industry of the state. For example, in the Imperial Valley, which is a very hot semi-desert region of the state, the development of an extensive irrigation system meant that crops could be produced on a year-round basis. The first irrigation systems in the valley were constructed by the Cocopas Indians of Mexico, between 1900 and 1910. Mexican labor was also used extensively in the clearing and leveling of the desert terrain in order to provide a seed bed for the perpetual garden of California.[24] The Imperial Valley soon became the cornucopia of the state.

The first successful commercial harvest of cotton in the valley occurred in 1909, and by the following year cotton had established itself as the "king of the valley." While it is a historical fact that Mexican labor was always present in the valley, it is also true that they were not used extensively until 1917, when the local agriculturalists turned seriously toward Mexican laborers. At about this time various immigration restrictions were placed on cheap Oriental labor, while Anglo laborers migrated to the industrial centers of the state, where they could take full advantage of the higher wages paid by the wartime industries. Other Anglos were drafted into the military services. To make matters even worse, the farmers in the valley expanded from cotton production to the year-round cultivation of cantaloupes, lettuce, tomatoes, and grapes. Obviously, the local growers were confronted with a very serious labor shortage.

Once again the American farmer looked south of the border for the solution to their critical labor shortage. By 1920 some 20,000 Mexican laborers were living and working in the Imperial Valley, out of a total population of 54,000.[25] In the late 1920s a number of Mexican communities were established in such cities as Brawley, Imperial, El Centro, Calipatria, and others. These laborers worked for eight to ten months out of the year, with a slack period during August and September. During this slack period, some would make their way to the citrus crops of Southern California, while others would cross the Tehachapi mountains and enter the great San Joaquin Valley.

The historical data indicate that Mexican agricultural laborers gradually moved from the Imperial Valley into the citrus groves of Southern California, then over to Oxnard, and into the San Joaquin Valley. Some settled in the Salinas Valley, while others moved further north into the great Sacramento Valley, and still others settled in the Napa Valley.

MEXICAN LABORERS IN CALIFORNIA: 1920–65

By the late 1920s Mexican laborers constituted the primary source of labor in the agricultural industry, not only in California but in all of the greater Southwest. However, the 1930s brought hard times for the nation as a whole, and particularly for those hapless individuals who eked out their living from the land. The 1930s were marked by severe economic depression, social disorganization, and also witnessed the mass deportation of Chicanos. With the onset of the Great Depression Mexican agricultural laborers were rapidly replaced by the "dust bowl" refugees from Arkansas, Oklahoma, and Texas. Consequently, the unemployment rate among Chicanos was extremely high and times were particularly tough for those in the rural areas of the Southwest.

The mass unemployment suffered by Chicanos during the Depression was not only a result of the "last hired, first fired" policy but in fact serves as an excellent example of the "shock absorber" function of the "reserve army of labor," to which all Chicanos were relegated. In fact, they were, as a matter of common practice, fired from their agricultural and industrial jobs in order to provide jobs for unemployed Anglos. As is always the case, the social and economic effects of the Depression were felt most severely by those at the bottom of the economic heap, and particularly by the Chicano labor force.

Some 12 years elapsed before conditions improved in the United States, and before conditions began to improve for Chicanos in general. However, in view of the wartime crisis, and the resulting labor shortage, the agricultural interests in California were able to force the government to secure, supply, and guarantee a continuous source of cheap labor from Mexico, under the auspices of a program that came to be known as the "Bracero Program."

Under this program, the government entered into a formal agreement with the government of Mexico in 1942, allowing for the importation of "temporary" agricultural contract workers during the wartime emergency. By 1943, this program was in full force and some 52,000 Mexican aliens entered the agricultural fields of the Southwest; a vast proportion of these were assigned to growers in California. In the following year just over 62,000 were allowed to enter this country as contract laborers, and so their numbers continued to climb. However, the overall effect of this government policy was that the braceros were in fact taking jobs away from the local Chicano agricultural workers. What was worse was that the agricultural interests in the Southwest were able to force the government to continue this emergency wartime program long after the hostilities were over. Even as late as 1949, over 143,000 braceros were brought in as agricultural laborers, and this figure does not take into consideration all of those who entered without documentation.

This massive influx of contract laborers from Mexico not only displeased American citizens, but also meant that agricultural workers could not organize themselves to improve their working conditions, inasmuch as the growers could use braceros as a threat to worker organizations, and in some cases even as strike breakers. The deleterious effects of the Bracero Program were that Mexican-American agricultural workers suffered from very high rates of unemployment and underemployment, were not able to organize to improve their working conditions, and were unable to secure higher wages. Therefore, the Bracero Program not only guaranteed the growers of the Southwest an adequate supply of cheap and tractable labor, but also insured that agricultural wages would remain at the subsistence level and that farm workers would not be able to form labor unions and improve their working conditions.

In this regard growers were imminently successful inasmuch as they were able to forestall the organization of agricultural workers until 1965, when the United Farm Workers organized and struck for improved working conditions and higher wages. However, it was not long before the growers developed another tactic in their indefatigable efforts to prevent the organization of agricultural workers, as they secured a bountiful supply of "green card workers," who were brought into this country as "commuters," and as legal resident aliens. This meant that the growers could use these Mexican aliens as a threat to union organization, and in fact as strike breakers. In effect, the growers substituted the old Bracero Program, sponsored and organized by the U.S. government, for the available green card workers, and the endless number of undocumented workers, in order to achieve the same objective, that is, to insure the maintenance and availability of a cheap and tractable agricultural labor force.

NOTES

1. Lyle Saunders, "The Social History of Spanish-Speaking People in Southwestern United States Since 1846," Southwest Council on Education of Spanish-Speaking People (Albuquerque: 1950), p. 2.

2. Vincent N. Parrillo, Strangers to These Shores: Race and Ethnic Relations in the United States (Boston: Houghton Mifflin, 1980), pp. 469-70. In this regard Bogardus found that only 3,078 Mexicans arrived in this country between 1851 and 1860, 2,191 from 1861 to 1870, and only 8,000 immigrated between 1871 and 1900. See Emory S. Bogardus, The Mexican in the United States, Social Science Series No. 5, Los Angeles, University of Southern California Press, 1934 (reprint ed., New York: Arno Press, 1970), p. 13.

3. Elac expressed a similar opinion when he concluded that "Mexican immigration was of minor importance before 1900. The statistics on immigration show that between 1870 and 1899 the number of immigrants from Mexico did not exceed 700 in any one year." In John C. Elac, "The Employment of Mexican Workers in U.S. Agriculture 1900-1960," M.A. thesis, University of California, Los Angeles, 1961, p. 4.

4. The first railway line connecting Mexico City to Ciudad Juarez was completed on March 8, 1884, and gave the Mexican Central Railway direct connections with the U.S. Atchison Topeka and Santa Fe, the Texas and Pacific, and the Southern Pacific. In Elac, "The Employment of Mexican Workers," pp. 88-89. The most complete historical treatment of this subject can be obtained by reading David M. Pletcher's Rails, Mines and Progress: Seven American Promoters in Mexico, 1867-1911 (Ithaca: Cornell University Press, 1958; and John H. McNeely, The Railways of Mexico (El Paso: Texas Western College Press, 1964).

5. As Fernandez points out that, "Large-scale irrigation meant, additionally, a new and increased over-capitalization of the land. Heavy capital investment, in addition to creating 'agribusiness' by bringing banking capital into the agricultural enterprise, meant an increase in demand for ever larger pools of cheap labor." In Raul Fernandez, The United States Mexico Border: A Political Economic Profile (Notre Dame: University of Notre Dame Press, 1977), p. 97.

6. For a brief history of the development of the sugar beet industry in the Southwest see the work of Harry Schwartz, Seasonal Farm Labor in the United States: With Special Reference to Hired Workers in Fruit and Vegetable and Sugar-Beet Production (New York: Columbia University Press, 1945).

7. For a complete historical discussion of the government's support of the sugar beet industry in this country see Leonidas Polopolus, "United States Beet Sugar: A Study of Industry Structure and Performance Under Protection and Control," Ph.D. dissertation, University of California, Berkeley, 1961.

8. In fact, Taylor found that one labor agent sent his recruiters south of the border into Monterey, Mexico in search of cheap labor. In Paul S. Taylor, Mexican Labor in the United States: Chicago and the Calumet Region, Vol. 7, no. 2 (Berkeley: University of California Press, 1931), pp. 117-19. However, the Mexican government prohibited the recruitment of Mexican laborers by American labor agents, after 1917. See Arthur F. Corwin, ed., Immigrants and Immigrants: Perspectives on Mexican Labor Migration to the United States (Westport, Conn.: Greenwood Press, 1978), p. 179.

9. While the wages paid in the agricultural industry were low by American standards, they were considered high by Mexican standards. For example, in 1905 an agricultural worker in Jalisco could only expect to earn 12.5 cents per day, plus some maize. But if an entire Mexican family picked cotton in Texas, they could expect to earn as much as $5.00 per day, that is, during the peak of the harvest season. See Mark Reisler, By the Sweat of Their Brow: Mexican Immigrant Labor in the U.S. 1900-1940 (Westport, Conn.: Greenwood Press, 1976), p. 14.

10. Lawrence A. Cardoso, "Mexican Emigration to the United States, 1900-1930: An Analysis of Socio-Economic Causes," Ph.D. dissertation, University of Connecticut, 1974, p. 66.

11. John R. Martinez, "Mexican Emigration to the U.S. 1910–1930," Ph.D. dissertation, University of California, Berkeley, 1957, p. 9.

12. Carey McWilliams, North From Mexico (New York: Greenwood Press, 1968), p. 168.

13. Cardoso, "Mexican Emigration," p. 58.

14. An excellent historical source on the immigration and settlement of Mexican immigrants in northern cities is Paul S. Taylor's Mexican Labor in the United States: Chicago and the Calumet Region, cited above, and his Mexican Labor in the United States: Bethlehem, Pennsylvania, Vol. 7, no. 1 (Berkeley: University of California Press, 1931).

15. George O. Coalson, "The Development of the Migratory Farm Labor System in Texas, 1900–1945," Ph.D. dissertation, University of Oklahoma, 1955, p. 1.

16. Charles H. Hufford, "The Social and Economic Effects of the Mexican Migration into Texas," M.A. thesis, Howard Payne College, University of Colorado, 1929, p. 10.

17. Carey McWilliams, Ill Fares the Land: Migrants and Migratory Labor in the United States (New York: Barnes & Noble, Inc., 1942), p. 230.

18. McWilliams, North From Mexico, p. 157.

19. McWilliams, Ill Fares the Land, p. 241.

20. Paul S. Taylor, Mexican Labor in the United States: Valley of the South Platte–Colorado, Vol. 6, no. 2 (Berkeley: University of California Press, 1929), p. 105.

21. Schwartz, Seasonal Farm Labor, p. 117.

22. Ibid.

23. For a complete historical, geographic, and demographic study of the population growth of the state of California, with particular emphasis on ethnic groups, see Davis McEntire, "An Economic Study of Population Movements in California, 1850–1944," Ph.D. dissertation, Harvard University, 1947.

24. This is not to say that irrigation projects did not exist in California prior to the turn of the century, as Bancroft notes that irrigation was introduced into California during the first years of Spanish occupation. He further notes that by 1879 some 13,000 acres were under irrigation in the San Joaquin Valley. Hurbert H. Bancroft, History of California, Vol. 24 (San Francisco: History Company Publishers, 1890).

25. Paul S. Taylor, Mexican Labor in the United States: Imperial Valley, Vol. 6, no. 1 (Berkeley: University of California Press, 1928), p. 18.

2

The Mexican Agricultural Community in California: Some Preliminary Observations

As demonstrated in Chapter 1, the Mexican and Mexican-American population of the Southwest has always played a very important role in development of the agricultural industry, and particularly in California. As a result, several hundred Mexican agricultural communities have developed in the various agricultural regions of the state, with a majority exhibiting many of the same social and economic characteristics. The primary reason for the similarity in the organization of each of these rural communities is that they all depend on the agricultural industry for their existence and survival.

During the course of our investigation of the living and working conditions of Mexican agricultural workers in California it became clear that each of our research communities exhibited certain unique characteristics, while in general they all tend to share a good deal in common. With this sense of homogeneity clearly established as a common pattern in various Mexican agricultural communities, it is important to describe the historical origins and the day-to-day life in one of these typical rural communities. For this purpose we shall turn our attention to "Ciudad de Esperanza" (a pseudonym), which served as one of the first research communities surveyed during the course of this study.

THE HISTORY OF "CIUDAD DE ESPERANZA"

As is the case with many other agricultural communities in the state of California, Ciudad de Esperanza is

located in a county the major industry of which is agriculture. And, as is often the case with other agricultural
communities, Esperanza is also rather isolated. This community is located along a state highway between the
second-largest city in the county and the largest city in
the region, a university town with a population of approximately 40,000 people.

According to the county historical society, Ciudad
de Esperanza can trace its origins to 1905, when the di-
rectors of a large eastern sugar cartel decided to expand
their holdings and develop a new region for the production
of sugar beets. While the initial cultivation of sugar beets
on a commercial basis is said to have occurred in Alvarado,
California in 1870, this was only an experimental operation
and only functioned on a temporary basis. However, the
first successful sugar beet processing plant was constructed
at Watsonville, California in 1888.

In the fall of 1905, two of the company's representatives traveled to the northern Sacramento Valley and
selected a 5,000-acre site on the west bank of the Sacramento River as an ideal location for their new sugar beet
processing plant. Within the next few months, plans were
made for the construction of a 600-ton capacity plant,
while the original plans for the city were laid out by
three company representatives. However, the project was
plagued with difficulties and delays from the very start.
The motors and pumps ordered for the factory had arrived
in San Francisco according to plan, but were destroyed in
the earthquake and fire of 1906. Laborers were also difficult to obtain and the majority of Mexicans brought up
from Los Angeles did not remain in the area for very long.
One of the reasons for their departure was the difficulty
they were having with malaria. The Southern Pacific Railroad was supposed to construct a ten-mile line to the main
line but unfortunately they encountered a number of difficulties with right of way. Another obstacle was the un-
predictable seasonal flooding of the river, and their inability to establish a ferry system on the river. Most important, they found that the majority of farmers in the
area were very reluctant to convert to the sugar beet crop,
as they were not familiar with it and therefore refused to
sign leases or contracts with the company.

It was not until 1907 that the factory finally went
into production; however, the investors were still confronted
with transportation problems, irrigation problems, a white

fly infestation, labor shortages, land lease problems, and so on. As a result, the plant often remained open for several years, would then close for a few years, and then reopen for a number of years. Overall, the investors were not very successful in their venture. As it turned out it was not until 1936 when the factory and lands were sold to the Holly Sugar Company that success and stability were finally established.

During World War II the Holly Sugar Company expanded its production in order to supply the needs of a wartime economy. Naturally, this meant that they needed more laborers, and, for this purpose, they turned to the available Mexican agricultural laborers, mostly undocumented workers and braceros. Following the war, the Mexican population established itself in Ciudad de Esperanza on a permanent basis and soon became the largest community in the city's population. The Mexican agricultural laborers were primarily employed as field workers in the sugar beet fields and in the various fruit, citrus, and nut orchards in the region, while only a few were hired by the factory. Although many were migratory workers, a rather significant proportion established themselves as permanent residents in Ciudad de Esperanza by the late 1950s.

CIUDAD DE ESPERANZA TODAY

Ciudad de Esperanza remains an agriculturally based community, with the major difference being that its economy is not totally dependent on the agricultural industry or the production of sugar beets. The agricultural economy of the area has diversified beyond sugar beet production, and now includes such major crops as citrus, nuts, and horticultural products.

According to the United States Census, the permanent population of Ciudad de Esperanza was 956 in 1970, and increased to 1,301 in 1976. However, it can be assumed that the actual population of the community is larger than these official statistics would lead one to believe. In the household census conducted as part of this study in 1977, there were a total of 360 single-family dwelling units in the community, excluding approximately 41 multiple dwelling units. Of these 360 units, 101 (28%) were designated Mexican or Mexican-American families, while the remaining 259 units (71.9%) were designated Anglo households. If we consider that the average family size in California in 1970, according to the United States Census was 3.47 then a total Anglo population of 899 can be calculated. While the average family size among Hispanics in 1970 was 4.2, the results of this study among Mexican agricultural workers found that the average family size was 6.5. Now we can multiply the total number of Hispanic households in the community (101) by this figure and estimate a total Hispanic population of 657. When the Hispanic and the Anglo population estimates are combined we arrive at a total estimated population for the community in 1977 of 1,556, with Hispanics representing 42.2 percent of the total. The difference between our estimated population figure and the official census figures can best be explained by the traditional undercount that occurs among the Hispanic population and other ethnic minorities.

In actual fact the Mexican and Mexican-American population of Ciudad de Esperanza is really larger when we consider that the majority of the residents in the 41 multiple dwelling units are of Hispanic origin. In addition, during the harvest season the community undergoes a radical transformation in character as it adapts to the mass influx of migratory workers, consisting mainly of single or unaccompanied Mexican aliens. Given our knowledge of the community we can estimate that the Hispanic population of Ciudad de Esperanza accounts for approximately 60 to 65 percent of the total year-round population.

The results of the 1976 special census of the community reveal the strong Mexican influence, in that the largest occupational category consists of agricultural workers, at 45 percent of the total. It can safely be assumed that the vast majority of these agricultural workers are of Hispanic origin. Craftsmen accounted for 13.8 percent of the total, and operatives were next in order of significance with 11.8 percent. Overall, 80 percent of the labor force can be classified as blue collar, 14.9 percent as white collar, and only 7.0 percent as professional workers. These percentages reflect the strong dependence of the community on the agricultural industry. During the course of my field observations in Ciudad de Esperanza I found very few Mexicans or Mexican Americans employed outside of the agricultural industry. Only a handful were employed as laborers at a local cement factory, a few were hired by the sugar refinery, and a few were employed at the local Mexican restaurant. Overall, the stereotype persists that Mexicans or Mexican Americans are simply agricultural workers.

As previously stated, the community of Ciudad de Esperanza is relatively isolated from all of the other agricultural communities in the surrounding area, as it is located midway between two larger cities on a two-lane state highway. In terms of total land area, the community covers approximately one square mile, bounded by an almond orchard on the east, a major irrigation canal on the west, the state highway to the north, and the sugar factory to the south.

Although the community is relatively small in geographical area and in population, it does have a grade school, a high school, a one-block-square park, two Protestant churches, one Catholic church, two bars, three restaurants, three grocery stores, two service stations, two liquor stores, a post office, a small library, and a sheriff's substation. As is often the case in agricultural communities heavily populated by Hispanics, these various services and businesses are either used exclusively by the Hispanic population or exclusively by Anglos, and only rarely are they utilized by members of both groups.

While Hispanic families live on virtually every block of the community, it is true that the greater proportion live on the east side of town, literally on the other side of the tracks. Those Hispanics who do live on the better side of town tend to be the long-term settled residents of the community, and they live in nicer homes and enjoy a higher standard of living. Conversely, those living across the tracks are less well off economically, tend to be short-term residents, live in deteriorating housing, and most are migratory agricultural workers.

In accordance with federal law, the grade school and the high school were integrated and are used by the children of both the Mexican and Anglo populations, but not without certain problems. In the grade school it was common to find that the Mexican and Mexican-American children were frequently segregated into separate groups, primarily because of language difficulties encountered by Hispanic children. This meant that Anglo and Hispanic children did not have many opportunities to associate with one another, except on the playground. At the high school level, I observed a voluntary segregation of the two groups

as various difficulties in the past have made harmonious
relations among Anglo and Hispanic children difficult if
not impossible. Some of these problems can be attributed
to the social class differences that exist in all rural
schools, that is, the difference between the children of
agricultural workers and the children of growers. To
their credit, school officials have tried to address the
issues and solve the problems of these students.

While the public park is located in the predominantly
Anglo section of the community, it is used primarily by
the Mexican and Mexican-American residents. The park is
heavily used during the hot summer evenings by the local
agricultural workers and their families as most of their
homes do not have air conditioning. However, family use
is the greatest on Sundays, while weekday evenings are
generally reserved for adolescent males and the Hispanic
men of the community. For the most part, the Anglo residents have given the park over to the Mexicans, and most
Hispanics recognize it as their "turf." Some problems have
developed in the park as a result of alcohol abuse and
fights. The police have banned alcohol in the park and
this measure has reduced the number of problems, but the
law is not always observed or enforced.

For its part the Catholic church has a virtual monopoly on the Hispanic population, and offers four masses
on Sundays, three of the services conducted in Spanish.
The English language mass is primarily attended by local
Anglos; however, they represent a small proportion of the
total Anglo population of the community. The Protestant
church, located on the opposite corner from the Catholic
church, caters to the religious needs of the major proportion of church-going Anglos in the community. Hence, the
Protestant church serves as a very strong bonding agent
among the Anglos in the community. The other church in
Ciudad de Esperanza is more of a "store-front" affair, and
is of the evangelical variety. This church seems to attract
a mixed group of people from the community, but primarily
from the lower socio-economic strata.

As is true of most small communities, the locals
have their favorite bars which tend to be highly segregated, and so is the case in Ciudad de Esperanza. The
local Mexican bar is located out on the main highway running along the edge of town, while the local Anglo bar is
located at the opposite end of town, by the sugar mill.
While the Mexican bar is totally segregated, this is not

the case with the Anglo bar. Patrons in the Anglo bar
are primarily farm hands, foremen, growers, ranchers,
truck drivers, and laborers from the local sugar refinery.
The Mexicans and Mexican Americans who frequent the
Anglo bar are usually bilingual and are not generally
agricultural workers, but rather are employed in the sugar
refinery or in some other local industry. Those who do
work in the agricultural industry are usually long-term
skilled agricultural workers, agricultural foremen, or labor
contractors. For the most part, both groups enjoy themselves in the Anglo bar in a rather harmonious atmosphere,
although they mix only infrequently and social contact is
usually limited to salutations.

　　　　While the results obtained in this study are based
on field observations and interviews conducted in selected
communities in eight different counties of northern California, it is also the case that original field experience in
Ciudad de Esperanza was very similar, in most respects,
to the social and economic conditions encountered in other
areas. Therefore, the ethnographic study conducted in
Ciudad de Esperanza can serve as a model for other agricultural communities studied as part of this project. The
most common characteristics found in Esperanza were also
found to be a part of the community life in the other
study areas, with only a slight variation in some cases.
Hence, the Mexican and Mexican-American agricultural communities are typically recognized for their lower socio-
economic status, their social isolation, their geographic
segregation, their ethnic and class barriers, their seasonal
fluctuation in population size, and their total dependence
on the agricultural industry for their livelihood.

3

A Typology of Mexican Agricultural Workers

There are a variety of methods by which Mexican agricultural workers can be studied and understood as individuals who make a substantial contribution to the economic well-being of society. But what is required is an analysis of the more fundamental terms that are applied, and often misapplied, to the various groups within the agricultural labor force.[1]

SEASONAL AND MIGRATORY AGRICULTURAL WORKERS

When the term seasonal is used with reference to the agricultural force, it implies that certain laborers work a particular crop during designated periods of the year. This concentration of effort results from the fact that every crop reaches a particular period when it requires the complete attention of a small army of agricultural workers. For example, during the life cycle of any given plant, it requires plentiful amounts of water, it has to be thinned, cultivated, treated with insecticides, and eventually harvested. This crop may require 200 farm workers for the thinning-out process, which may last only a week, and thereafter may require just four agriculturists for the cultivation of the soil and the spraying of insecticides. During the harvest season, the same crop may require the toil of 200 farm workers for a relatively short period of time. Therefore, the two peak periods in the life cycle of a particular crop refer to the seasonal needs and manpower requirements placed upon the agricultural labor force.

Briefly, seasonal farm workers are those whose livelihood revolves around the peak periods in the life cycle of each crop, which, in turn, determine the need for their labor. Consequently, there are periods in the year when they have little or no opportunity for employment because certain crops can be planted only at designated times of the year and come to fruition at other set times of the year. There are also periods during the harvest season when agricultural workers have more work than they can manage in a single day. However, this pattern does appear to be an inherent characteristic of agricultural work, which is based on the life cycle of certain crops.

Logically, it would appear that any given agricultural worker would be exposed to a variety of employment opportunities due to the abundance of agricultural products found in most rural communities. Also, it would appear that the selection of five to ten different crops within a 15-mile radius of his home would certainly keep an agricultural worker occupied for the greater part of the year. However, the major difficulty with this reasoning is that crops in any one agricultural region of the state do not come to fruition in exact numerical sequence; consequently, there will always be gaps in the agricultural labor market. Thus, the real situation is represented by periods of seasonal unemployment for the majority of agricultural workers. Additionally, the low rate of pay for these workers leaves them at the subsistence level of existence. As a partial remedy, they often look for work in agricultural areas outside of their immediate communities. This movement outside of their immediate employment sectors has a long-term deleterious effect on adjacent agricultural labor markets, resulting in an economic domino effect within the agricultural labor market. Therefore, once they begin to move into adjacent agricultural areas, an automatic glut is caused in a previously stable agricultural labor market. This process continues and more and more agricultural workers are forced to take to the road.[2]

This forced migration results in the creation of a new set of social and economic problems for the agricultural worker and his family. In many cases they are required to leave their wives and children at home and embark on a migratory search for employment opportunities in

unfamiliar labor markets. In effect, the migratory farm
worker is simply an individual who is unable to find sufficient employment opportunities in his home community.
He is forced to travel or migrate in order to feed, clothe,
and otherwise maintain his family.[3] Clearly they are vic-
tims of the cyclical nature of the agricultural environment.
In a geographic and deterministic sense, the agricultural
worker is forced to extend his original employment radius
of ten or 15 miles to perhaps 200 to 400 or more miles.[4]

Over the years, seasonal migratory farm workers
have developed certain patterns of behavior and certain
geographic routes which have matured into established
migratory streams. In practice, the seasonal natures of
the various agricultural crops determine these routes, and
the workers' time of arrival and departure from the most
lucrative agricultural areas of the state. The seasonal
migratory farm worker always has the personal consolation
that he has a place that he can call home when the agricultural season has ended.

Historically, certain agricultural workers do not
have a community that they can rightfully call home at
the end of the season. This group will be referred to as
continuous migratory farm workers. When the harvest
season is over, they remain in the vicinity of their last
place of employment. In most cases, this is not a matter
of personal choice or convenience but results from the fact
that they do not have the funds or reliable transportation
to make the trip to their point of origin. They are relegated to a nomadic lifestyle as a direct result of the
vicissitudes of the agricultural industry.

FARM WORKER TYPES

While the seasonal and migratory concepts provide an
indication of the general instability of agricultural work
and the geographic mobility that is often required, there
are also concepts that account for the agricultural workers'
participation in farm work according to their degree of
personal involvement with, and their immediate dependence
on, this type of work for their livelihood. Given these
observations, it appears that agricultural workers can be
understood best in terms of their personal dependence on
work in the fields for their main source of income. Their
variable level of dependency can be measured and described

in a number of ways. For example, one can assess whether agricultural work is their principal source of income on a year-to-year or a month-to-month basis. In this manner, a host of sociological categories can be generated to describe and analyze their fluctuating level of dependence on agricultural work.

THE PROFESSIONAL FARM WORKER

The discussion of farm worker types will initially begin with a description of those individuals who are most intimately involved in agricultural work, the professional farm worker. They are completely involved in agricultural work on a full-time basis and it serves as their only means of support. This is the sense in which the term professional is used. But, this does not imply a personal dedication to agricultural work as a viable career option, rather, indicates a high level of dependence on farm work as a direct result of the lack of appropriate skills and/or opportunity to become involved in other aspects of the American economy.

Perhaps the most prominent characteristic of the professional farm worker is the fact that he works directly for the grower. He takes his orders from the grower and is required to answer to him for the proper performance of his work assignments. This direct contact stems from the fact that he is hired directly by the grower and is often referred to as the grower's hired hand.[5]

Often, the grower will place a good deal of responsibility for the operation of the farm in his hands; this is particularly true when the grower is absent for a few days. In many situations, the professional farm worker will actually run the complete outdoor operation of the farm, whether the grower is present or not. In these situations, the grower attends to the business and administrative matters and his hired hands oversee the daily operation of the farm. Needless to say, professional farm workers are very conscientious in the performance of their duties and the grower can depend on their dedication to the completion of an assigned task.

The professional farm worker also has the requisite knowledge and skill level to operate every piece of farm equipment and machinery. A high degree of mechanical ability is required of someone in this position as he will

generally perform the major portion of the scheduled maintenance on all agricultural equipment. In addition, during the slow periods of the winter months he is occupied,
on a full-time basis, with engine overhauls and other
major maintenance projects. It is also his duty to supervise fellow workers who are hired on a temporary basis
during the busy harvest season. In this capacity he
serves as the grower's foreman in the supervision of all
temporary help.

In many cases the professional farm worker and his
family will live in housing provided by the grower and
this is economically advantageous because in some cases he
is not required to pay rent. This provides an additional
benefit inasmuch as he does not have to be concerned with
transportation to and from the job site. This also means
that he can take all of his meals at home, which is an
additional saving. Living on the farm also means that he
can work longer hours on any given day. And it is not
unusual to find that he will work an average of 12 to 14
hours a day, six to seven days a week for eight to nine
months of the productive agricultural season. During the
off season, he may only work five days a week, eight
hours a day.[6]

Another important characteristic of the professional
farm worker is that he is often employed by the same
grower for a number of years and consequently develops
a close relationship with his employer. Some have worked
for the same grower for 15, 20, or more years. Many
began their employment with a grower as a bracero and
have continued working for the same person for all of
these years.

THE SEMI-PROFESSIONAL FARM WORKER

Generally, the semi-professional farm worker spends
the majority of his time working in the agricultural industry and farm labor is the major source of economic support
for his family. However, he will seek out other employment opportunities during the slack periods in the agricultural season. For example, he will work in agriculture
for eight or nine months out of the year and during the
other three or four months, he will secure a temporary job
as a mechanic's helper or as a delivery truck driver in
one of the local communities. He is very ambitious and

will invariably look for nonagricultural employment when the seasonal unemployment rate is high in the local agricultural job market.

The most obvious difference between the professional and the semi-professional farm worker is that the latter will generally find work in a nonagricultural environment during slack periods of the year. The professional farm worker does not need to look for work outside of agriculture during these slack periods because he has a steady source of income.

Like the professional farm worker, the semi-professional worker is very conscientious in the performance of assigned duties and occasionally will also supervise the work of temporary farm hands. The major difference between the two types is that the semi-professional farm worker has not been employed by the same grower for as long a period of time as has the professional farm worker, therefore, he has not acquired all of the skills and responsibilities of the professional farm worker. And he does not have the job security achieved by the professional farm worker. However, with an increase in tenure and the availability of a permanent full-time position, he will obtain job security and associated responsibilities connected with the position of professional farm worker.

The configuration of duties and responsibilities that adhere to the positions of professional and semi-professional farm workers reveals the existence of an occupational hierarchy within the agricultural labor force. Here, job advancement, job tenure, job security, and the delegation of responsibilities are determined on the basis of the length of time on the job, the development of occupational skills, and the ability to work independent of direct supervision. In effect, occupational mobility in the agricultural industry is based on longevity and the ability of the agricultural worker to execute the duties and responsibilities at each level of the occupational hierarchy.[7]

THE AMATEUR FARM WORKER

The amateur farm worker spends approximately half of his time working in agriculture and the remainder of his time employed outside of agriculture. For all practical purposes, he is caught between his involvement in agriculture and his participation in some other industry; in a peculiar sense, he is a "marginal man" to the agricultural sector. In most cases, the amateur farm worker will work in agriculture during the more lucrative periods of the year, during the harvest season. This convenient arrangement allows him to log the maximum number of hours on the job thereby earning the most money for his time in the agricultural labor force. During the slack and off-season times, he will seek out employment in other areas, such as in the service or industrial sectors of the economy.

The amateur farm worker may work in a variety of crops for five or six months of the year and spend the rest of his time working at a variety of odd jobs such as in an auto body repair shop, a service station, or in a warehouse. In the spring, when employment opportunities begin to develop in agriculture, he will leave his temporary job and earn more money picking fruit. The fact that he can earn a better income in agriculture during the peak season does not mean that agricultural employment pays more; it simply indicates that he can work more hours per day and, as a result, he can earn more money on a weekly basis than he could expect to earn at a nonagricultural job. This yearly transition into agriculture is also spurred on because more money can be earned if harvest laborers are paid on a piece rate basis.

While the amateur farm worker may be hired directly by the grower, he usually receives his orders and works directly under the supervision of a professional farm worker. Generally, he is well versed in the fundamental aspects of agricultural work and has the basic skills necessary to operate farm tractors, loaders, trucks, and other pieces of agricultural equipment. However, his knowledge does not encompass the general maintenance required to keep such machinery in operating condition.

One of the most outstanding characteristics of the amateur farm worker is that he will usually work for a variety of growers during his brief tenure in the agricultural industry. Therefore, he will continually strive to maximize his income within this short period of employment and understandably is very selective in the type of agricultural employment he will accept. For the most part, he prefers to work deciduous crops during the harvest; however, he will work as a tractor operator or find employment in one of the local canneries.

THE DILETTANTE FARM WORKER

The dilettante farm worker is distinguished by the fact that he has a regular source of employment or some other obligations outside of the agricultural industry but nonetheless manages to take two or three months away from his regular job to work full-time in agriculture. For the most part, high school students, college students, and housewives fit into this category. Students will often work in the fruit and vegetable harvests during the summer months and return to school in the fall. Likewise, many housewives work exclusively during the tomato harvest or in one of the local canneries. Consequently, they only work three or four months out of the year in the agricultural industry. This group does represent a very important segment of the total agricultural labor force despite the fact that they are only part-time workers. Overall, they seem pleased with this arrangement as this type of work fulfills their need for extra income during specific periods of the year.

DISCUSSION OF IDEAL TYPES

Thus far we have focused on a set of general agricultural terms that are useful if one wishes to gain a fundamental understanding of the agricultural labor force. Terms such as seasonal migratory farm worker and amateur farm worker describe the agricultural labor force according to the various levels and degrees of involvement and participation by certain individuals. However, now the Mexican and Mexican-American agricultural worker in California will be studied in more detail with regard to his distinctive characteristics.

Undoubtedly, there are a variety of ways to describe and categorize the agricultural labor force of California. Perhaps the analysis should be made within the context of the most pervasive issue involving the agricultural worker, whether he is legal or illegal. This approach seems very appropriate since the popular stereotype is held that the majority of Mexican farm workers are illegal aliens. By confronting this issue directly, I hope to demonstrate the overall complexity of this issue and, as a result, make this old stereotype meaningless.

The overall discussion and analysis of Mexican farm workers will be based on three broad categories: (1) the illegal Mexican national farmworker, (2) the legal Mexican national farm worker, and (3) the Mexican-American farm worker. Within each of these categories, I shall provide an examination and sociological analysis of specific types of Mexican agricultural workers, not only in terms of their legality or illegality but also according to their degree of participation in the agricultural force.

ILLEGAL MEXICAN NATIONAL FARM WORKERS

These shall be defined as individuals who immigrate to this country to work in the agricultural industry but have chosen illegal means to do so. These agricultural workers are commonly referred to as illegal aliens and, in more sympathetic circles, are referred to as undocumented workers.[8] As a group they have few legal rights in this country and are subject to arrest and deportation at any time. Four distinct categories of subclassifications have been developed that best describe this group of illegal Mexican farm workers: the Border Jumpers, the Adventurers, the Innovators, and the Social Climbers.

THE BORDER JUMPERS

This particular group of illegal Mexican farm workers crosses the border illegally, works in an adjacent agricultural area, and then returns home to Mexico at the end of a day's work—hence, the appellative, Border Jumper. The individuals usually live with their families in one of the twin cities found along the United States-Mexican border—San Diego-Tijuana, Calexico-Mexicali.

Access to the plentiful job opportunities in the United States labor market, particularly in California agriculture, presents no significant problem for these Border Jumpers as they have a variety of established methods, both legal and illegal, of penetrating the international border. One of the most popular legal methods of crossing the border is to obtain a 72-hour visitor's pass.[9] The intended purpose of this pass (which can be obtained at any official border crossing point) is to allow Mexican nationals to visit their friends and relatives in this country and to purchase products on this side of the border. However, the Border Jumper often will use his visitor's pass to obtain legal entry into this country to work for a few days in the agricultural fields of southern California. In fact, the visitor's pass as an Immigration and Naturalization Service (INS) policy has been viewed by some as " a back door bracero program to benefit employers at the expense of the resident poor."[10] But this practice is blatantly illegal since a person who holds a visitor's pass is strictly prohibited from working while visiting in the United States. Commenting on this point, "Sheldon Green, counsel for California Rural Legal Assistance, has estimated that it is used for 70–80 percent of all illegal entries and legal entries for an illegal purpose."[11]

Generally, the Border Jumper will enter the United States in the prescribed legal manner and, once on this side of the border, he will mail his 72–hour visitor's pass to his home address in Mexico. By taking this precaution, he knows that his border crossing permit is in safe keeping at home. If he should have the misfortune of being apprehended by the INS, he can always testify that he entered the United States illegally and the INS will automatically send him back across the border. By this method, he only suffers a temporary inconvenience and is able to use his visitor's pass to gain legal entry into the United States and begin the same procedure over again. Actually, "Aliens who enter the United States illegally are subject to criminal penalties, but they are rarely applied against them. The first violation calls for a $500 fine and up to six months' imprisonment. A second offense is a felony, punishable by up to two years' imprisonment and a fine of $1,000."[12] But Vernon Briggs, a noted authority, points out that, "Over 95 percent of those aliens who are apprehended by the INS are simply returned to Mexico by the most expedient form of transportation. Less than 5 percent of the illegal Mexicans are subjected by the INS to formal deportation proceedings that would render any subsequent entry a felony."[13]

The most popular illegal method of entering the United States is simply to walk across the border, using one of the well–marked foot paths. This jaunt is usually taken in the early morning hours to avoid detection and apprehension by the INS forces and to insure the ready availability of transportation to the tomato and lettuce fields of California and Arizona. This is a relatively simple process as the Border Jumper knows from years of experience. Some American growers have made all of the necessary arrangements to have buses and/or trucks waiting for his entry into this country at predetermined locations.[14] The Border Jumper can leave his home in Mexico at 4 a.m. and be assured that he will be working in the fields of California or Arizona by 5:30 or 6 a.m. the same day.

For the most part, the Border Jumpers are men from the ages of 16 to 44, either married or single.[15] One authority has estimated that "About half of the Mexican illegals are married and almost all support relatives living in Mexico."[16] In their study, North and Houstoun have estimated that for each illegal Mexican national working in this country, they are supporting an average of 5.4 dependents in Mexico.[17] While the majority of Border Jumpers are men, there does exist a very small percentage of single women who also make this trip to the agricultural fields of the North. In most cases they make this trip on a daily basis. However, there are others who have made the appropriate arrangements and are able to work for six days out of each week in the border areas of California, return home on Saturday afternoon, and prepare to start a new work week on Monday morning. But it does appear that the majority of workers prefer to commute on a daily basis and, in this manner, can have the best of both worlds.

Generally, they limit their work to a 75- or 100-mile radius of the border. This makes their commute easier and more practical. One of the most deleterious effects of their confinement to this agricultural corridor is that these workers have a depressive effect on the rate of pay for agricultural work in the areas. Wages keep to a minimum level and some growers pay their illegal Mexican workers below the prevailing minimum wage.[18]

In his recent study of labor conditions in the greater Southwest, Fogel found that "The lowest wages and the greatest concentrations of illegal employment are found in agriculture and in nonfarm firms which are likely to be small, nonunion, and either not covered or in frequent violation of fair labor standards law."[19]

A second consequence of their illegal activities is that they usurp job opportunities that would normally be available to local legal residents who desire to work in agriculture but are systematically denied their legitimate right to work. However, the principal culprits are the local growers and the labor contractors who prefer to hire Border Jumpers over the available legal residents. Their preference for hiring them stems from the fact that they will invariably work for less than the prevailing rate of pay acceptable to legal residents. An additional advantage to local growers and labor contractors is that they will rarely complain about working conditions or safety hazards on the job. By the same token, illegal Mexican farm workers are not likely to organize to secure a decent wage and demand humane working conditions, as would most probably be the case with legal residents in the same situation.

The case, as it exists today in the agricultural corridor along the United States–Mexican border, is such that job opportunities are often better for illegal Mexican nationals than for those who are here legally, are American citizens, and who desire to work in the agricultural industry. It is obvious that the presence of illegal Mexican farm workers stirs up a number of problems between themselves and those who are here legally and desire to work in agriculture. An additional problem is that the organization of farm workers into unions is made much more difficult since the most effective tool available to agricultural unions, the threat of a strike, is made ineffective. The growers in these border areas realize, through years of experience, that they can limit the effectiveness of any strike effort by importing anxious strike breakers from just across the border.

The Border Jumpers, as a group, are probably the most alien of all of the illegal Mexican nationals in our agricultural fields. They are socially isolated from the members of the local Mexican-American communities because they are often provided with substandard housing by the grower who employs them or by the labor contractor who hires them. As a result, they rarely leave the farm or labor camp; this is particularly true if they spend the entire week working in the fields and return home only on weekends. For the most part, they are not received very warmly by the members of the Mexican-American community for the above reasons.

THE ADVENTURERS

The Adventurers represent a group of illegal Mexican agricultural workers generally composed of young married and unmarried males between the ages of 16 and 30 who venture into the agricultural areas of the Southwest in search of employment opportunities. For the most part, they are most interested in earning the greatest amount of money in the shortest period of time. Consequently, they are willing to work long hours under difficult conditions. In many instances they will gladly accept less than the prevailing hourly wage for their labor; they are more concerned with the total number of hours that they can work per day and the number of days per week than with the hourly pay rate. In addition, they accept poor housing conditions willingly with few, if any, complaints.

Primarily, they reside on the property of their employer which is advantageous to both parties involved. This arrangement allows them to avoid detection for a greater period of time and results in a lower level of subsistence. It is not at all uncommon to find these Adventurers living in barns, outhouses, and converted chicken coops. Their housing is inexpensive and they manage to prepare their own meals, further reducing their daily living expenses.

Socially, the Adventurers are isolated from the established members of the Mexican-American community but nonetheless always live in a gregarious environment. Many prefer their isolation for a number of valid reasons. It protects them from the possibility of deportation but it also presents certain economic and social disadvantages. In many cases they must pay an intermediary for any social contact that may be required with the outside world beyond their labor camp. For example, they have to pay someone to go into town for food and supplies and they also have to pay someone to cash their checks or to help them buy money orders, and so on. In addition to the economic expense involved, a social stigma exists that is attached to the use of intermediaries. The employment of an intercessor draws attention to the Adventurers' presence in areas where they are required to conduct economic transactions, such as in banks, post offices, stores, and other places. Therefore, they often place themselves in jeopardy of being detected when they must leave the security of the grower's property.

In the opinion of many of the legal resident agricultural workers, the Adventurers are often looked upon with disdain. In many cases these single or unattached males who are working here illegally are viewed as the principal cause of the prevailing subsistence wages paid in the agricultural industry. In numerous conversations with legal resident farm workers time and time again it was found that one of the major reasons for their low rate of pay, in their opinion, was the fact that the illegal Mexican farm workers were willing to work for less than the prevailing wage. Additionally, many felt that the illegal farm workers also deprived them of their own job opportunities.

Along with being blamed for the low rate of pay in the agricultural industry, and usurping of unskilled agricultural jobs, the Adventurers are ostracized for their misbehavior and scandalous conduct in the Mexican-American community. Since they are usually unattached or single, it is not uncommon that they are given to a great deal of heavy drinking. The prevailing community prejudice is that they drink and engage in violent behavior in local Mexican bars. The local Mexican-American residents resent this rowdy behavior and feel that the Adventurers give their community a bad reputation that leads to furthering the belief that all individuals of Mexican heritage are given to drunkenness and violent behavior.

One curious characteristic of the Adventurers is that they are not particularly concerned whether they are deported or not. It seems that the very threat of deportation lends a sense of excitement and intrigue to their daily existence; at least this is the general impression that one receives from conversation with them.[20] Practically speaking, one must consider that if an Adventurer has worked a minimum of three or four weeks in this country, then he has, according to his point of view, justified the trouble and expense involved in his illegal migration from Mexico. This is particularly true in agricultural areas where a specialty crop is produced. In this case he can plan his sojourn to California so that it will coincide with the harvest of a particular crop, as frequently occurs with the grape harvest in the Napa Valley. During the grape harvest he can earn anywhere from $65 to $75 a day, and even more with experience, on a piecework basis. Since he is required to work every day during the grape harvest, it is easy to understand how an Adventurer could earn a sizable income in three or four weeks.

It is common knowledge in the various agricultural areas of California that the INS rarely makes an appearance

in the Mexican agricultural community during the critical
harvest season. In fact, the local lore has it that the
INS serves as a transportation department for the illegals
at the end of the harvest season. If the Adventurer is
deported before his time, it is a relatively simple matter
for him to return to his place of employment in a matter
of days. A variation occurs when an Adventurer who is
ready to return to Mexico will purposely walk along a main
highway with full knowledge that the California Highway
Patrol will stop and detain him until the INS agents arrive
and provide him with free transportation to la frontera
(the border). Recently it has become common practice for
them to secure transportation to the San Francisco Airport
and purchase a ticket on the midnight flight to either
Guadalajara or Mexico City. In this manner, they can be
home after a successful harvest season in a matter of
hours.

THE INNOVATORS

The most conspicuous characteristic of the Innovators
is that they travel and work in family groups. For the
most part, they are primarily migratory and strictly seasonal in their illegal endeavors. They travel from one
agricultural region to another, following the crops as they
come into fruition. Some track the seasonal cycle of specific crops on a yearly basis, while others resort to this
pattern only when there is some pressing financial need in
the family.
While they do travel in family groups, this does not
necessarily indicate that all of the members of each family
participate in work-related activities or that the traveling
group constitutes one nuclear family. Generally, only
those who are old enough and mature enough to work in
the fields are allowed to make the long and arduous trip
to the North. As a result, the Innovators usually consist
of adults and any older children who are capable of working in the fields, while the younger family members are
left at home with relatives or compadres. As a group,
they constitute a very efficient economic unit.
In situations where husband and wife travel together,
both male and female children are allowed to accompany
them provided they are old enough and physically capable
of working in the fields. Usually when the mother is not

able to travel, only the husband and his mature sons will make the pilgrimage. Without the presence of the female head of household, a very sharp sexual division of labor develops. In other variations, certain members of the extended family will also participate in this economic venture. It is not uncommon to find situations where the male members of two or three related families will make the trip North as one cohesive economic unit. In other situations, two brothers will bring their families with them and work the season as a communal group.

In some instances, Innovators are actually recruited for agricultural work in California while still in their home communities. One crew leader can bring several families with him from Mexico and follow the crops on a seasonal basis.[21] In other situations, one family member may have the necessary vehicle for transportation, the experience, knowledge, and proper connections necessary to find suitable employment for members of such an expedition. By this method, all of the required economic transactions are retained within the family.

Usually the Innovators are isolated from the members of the local Mexican-American community as they are provided housing by the grower for whom they work, or by the labor contractor who initially recruited them in Mexico, or by one of the local labor contractors. Otherwise, they will locate housing in an established government camp which is the very best in terms of maintenance and general availability of facilities. An additional reason for their isolation is that they rarely have their own means of transportation and therefore must rely on other people for their transportation needs. Consequently, they frequently pay someone to take them into town to buy food and to secure other essential items.

As is the case with other illegals, the Innovators are not looked upon favorably by the local legal resident farm workers. Once again, they are viewed as individuals who take jobs in the agricultural industry at the best hourly wage or piece rate that they can negotiate, whether it conforms to minimum wage or not. In many cases they will accept less than the minimum wage, contributing to the general depression in local wages and, in the process, drive local agricultural workers out of their own labor market. This partially explains why they are not held in high esteem by local farm workers.

One of the reasons that they are able and willing to work below the minimum wage is that the cost of living in Mexico is so much lower than it is here and therefore the United States dollar is worth a great deal more in Mexico. Another important consideration is that their dependency ratio is kept very low or nonexistent during their stay in this country. Most illegal farm workers are able to earn a relatively high income (by their standards) and are simultaneously able to survive on a small budget. This means that they are able to save a substantial portion of their income, which they usually send to their families in Mexico. This situation frequently occurs among Innovators as most are self-supporting wage earners and are members of a nuclear or extended family. Consequently, their overhead and their subsistence level while they are in this country are very low and they can save a large portion of their weekly income. It is easy to see that if a couple and their three mature children work for ten hours a day, six days a week, for three months, they can build up a substantial savings, even at $3.00 an hour.

THE CLIMBERS

This group of illegal Mexican farm workers is generally composed of men between the ages of 30 and 50. Most are married and have large families in Mexico but work in the agricultural fields of this country on a regular, seasonal basis. Their most distinctive characteristic is that they work in the United States in order to improve their economic situation in Mexico; hence, the name, the Climbers.

They are a very serious group of individuals as they are ambitious, goal-oriented, and are determined to improve their lot in life. They are willing to leave their families in Mexico and work in the agricultural areas of the Southwest for three to seven months of the year. However, some do spend nine or ten months working in this country. One of their most distinctive characteristics is that they invariably return to their agricultural jobs year after year and, as a result, have established a certain degree of job security with particular growers; therefore, many can rely on having a steady job when they return from Mexico each year. I encountered one Climber who has spent nine or ten months out of each year working in

the vineyards of the Napa Valley for the past 20 years.
This individual has ten children and a wife to support in
Mexico. He is a fairly well-to-do person in his native
village and has a nice home with modern conveniences, two
cars, acreage (he pays several members of his village to
operate and maintain his farm), and two sons away at
college.

An outstanding trait of the Climbers is that they
spend their time in California with relatives, close friends
(amigos de confianza), or compadres. They live in a
stable family environment while they are working in the
agricultural industry--usually with a brother, a first
cousin (primo hermano), or a close friend who has obtained
legal status in this country and also has a steady and
secure job (probably in agriculture) and has a relatively
permanent residence. Given these domestic ties, they blend
into the family environment and actually become a part of
the community in which they reside for a major portion of
the year and generally lead a very sedate and sober existence.

There are a number of means by which they are able
to maintain a regular source of employment despite their
illegal status in this country. One important source of
security against detection by the INS is that they are
actually members of an established family in the local
Mexican-American community. Consequently, they are not
easily detected by the authorities. Another important consideration is that they have regular employment with one
or two employers, whom they have probably known and
trusted for a number of years. This synergistic relationship between the Climber and his employer provides a high
degree of job security resulting in a low probability that
his illegal status will be detected in this country.

In addition to blending into the Mexican-American
community and having a steady source of employment with
one or two local growers, many function very well in an
Anglo environment and do not call undue attention to themselves. In many cases, Climbers speak and understand
enough English and therefore conduct the majority of social and economic transactions that are essential to survival in this society. They can undertake such basic
transactions as marketing, cashing a check at the bank,
purchasing money orders, and so on, all without outside
assistance. Climbers do not appear anomalous in public
places. Sometimes they have developed so much self-

confidence that they have opened savings accounts, purchased used cars, obtained valid drivers' licenses, and
attend and participate in various meetings of the local
Mexican-American community.

In addition to these social and economic characteristics, which tend to make the Climbers inconspicuous in
public and to the local authorities, it is also true that
many have a variety of illicit means by which they can
avoid detection. Of primary importance is the availability
and purchase of falsified documents which provide them
with an aura of legitimacy. The most important counterfeit document available to these illegals is the so-called
"green card" (actually it is INS document #I-151). This
bogus document can be purchased in most Mexican-American
communities and elsewhere in the Southwest. The cost will
range from a low of $150 to a high of about $300. But
this is a relatively small amount to pay for the security
and the protection that the green card provides the illegal
agricultural worker.[22]

Socially, the Climber is acceptable to the members
of the agricultural community since he blends in well, one
might say "passes" with the established members of Mexican-
American society. This is particularly true since the
Climber is a hard worker, a responsible person, and,
most important, he does not create any problems for his
employer or for the members of the local community. However, the most significant factor, relative to the local labor
market, is that he does not work for less than the prevailing wage scale. Climbers expect to receive, and indeed
do receive, the usual wage rate for their labor in the
fields, just as the local Mexican-American farm workers
maintain this expectation. Furthermore, they will rarely
work as strike breakers; in fact, most are adamant supporters of the unionization of all agricultural workers.
This is a very important consideration in understanding
their general acceptance in the Mexican-American agricultural community, particularly in view of the fact that illegals are often accused of depressing wages in the agricultural industry, taking jobs away from local legal residents, and serving as strike breakers.

The sociological vignette of the Climber as simply
an illegal agricultural worker appears, on the contrary,
to represent a situation in which this individual has
assimilated and has accepted the American middle-class
ethos of "deferred gratification" to the nth degree. This

assertion is supported by the following sociological observations: They are industrious, ambitious, self-confident,
goal-oriented, basically upwardly mobile, and more than
willing to make whatever sacrifices are necessary to improve the socio-economic position of their families. These
observations are sustained by the fact that they willingly
make an annual pilgrimage to the agricultural areas of
the Southwest, work for six or seven days a week, six to
ten months out of each year, live at a subsistence level,
and send the major portion of their weekly income to their
families in Mexico. In addition, they willingly endure
all of the back-breaking work in agriculture, not to men-
tion the loneliness of separation from their families, in
order to provide them with a better standard of living and
prepare their sons and daughters for a brighter future in
Mexico. In effect the climbers epitomize Schneider and
Sysgaard's portrayal of deferred gratification.[23] In her
firsthand study of Mexican agricultural workers in this
country, Sasha Lewis has also taken note of the immense
personal sacrifice that these Climbers must make but has
also observed that the immigration process can become a
vicious circle. That is, once a migrant worker has married and established a family, he must go to the North
and work in order to support his family and perhaps even
his aged parents. She makes the observation that the
migrant worker or Climber

> returns once a year, or more frequently if
> he can afford it, to visit his family, espe-
> cially for the Christmas celebrations. He
> will spend the next ten or twelve years
> mostly working in the United States, sending
> money back to his family and hoping to earn
> enough money perhaps to buy a small farm
> of his own.[24]

LEGAL MEXICAN NATIONAL FARM WORKERS

Thus far this discussion has focused on the various
groups of illegal Mexican nationals employed in the agricultural industry; however, we shall turn our attention to
that broad category of individuals whom we shall refer to
as Legal Mexican national farm workers. These are Mexican nationals who are in the United States legally and

have a legitimate right to live here and work in the agricultural industry. In common phraseology, they are referred to as "green card workers" or "documented Mexican
nationals." Within the broad category of legal Mexican
national farm workers three distinct subcategories will be
differentiated: the Commuters, the Opportunists, and the
Loyalists.

THE COMMUTERS

The term <u>Commuters</u> refers to those who have chosen
to live in Mexico and still maintain the legal right to
work in the United States as a result of their green card
status. It is a relatively simple matter for Commuters to
arrive at an official border crossing station, display their
green cards, and arrive at their regular place of employment right on schedule each morning. When the work day
is completed, they cross the international bridge and
spend their evenings with their families. In the 1970s
when the INS conducted a study of this situation, they
found that the "number of green carders who cross the
border 'daily' to work in the United States have ranged
from 50,000 to 70,000 people."[25]
Various studies indicate that the greater proportion
of Commuters have jobs that are directly related to agriculture, while a smaller percentage hold jobs as domestic
workers. Still others are employed in various factories
and assembly plants on this side of the border. However,
once they develop certain occupational skills and a greater
facility with the English language, they will gradually
make the transition from agricultural work to the better
paying jobs with the attendant employment security available in the industrial sector of the American economy.
Without doubt, Commuters have their greatest impact
on the agricultural labor force within a 100-mile radius of
the U.S.-Mexican border.[26] The result is that a large
proportion of the agricultural workers in the Imperial and
Coachella Valleys are Mexican nationals with green card
status who work in the California agricultural industry
and live in the various border towns.
The Commuter's trip from Mexico to the United
States is greatly facilitated inasmuch as transportation
from the border crossing station to his place of employment is often provided by local growers or by local farm

labor contractors. In other instances, they will car pool to the various agricultural areas, and in some cases they will make arrangements to stay in housing provided by the grower or the labor contractor during the week and return home on weekends. With the income earned in this country, the Commuter provides a rather comfortable living for his family in Mexico.

While a good deal of controversy centers around the negative effect of Commuters on local wages, it appears that they do not necessarily have a negative impact on the wage scale in the local agricultural areas along the U.S.-Mexican border. They realize that they must provide a living for their families on a year-round basis and are primarily interested in obtaining the maximum amount of money for their labor in the agricultural industry. Commuters have been strong supporters of recent efforts to unionize agricultural workers and many are active members in the United Farm Workers Union (UFW). This is probably one of the principal reasons why the UFW has been so successful in its unionization efforts in the Imperial and Coachella Valleys in recent years. It is certain that without their ardent support, the efforts of Cesar Chavez to organize agricultural workers in these areas of California would have gone down in certain defeat.

For the most part, Commuters have remained relatively isolated from the local Mexican-American communities. The reason is that many return home daily or else live in farm labor camps or on the property of local growers and return home on weekends. However, since they do not have to contend with the constant fear of detection and deportation, they are prone to patronize local bars, stores, and restaurants to a much greater extent than would be the case among illegal agricultural workers. They are also more likely to put a greater percentage of their income back into the local economic market, than would be true among illegals.

Commuters are generally married men with families to support and are between the ages of 25 to 54.[27] They are, for the most part, very mature, conscientious, dependable workers without whom the agricultural industry, particularly in the border areas, would suffer greatly. One important reason they are such good workers is that they have had to endure a certain amount of bureaucratic red tape and personal sacrifice to obtain their cherished green card status. This sets them off as an elite group of farm workers among Mexican nationals.

THE OPPORTUNISTS

The term Opportunists refers to a group of Mexican nationals who have managed to obtain the appropriate documents and prefer to live and work in Mexico for most of the year but travel to the United States and work in the agricultural industry for a few months out of each year.

The most marked characteristic of the Opportunist is that he is a very hard working and ambitious individual who is not satisfied with what he has at the present time and is determined to improve his situation in the future, and thereby provide even greater opportunities for his children. The typical Opportunist is married and has several children and perhaps is in the process of buying and/or building a house for his family. It is also likely that he has a small business in Mexico or is a skilled craftsperson. In addition, he probably owns several plots of agricultural property which he tends diligently in his spare time. During the cultivating and harvest seasons, he hires extra help as needed.

His presence in his community in Mexico is also conspicuous as he owns a station wagon or a truck and is one of the few individuals who can afford to send his older children to la secundaria (high school), which, in most cases, is a boarding school in a distant town. In their study of Mexican agricultural workers in California, Sultan and Enos point out that they "have established themselves as community leaders and major land owners with investments made from earnings in this country."[28]

The key to their success is that they have taken the necessary steps to secure green card status for themselves and certain members of their family, permitting them to travel to the agricultural fields of the Southwest. Their trip north will usually begin around mid-April and they will work the various crops as they come into season. Generally they will return to Mexico in late September or early October when the harvest season is virtually past. Of greater importance is the consideration that many return by September in order to supervise and work the harvest of their own crops.

The Opportunist will invariably travel north as part of a family unit or in groups, particularly if they are members of an extended family from the same community. Sometimes the entire family will make the trip, but in most cases the dependent children are left in the care of relatives. Their homes and property are also maintained and protected by their relatives; consequently, they have no need to be concerned about their worldly goods while they are working in the North.

Once they arrive in the agricultural fields, they can be divided into two distinct groups: those who follow the crops in a migratory pattern and those who travel to one particular agricultural area where they are well known and return yearly. Since a detailed description of the migratory Opportunist has already been provided, we shall focus here on the stationary Opportunist.

The most significant characteristic of the stationary Opportunists is that they specialize in one or two crops and return to one particular agricultural area each year. They have established close ties with local growers and are guaranteed regular employment year after year. In some cases the grower provides them with housing; otherwise, they are familiar with the local housing market and locate appropriate housing with little difficulty. Generally the first family to arrive in the area will secure housing for the other families who will arrive a week or so later. This is particularly true in both government-sponsored and private labor camps.

For the most part, the Opportunists are not socially isolated, particularly if they locate housing in a Mexican-American community. The principal reason for their gregarious nature is that their family structure requires that they not only associate with members of the Mexican-American community but also with the institutional representatives of Anglo society. The most common social contacts occur when they purchase household staples, attend church services, and, in certain situations, when their children attend school in the local community. For these and other practical reasons they frequently communicate and interact with members of the host community. In the process of social intercourse many are accepted by the established members of the community and those with authority in the Anglo world.

The Opportunist has not acquired a reputation for working for less than the prevailing wage and so has not encountered the stigma that is often attributed to those who do. He considers himself to be a man of honor and is willing to do an honest day's work, but he also expects to be paid a decent wage for his assiduous devotion to the task. Following along in this philosophy, Opportunists are generally in favor of the unionization of agricultural workers and can usually be depended upon to support a farm worker's union. However, some do not take a particularly favorable view of unionization. This attitude stems from the fact that they reside in Mexico for the major portion of the year and are, hence, unable to obtain seniority in the union. As a result, they often feel locked out by established agricultural unions.

Briefly, they have obtained a legal standing in this country and return year after year to work in the agricultural industry with the idea that they will return home with a substantial savings. However, their main objective and their raison d'etre in the fields is to improve their own socio-economic conditions in their home communities and to provide more opportunities and a brighter future for their children.

THE LOYALISTS

The appellation Loyalists has been reserved for those Mexican nationals who have obtained green card status and who have made their homes in the United States and present themselves as legal resident aliens. The Loyalists are content to spend the major portion of their time living and working in the agricultural industry and have decided to become permanent members of the Mexican-American community.

For the most part, they have spent a number of years working in the Southwest, usually a minimum of eight to ten years. In addition, some of their children are American citizens by birth and in many instances their offspring have received all, or at least most, of their education in local schools. In some cases they are also making mortgage payments on a home. Briefly, the Loyalist has established firm roots in American soil and views his future and the future of his children in terms of the development of American society.

Perhaps the most important reason that they remain in this country is that they have a permanent and secure job that provides them with a source of regular income. This links closely to their diligence and dependability as workers and as a result they have no problems locating permanent employment with local growers who are eager to attract and keep workers of their caliber and potential. Many growers pay them a better than average wage which enables the Loyalists to provide a higher standard of living for their families.

The Loyalist soon discovers that he has two very important advantages over other agricultural workers and over his friends and relatives in Mexico. He has developed job security; therefore, he can count on a regular monthly salary. Over the years the Loyalist determines that his lot in life is much improved by his continuous employment in Southwestern agriculture and, in time, a reversal of original employment patterns occur. The Loyalists spend the major portion of their time living and working in the United States and return to Mexico for short visits.

In addition to the advantages of job security and a regular salary, the Loyalist is also pressured into prolonging his stay in this country by his children who like their situation here much better than they did in their native villages in Mexico. Sometimes half of the children (if not all) were born in the United States and have received most of their education in local schools. Hence they are accustomed to the American way of life. The familial pressure from these children to remain in the United States becomes particularly strong and most apparent during adolescence. This reaction is largely due to his children having developed a complete network of friends and acquaintances whom they have no desire to leave. The Loyalists' offspring serve as a social anchor for his continued residence in this country.

Loyalists do not adversely affect the prevailing wage scale as they often receive a salary above the wage scale of other agricultural workers. This is primarily a result of the stable relationship developed with their employers over the years. They have proven time after time that they can accept and manage responsibility on the job; consequently, their remuneration is concomitantly higher than that of the typical agricultural worker.

Of all the workers in this typology, the Loyalist has the greatest potential for becoming an American citizen. After years of living and working in this country, he and his wife realize that they have become an integral part of a new community and that their children are also attached to the American way of life; often, they have only vague childhood memories of life in Mexico. It is at this point that they make a decision, with the encouragement of their American-born children, to become American citizens.

MEXICAN-AMERICAN FARM WORKERS

A final broad category of agricultural workers in the Southwest will focus on those who are of Mexican ancestry but who are native-born American citizens or are naturalized American citizens, the Mexican-American Farm Worker. This group represents the smallest proportion of the total number of laborers who are dependent on agriculture for their source of economic support and livelihood.

In the discussion and analysis of Mexican-American Farm Workers, two main categories will be utilized within this broad classification--the Native Born Farm Worker and the Naturalized Farm Worker. Each of these categories can also be divided into two subcategories, Native Residents and Native by Birth for the former main category and Resident Naturalized and Adult Naturalized for the latter category.

NATIVE RESIDENT FARM WORKERS

In this section, emphasis will be placed on those who are of Mexican ancestry and are also native-born citizens of the United States but were subsequently reared in Mexico, and secondly, those who were born and raised in this country. The former group will be referred to as Native Resident Farm Workers and the latter group will be referred to as Native By Birth Farm Workers.

The Native Resident farm workers constitute a very small proportion of the total agricultural labor force in the Southwest and are somewhat an anomaly in the industry. The primary reason for their underrepresentation is that they were born and raised in the midst of the American socio-cultural environment and have many of the expectations and opportunities available to the typical Anglo-American. They possess many of the social and

cultural skills that are essential for advancement within
agriculture or, if the opportunity presents itself, for
movement out of agriculture. Actually, a large proportion
are only working in the industry on a short term basis,
that is, only as long as they have to before finding something better in another industry. Their strong desire to
leave agriculture accounts for their low level of participation in this industry.

They only remain in agriculture on a temporary
basis because they possess the basic social, cultural, and
educational skills required by employers in other industries; they move upward and out at the first opportunity.
They find agricultural work arduous, dirty, insecure, and
it offers a very low wage in comparison to the wages offered in other industries. Those who do remain in agriculture usually occupy positions of authority such as foremen, crew leaders, or labor contractors. Frequently they
serve as middlemen between the grower and the field hands
and are well suited for this role as they are bilingual
and educated. They function very effectively in both the
Anglo-American setting and in the world of the Mexican
agricultural worker.

In other situations, they will work in the agricultural industry only on a temporary basis. To illustrate
this point, it is not unusual to find housewives, who are
second-generation Mexican-Americans, working during the
thinning and harvest season or temporarily employed by a
local cannery. Additionally, some Mexican-American high
school and college students spend the entire summer working in the fields, in order to earn money for themselves
and to aid in the support of their families. But it must
be stressed that they are participating in the industry on
a temporary basis and have no intention to remain there
any longer than is absolutely necessary.

Those who have made careers out of their work in
agriculture come from families with a background in agriculture. Often they have lived and worked in the same
agricultural community since childhood; consequently, they
are usually well known in the Mexican-American community.

NATIVE BY BIRTH FARM WORKERS

The term Native by Birth Farm Worker designates
those individuals who are American citizens of Mexican

ancestry, born in the United States but reared in Mexico. They hold dual citizenship status since their parents are Mexican nationals. This situation occurs when Mexican nationals, who have come to this country legally or illegally to work in agriculture and other American industries, bear children during their stay in this country. When their work is completed, they return to Mexico with an infant who was born here and is therefore an American citizen.[29] This situation may take place several times in the life cycle of one family, or it may happen only once. It really depends on the migratory patterns of Mexican nationals who come to the United States to work. The result is a child who is raised and socialized in Mexico and who feels and acts like any other Mexican but as a result of his or her birth in the United States is an American citizen.

The Native by Birth Farm Worker, as a matter of birth, is legally and rightfully an American citizen and is entitled to all of the rights and privileges of American citizenship. Most are content to work in the agricultural industry without fear of deportation. But many work under the same handicaps that plague the majority of illegal and green card workers because they cannot communicate in English and are ignorant of the cultural expectations of American society. The result is that the Native by Birth Farm Worker does not always assert his or her rights as an American citizen and is often the victim of the inhumane treatment that is normally reserved for illegal and green card workers.

For the most part, Native by Birth Farm Workers adapt to the living and working conditions in this country in much the same fashion as do green card workers who decide to stay in California, but with one important exception and real advantage, they can assert their rights as American citizens, if the need or situation should call for this acknowledgment.

THE NATURALIZED FARM WORKERS

Naturalized Farm Workers can best be analyzed as dichotomous groups. Some were born and raised in Mexico and came as adults to live and work in the United States. After a period of time, they decided to become citizens and are referred to as naturalized citizens (Adult Naturalized).

Others were brought to the United States as infants or small children and have spent most of their lives here, and as adults became naturalized. The concept of Naturalized Farm Worker represents two very different groups of people who have chosen to become citizens of the United States.

For the most part, the Naturalized Farm Workers who come to the United States as adults and become citizens in later life will follow the pattern previously described for the Loyalist. That is, they have lived and worked in the Southwest as green carders and have several native-born children, and have decided to spend the remainder of their lives in this country. Citizenship is in order, and they decide to take this step as a result of the social pressures exerted by their adult children, who are, in many cases, native-born American citizens.

Those who were raised and socialized in the United States will often follow the pattern of the agricultural workers who are described as Native Born, Native Resident Farm Workers. In both situations reference is made to persons who were educated and socialized in the United States and who are bilingual and bicultural in their background. These agricultural workers have many of the advantages and exhibit the same patterns of social adaptation to their marginal situation in the agricultural industry of the Southwest.

GENERAL OBSERVATIONS AND CONCLUSIONS

In conclusion, there are three major groups of agricultural workers of Mexican ancestry who provide the primary source of labor for the total industry. We have demonstrated the diversity and complexity of each of these groups of agricultural workers and in the process drawn attention to the inherent weaknesses and pitfalls involved in the use of simplistic terms and general categories that attempt to describe and otherwise explain the sociological characteristics of Mexican and Mexican-American agricultural laborers. In an effort to summarize the unique characteristics of each agricultural type I have prepared this typology in a basic outline form (see Table 1).

One noteworthy characteristic of this outline is that as one moves from one category to the next, a cumulative increase in the level of legitimacy for each for the agri-

cultural types is noticed. Those with the lowest level of
legitimacy are the Border Jumpers and those with the highest level of legitimacy are the Mexican-American Farm
Workers. From this observation a number of hypotheses
can be made. For example, the lower the level of legitimacy, the lower the level of education, occupational
status, and income. Concomitantly, the higher the level of
legitimacy, the higher the level of education, occupational
status, and income. As the level of legitimacy increases,
so does the level of social influence and economic affluence.

TABLE 1 A Typology of Mexican and Mexican-American Farm
Workers in California

A. Illegal Mexican National Farm Workers
    1. The Border Jumpers
    2. The Adventurers
    3. The Innovators
    4. The Social Climbers

B. Legal Mexican National Farm Workers
    1. The Commuters
    2. The Opportunists
    3. The Loyalists

C. Mexican-American Farm Workers
    1. The Native Born Farm Workers
      a. Native Residents
      b. Native by Birth
    2. The Naturalized Farm Workers
      a. Adult Naturalized
      b. Resident Naturalized

D. General Agricultural Terms
    1. Seasonal Farm Workers
    2. Migratory Farm Workers
    3. Seasonal Migratory Farm Workers
    4. Continuous Migratory Farm Workers

E. Levels of Personal Involvement in Agriculture
    1. Professional Farm Worker
    2. Semi-Professional Farm Worker
    3. Amateur Farm Worker
    4. Dilettante Farm Worker

Source: Compiled by the author.

Turning our attention to Table 2, we can see how
each of the agricultural types compares one with the others.
At the same time the table confirms the validity of the
hypothesis concerning the direct relationship between the
level of legitimacy and the socio-economic status of the
various Mexican and Mexican-American agricultural groups.

One important aspect of this table is that it does
support the initial assertion that Professional Farm Workers, those who spend all of their time in agricultural work,
as a group, live on a higher socio-economic level and
demonstrate the greatest potential for upward mobility.
They score high in all of the indexes of education, occupation, and income. In addition, they also indicate a
high level of assimilation, have the greatest command of
the English language, identify closely with agricultural
work and the agricultural community. They have better
housing, demonstrate a strong potential for upward mobility, register the greatest interest in citizenship, are most
interested in learning new skills, and have the most favorable attitudes toward the unionization of agricultural workers. Whereas the Illegal Mexican National Farm Workers,
with the exception of the Climbers, as a group, score the
lowest in all categories.

At this juncture it should be pointed out that these
categories are not necessarily limited to the verbatim de-
scriptions. What have been presented are ideal types and
the analysis is based on a set of frequencies and probabilities that each of the types will have the general characteristics of certain groups of agricultural workers. The
expectation is that a majority of them will fall into the
sociological categories that have been created. Caution
must be taken against any rigid application of these ideal
types to agricultural workers in the real world and thereby
it is hoped one will avoid the undesirable reification of
this typology. The fundamental purpose is to provide de-
scriptive categories that will serve as sociological tools
for the analysis of agricultural workers and that will
lead to a clearer understanding of their plight.

These sociological categories are unique in that
they are not based solely on static models of reality but
have been developed and formulated with a view toward
the dynamic aspects of reality. It is conceivable that a
Mexican agricultural worker might begin working at the
lowest level of legitimacy and, with time and ambition,
progress to a more acceptable level. To illustrate this
point, he could begin as a Border Jumper, become an

TABLE 2 Summary of General Characteristics of Mexican and Mexican-American Farm Workers in California Agriculture

| | Illegal Mexican Nationals | | | | Mexican-Americans | |
Characteristics	Border Jumpers	Adventurers	Innovators	Climbers	Naturalized	Native Born
Level of personal involvement	25%	25%	40%	100%	100%	100%
Number of months worked/year	3-4	3-4	5-6	10-12	10-12	10-12
Occupational status	Dilettante	Dilettante	Amateur	Professional	Professional	Professional
Level of education	0-4	0-6	3-6	3-8	3-9	6-12
Income level	Poverty	Poverty	Subsistence	Minimum comfort	Good comfort	Good comfort
Age level	16-44	16-30	30-50	30-50	16-65	16-65
Family size	0-12	0-5	3-12	5-12	2-5	2-5
Skill level	Very low	Low	Medium	High	High	High
Generation level	First	First	First	First	First and second	First and second
English usage	None	None	Little	Moderate	Moderate	High
Assimilation level	Not assimilated	Not assimilated	Not assimilated	Moderate assimilation	High assimilation	High assimilation

| | Legal Mexican Nationals | | |
Characteristics	Commuters	Opportunists	Loyalists
Level of personal involvement	25%	75%	100%
Number of months worked/year	3-4	7-9	10-12
Occupational status	Dilettante	Semi-professional	Professional
Level of education	3-6	3-6	3-8
Income level	Subsistence	Good comfort	Good comfort
Age level	25-54	30-50	35-65
Family size	3-12	4-12	3-6
Skill level	Low	Medium	High
Generation level	First	First	First
English usage	None	Little	Moderate
Assimilation level	Not assimilated	Not assimilated	High assimilation

Source: Compiled by the author.

Adventurer, and subsequently obtain green cards for himself and the members of his family, and advancing to the
level of Opportunist. After a few years he might decide to
become a permanent resident and consummate the transition
from his status as Opportunist to that of Loyalist. If conditions are suitable, he may decide to become a Naturalized
Farm Worker and thereby an American citizen.

This scenario is appropriate given the reality of the
situation, particularly when many of the Loyalist and some
of the Naturalized farm workers in this study actually began their careers as illegal farm workers.[30] Subsequently,
many of them have taken the steps as outlined above and
have legalized their status in the California agricultural
industry. But the conclusion must not be drawn that once
this dynamic process is set in motion it will ultimately
result in a complete legalization of all Mexican agricultural
workers. Rather, the study indicates that stability and
loyalty are goals for a certain percentage of agricultural
workers in this state.

An important characteristic of this paradigm is that
it can serve as a guide for those who wish to formulate
plans with a view toward the eventual stabilization of the
agricultural labor force, taking into consideration that certain agricultural groups would be more amenable to legalization and eventual stabilization than others. For example,
if one wishes to incubate and nurture a stable agricultural
labor force in a designated target area, it would be most
productive to focus attention on the Loyalists and Mexican-
American Farm Workers. Depending on the situation and
the availability and allocation of resources, one might consider attracting the Opportunists to the munificent benefits
of such a stabilization program, particularly because they
seem to have the greatest potential for social advancement
and eventual assimilation into American society.

One of the most serious stumbling blocks in such an
enterprise is the fact that no one person, organization, or
agency has the essential hard data to substantiate the
typological makeup of the agricultural labor force for any
specific region. As previously indicated, it is absolutely
impossible to obtain accurate and reliable figures for the
agricultural force. Consequently, the demographic data
available for the agricultural labor force is based on various underlying assumptions and probabilities. The data
does not represent the actual number of workers in the
agricultural industry. For example, two of the most difficult problems in this area are, first, that no one has been

able to devise a reliable method whereby they can locate, count, and verify the total number of legal and (more important and also more difficult) illegal agricultural workers; second, there is always the problem of counting the same group of agricultural workers more than once, since they are known for their geographic mobility.

It can be assumed that in all situations where one is dealing with numbers and statistics, particularly when applied to agricultural workers, one is really dealing with hypothetical or reified figures in the sense that these figures can never really represent the actual situation. However, we feel that the social hierarchy and the accompanying figures presented in Figure 1 represent a close approximation to the real situation in the sense that the categories and figures do provide a clear view of the actual situation in the agricultural labor force (see Figure 1).

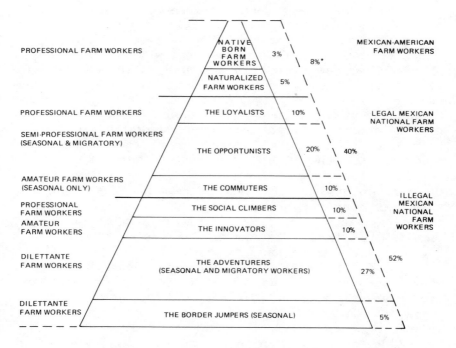

*Percentages are based on a rough estimate of the number of individuals involved in California agriculture for a one-year period of time.

FIGURE 1   Participation of Mexican and Mexican-American Agricultural Workers in California

NOTES

1. For example, see Where Have All the Farm Work-ers Gone? (Washington, D.C.: Rural America, Inc., 1977), p. iv. A statistical study points out that "None of the five statistical services employ the same definition of 'Farmworker,' 'Migrancy,' or "Seasonality' in describing the farmworker population. The confusion produces a situation where all statistical services use the same terminology to describe and count substantially different populations."
2. In her study, Hayes observed that "Ninety-three percent of the United States hired farm labor force was considered nonmigratory in 1971. . . ." Sue E. Hayes, "Seasonal Workers in Extended Employment: Implications for Agricultural Labor Policy," Ph.D. dissertation, Agricultural Economics, University of California, Berkeley, 1975, p. 11.
3. From the historical perspective, the Mexican agricultural worker has followed a migratory lifestyle for approximately 100 years. The result is that "migrancy" has become a significant aspect of the Mexican cultural tradition.
4. To make matters even worse, the agricultural worker must deduct his travel and lodging expenses from whatever income he is able to earn once he does find work. In addition, these expenses do not include the days of work that are lost while he is out looking for work.
5. In their study, Padfield and Martin have elaborated on this concept of "hired hands." See Harland Padfield and William E. Martin, Farmers, Workers and Machines (Tucson: University of Arizona Press, 1965), in particular, pp. 267-75.
6. However, it should be pointed out that the percentage of professional farm workers engaged in the overall labor force is rather small. Hayes has estimated that "Only about 15% of the farm workers employed in California can be considered year-round employees of a single farm or other agricultural employer." See Hayes, "Seasonal Workers in Extended Employment," p. 8. And it is to this group of agricultural workers that I refer.
7. Of course, this view of occupational mobility in the agricultural industry overlooks the impact of ethnic and class divisions that are inherent in the social organization of this industry. Consequently, one might point out that prejudice and ethnic discrimination in the allocation

of occupational positions and opportunities for occupational mobility play a critical role in the overall social welfare of Mexican agricultural workers.

8. From the nationalist perspective, some would refer to it as the "jingoistic" view, the idea of an "illegal Mexican alien" in this country is really a contradiction in terms since the Southwest was usurped from the Mexican people in a war of blatant aggression that was terminated by the Treaty of Guadalupe Hidalgo in 1848.

9. For examples of how this pass can be obtained and used by Mexican nationals when crossing the border, see the following sources: Grace Halsell, The Illegals (New York: Stein and Day, 1978), pp. 67-79; David North and Marion F. Houstoun, The Characteristics and Role of Illegal Aliens in the U.S. Labor Market (Washington, D.C.: Linton and Company, Inc., 1976), pp. 88-89; Julian Samora, Los Mojados: The Wetback Story (Notre Dame, Ind.: University of Notre Dame Press, 1971), pp. 76-80.

10. Vernon M. Briggs, Jr., Walter Fogel, and Fred Schmidt, The Chicano Worker (Austin: University of Texas Press, 1977), p. 85.

11. Walter Fogel, Mexican Illegal Alien Workers in the United States (Los Angeles: Institute of Industrial Relations, University of California, 1978), p. 44.

12. Ibid., p. 70.

13. Vernon M. Briggs, Jr., "Statement of Vernon Briggs, Jr." in Undocumented Workers: Implications for U.S. Policy in the Western Hemisphere, Hearing before the Subcommittee on Inter-American Affairs (Washington, D.C.: U.S. Government Printing Office, 1978), p. 248.

14. In their study, North and Houstoun (The Characteristics and Role of Illegal Aliens, p. A-29) note that these Border jumpers (as I have described them) cross the border at Calexico and "walk from their homes to 'The Hole, which is the local farm labor shape-up site; they mount buses which will take them 90 to 100 miles before they can start work."

15. For a complete description, see ibid., pp. 68-71 and Samora, Los Mojados: The Wetback Story, pp. 89-90.

16. Fogel, Mexican Illegal Alien Workers in the United States, p. 77.

17. Ibid.

18. For documentation of this wage issue see David North, The Border Crossers: People Who Live in Mexico

and Work in the United States (Washington, D.C.: Trans Century Corp., 1970), particularly pp. 143-84; and also the work by Barton Smith and Robert Newman, "Depressed Wages Along the U.S.-Mexico Border: an Empirical Analysis," Economic Inquiry 15 (1977):51-66.

19. Fogel, Mexical Illegal Alien Workers in the United States, p. 88.

20. Samora, Los Mojados: The Wetback Story, pp. 96-97.

21. Actually, these crew leaders are smuggling illegal aliens into this country, which, of course, is against the law. But, in fact, smuggling is a very common practice in view of the fact that "31,000 Mexicans admitted being smuggled into the United States in 1973 at an average price of $350." Fogel, Mexican Illegal Alien Workers in the United States, p. 46. Without any doubt, the number of Mexican nationals that are smuggled into this country today is much higher, and so is the fee.

22. In fact, the use of bogus documents has been a widespread practice for a number of years. As Briggs points out, even as early as 1973, "federal authorities seized 60,000 counterfeit alien registration cards (Form I-151) and engraving plates in a bus station in Los Angeles, stating, 'They were so perfectly done that they would sell for $500 each in Mexico.'" Briggs et al., The Chicano Worker, p. 15. Similarly, Corwin and McCain observe that "The Immigrant Alien Receipt Card, I-151, issued to all legal immigrants including the so-called greencard commuter, has been so artfully forged that only a machine could detect the fact. The same is true for border-crossing cards and temporary permits to visit the interior." Arthur F. Corwin and Johnny M. McCain, "Wetbackism Since 1964: A Catalogue of Factors," in Arthur Corwin, ed., Immigrants and Immigrants (Westport, Conn.: Greenwood Press, 1978), p. 90.

23. Louis Schneider and Sverre Sysgaard, "The Deferred Gratification Pattern: A Preliminary Study," American Sociological Review 18 (1953):142-49.

24. Sasha G. Lewis, Slave Trade Today: American Exploitation of Illegal Aliens (Boston: Beacon Press, 1979), p. 81.

25. Briggs et al., The Chicano Worker, p. 85.

26. Support for this observation can be found in the work of North, The Border Crossers, pp. 143-82.

27. Ibid., p. 107.

28. Paul Sultan and Darryl D. Enos, Farming and Farm Labor: A Study in California, A Report Prepared by the Center for Urban and Regional Studies of Claremont Graduate School, National Technical Information Service, Springfield, Illinois, 1974, p. 96.

29. For example, Zarrugh became aware of this situation in her ethnography of a Mexican village when she observed that

> The return of many Jacalan families to the village during the 1930s is indicated today by the number of adult villagers who are American citizens by birth. Having spent part of their childhood in Illinois or Ohio, some of these individuals grew up in the village only to migrate again as adults to California.

Laura H. Zarrugh, "Gente De Mi Tierra: Mexican Village Migrants in a California Community," Ph.D. dissertation, Department of Anthropology, University of California, Berkeley, 1974, p. 20.

30. In his study of Mexican immigrants, Hirschman found that when he asked his respondents if they "had ever lived in the United States (not including visits), 62 percent said 'yes' and 31 percent indicated their stay(s) totaled three years or more." Charles Hirschman, "Prior U.S. Residence Among Mexican Immigrants," Social Forces 56 (1978):1179–1202. Consequently, a majority of legal Mexican immigrants do spend a number of years in this country as illegal aliens before they actually legalize their status.

4

Working Conditions among
Mexican Agricultural Workers

GENERAL DEMOGRAPHIC CHARACTERISTICS

One of the primary objectives of this study was to
collect data concerning the social and economic characteristics of the Mexican and Mexican-American agricultural
laborers in northern California. For this purpose the
"Farmworker Interview Schedule" was administered to qualified agricultural workers. Additional data was obtained
from the administration of the "Key Informant Interview
Schedule."

Among the various criteria used in the selection
process of our interview subjects was the stipulation that
they must have worked full time in the agricultural industry for a minimum of ten years. Consequently, our respondents have had a good deal of experience working in
the agricultural industry, as they averaged 27.1 years of
experience in agriculture. While our results are not absolutely clear on this point, it does appear that our respondents lived in this state for a minimum of four and
one-half years and many have lived in California for more
than ten years. Clearly our sample represents a very
stable group of agricultural workers.

As a result, it is not surprising to discover that
our sample is made up of a mature group of individuals
who have settled into their agricultural lifestyle. For
example, the average age of our respondents was 41 years,
the youngest 23, the oldest 68. Since the majority of our
respondents were males (92.3%), a very familiar demographic

pattern revealed itself, that is, their wives were somewhat younger. The average age for their spouses was 36, with a minimum age of 18 and a maximum age of 61.

Our results also reveal that 89 percent of our respondents were born in Mexico, while the remainder were born in this country. Of those born in Mexico one in five (20.9%) were born in the state of Jalisco, one in five (22%) in Michocan, one in eight (13.2%) were from Guanajuato, and one in 11 (8.8%) were from Zacatecas.[1] Of those born in this country four were from Texas, three from California, one from Colorado, and two from the north central states. In comparison, 15 of their spouses were born in this country, while the majority (82.4%) were born in Mexico. Of the women born in Mexico, the majority were born in the same states as their husbands. For example, one in four (23.1%) were born in Michocan, one in six (16.5%) in Jalisco, one in eight (12.1%) in Zacatecas, and one in 11 (8.8%) in Guanajuato. Of the 15 born in this country, four were from Texas, seven from California, and one each from Arizona, New Mexico, and Oregon.

Overall ten of our respondents and 15 of their spouses were born in this country and are therefore citizens. This finding of course is simply indicative of the fact that only a small proportion of native-born citizens are occupied on a full-time basis in the agricultural industry, while the majority of agricultural workers consist of legal resident aliens, or naturalized citizens, or undocumented workers from Mexico.

As anticipated, the majority of our respondents' parents were born in Mexico (96.7%), as only three respondents had parents who were born in the United States. Hence the greater proportion of our respondents were first-generation immigrants to this country. These results seem to confirm our suspicions that a significant proportion of the laborers involved in the California agricultural industry are first-generation immigrants from Mexico. In effect the majority of our respondents were socialized in Mexico, as four out of five (82.4%) received their primary educations in Mexico, while only one out of six (17.6%) were educated in this country. Of those educated in Mexico, half (50.6%) received their primary instruction in the state of Jalisco (25.3%). In addition, one out of ten (10.7%) were educated in Guanajuato and only eight in Zacatecas.

In terms of their educational achievement almost two-thirds (62.6%) of our respondents had six years or less of formal education. Five respondents said that they were illiterate and had never received a formal education. Six others said that they were literate but had never attended school. Only three of our respondents indicated that they had completed high school (in California) and two said that they had taken courses at a community college.

While the majority of interviews were conducted in Spanish (only two were partially conducted in English) our results indicate that one in four (24.2%) of our respondents considered themselves bilingual. On the other hand, three fourths (73.6%) stated that they could only speak Spanish.

The average estimated income for the members of our sample for 1978, before taxes, was $8,773. The minimum income was reported by a female agricultural worker at $2,131; and the maximum income was reported by the foreman of a large vineyard in the Napa Valley, at $16,632 per year, that is, in 63.7 percent of the cases, the total family income was somewhat higher than the individual mean income for the year.

Our survey results also reveal that the majority of our respondents were married (96.7%), with the exception of one bachelor, one divorcee, and one respondent who was separated at the time of the interviews. All of our male respondents (92.3%) were heads of households, with the exception of one bachelor who was living with his brother; but only one of the women in our sample was the head of household, as she was divorced. While one of our couples had been married for a little less than a year and another couple had been married for 42 years, the total sample had been married a mean of 16.3 years. Those who were married, or who had been married, had an average of 4.5 children. Three respondents were childless, while, at the other extreme, one couple had 13 children.

A brief survey of their housing conditions revealed that just over one third (37.4%) were able to save enough money to begin making mortgage payments on their own homes. Needless to say these individuals were fairly well settled and were probably setting a trend for the others who were renting at the time of the interviews. Only three respondents reported that they were living with relatives.

When asked, nine out of ten of our respondents (91.2%) said they still had relatives living in Mexico. Of these, two out of five (39.8%) had parents living there and half (53%) indicated that they had one or more siblings living south of the border. Therefore, while the members of our sample have lived and worked in this country for many years, they nonetheless maintain social ties with their relatives living in the country of origin.

From this brief overview of the key demographic characteristics of our sample it is obvious that they do not conform to the typical stereotype of the Mexican or Mexican-American farm worker. Rather these results lend further support to our position that the "professional" farm worker, who forms the backbone of the agricultural labor force in California, is very different in many ways from the migratory or seasonal farm worker. Indeed, these individuals depend on their work in the agricultural industry to support their families, to pay their rent, and to survive as best they can.

LEVEL OF PARTICIPATION IN THE AGRICULTURAL LABOR FORCE

While it is virtually impossible to determine the number of laborers employed in the agricultural labor force, it is a much more formidable task to estimate the number of Mexicans and Mexican Americans involved in the California agricultural industry. However, regardless of the severe limitations of the available data, all authorities on this subject seem to agree that the majority of agricultural workers in this state, and in the greater Southwest, are of Mexican heritage.

In reality, their level of participation in the agricultural labor force is so ubiquitous and pervasive that over the years a very popular stereotype has developed that has painted an image of the Mexican as purely and simply an agricultural worker. In fact, this popular stereotype prompted Briggs to observe that

> The vast majority of the Mexicans who migrated into the Southwest in the twentieth century came from a rural agricultural background. Many of the illegal aliens continue to follow this route. Speaking little English and having few skills to offer an urban labor market, most of these immigrants and

aliens have become trapped in working for
America's most exploitive industry.[2]

Other social scientists have provided estimates of
the number of Mexicans and Mexican Americans who are
active in the agricultural economy of the Southwest. For
example, Fogel has observed that "53 percent of Mexican
American employed males who live outside of urban areas
in 1959 were farm laborers, owners, or managers, as compared to only 26 percent of all rural males in the United
States."[3] In effect, their participation rate is twice as
high as that found among rural adult males in the general
population. But in reality Fogel's figures are rather conservative, as official agricultural labor statistics have
historically suffered from the conservative malady of under-
counting the Spanish-speaking population in general.
Therefore, we suspect that the participation among Mexican
Americans in the agricultural labor force is actually
higher than the official figures would lead us to believe.
A 1975 Department of Agriculture survey found that
of 18,739 migrants studied in six states that 80 percent
working in California and Washington were of Hispanic
origin; 75 percent working in Michigan were thus classified, as were 70 percent in Oregon.[4] While these figures
may represent a slight exaggeration in the total percentages obtained, since the data were based on the participation rate of migrant agricultural laborers, they nonetheless serve to shed a good deal of light on the ethnic
makeup of the agricultural labor force in the greater
Southwest. Consequently there should be little doubt that
the vast majority of agricultural workers in this state are
either Mexicans or Mexican Americans.
Having established this premise, it seems appropriate
to examine some of the occupational characteristics of our
sample of "professional" farm workers, and, one hopes,
gain a better understanding of their plight. Of our total
sample almost three out of four respondents (72.5%) were
employed on a full-time basis when they were interviewed,
while one out of ten (9.9%) were unemployed and actively
looking for work. An additional 7.7 percent reported that
they were not working at the time of the interview as a
result of being out on disability. The remaining 9.9 percent provided a variety of miscellaneous responses. However, even those who were unemployed had a long history

of agricultural employment and viewed their displacement
from the agricultural labor force as a temporary state of
affairs.

When asked what type of work they did within
agriculture, half of our respondents (48.4%) reported that
they were skilled agricultural workers. From their interpretation this usually meant that they were machine operators, machine maintenance men, mechanics, welders, or
possessed any combination of these skills. One in four
indicated that they were "general agricultural workers,"
which meant that they performed a variety of agricultural
tasks that did not necessarily require any special skill or
technical knowledge, such as operating a small tractor,
harvesting crops, disking, fertilizing, and so on. Other
respondents gave more specific answers: supervisor, agricultural tractor operator, general agricultural mechanic,
to name a few. In addition, half of our respondents
(52.7%) said that they were working at a job that they
considered to be permanent. Generally this meant that
they had worked for the same employer for several years
and therefore could depend on having a job year after
year, that is, so long as their performance continued to
satisfy their employer. In addition, their permanent
status also meant that they could expect to be employed
for ten or more months out of the year. However, given
our overall results, the actual percentage of "permanent"
agricultural workers would be closer to 70 or 75 percent
of our sample.

When asked where they were working at the time of
the interview, nine out of ten of our respondents (92.3%)
indicated that they were actively working in the agricultural industry. The others reported that they were out on
disability, participating in a job training program, or
temporarily employed outside of agriculture. Upon further
investigation it was discovered that those who were working in nonagricultural jobs viewed their unconventional
employment as ephemeral and expedient to their current
economic situation. In effect, they were only working at
these odd jobs until they could secure a regular source of
employment within the agricultural industry.

When asked for their previous source of employment,
fully nine out of ten (92.3%) reported that they had worked
for another employer within the agricultural industry.
Others listed such miscellaneous jobs as employment in a
food processing plant, dairies, hospitals, and so on.

Once again these appear to be transitory jobs that were only taken in an effort to make ends meet while they were unemployed from their regular agricultural positions. However, regardless of these temporary divagations from their regular sources of employment, the majority were dedicated to their jobs in the agricultural industry, that is, they were "dedicated" in the sense that they viewed agricultural work as their principal source of sustenance and personal identity.

When asked about their previous jobs in the agricultural industry, seven out of ten (69%) said that they had worked as "general agricultural laborers" and additionally one out of five (19%) said that they had worked as "skilled" agricultural workers. The remainder indicated that they had worked as temporary harvest "pickers," unskilled agricultural laborers, and one reported that he had worked as a supervisor. Again our results reveal that they have had a clear pattern of continuous employment, except for occasional periods, in the agricultural industry over a period of many years. Any deviations from this overall pattern can be viewed as "occupational sojourns" in which these hapless individuals attempt to make the best of a bad situation; in other words, they always manage to find ways to bridge the gap between periods of full employment, year after year.

A review of our data concerning job tenure might lead us to believe, at first glance, that our findings are somewhat anomalous inasmuch as the average number of years of their personal involvement in agriculture is 27 years. This inordinate number of years of experience in the agricultural labor force can be partially explained by our sampling process, as our respondents were required to have a minimum of ten years of job experience in the industry. Therefore, this stipulation would account for the many years of experience of our respondents, as opposed to the findings of other researchers. For example, of the 600 agricultural workers in their southern California study, of which the majority (88.7%) were Mexican Americans, Sultan and Enos found that half (50.2%) had been in the agricultural labor force for ten years or less and only 4.9 percent had between 26 and 30 years of experience.[5] However, their study included many agricultural workers who were migratory or seasonal workers. Consequently, the range of experience of our respondents, that is, from 10 to 56 years, gives us a view of a group of individuals who have had a substantial number of years of experience in the agricultural labor force of California.

Obviously, the number of years of experience in the agricultural labor force is directly related to their age. The mean age of our sample was 41.4 years, in spite of the fact that the Mexican agricultural labor force tends to be a rather young population group. For example, Sultan and Enos found that 70 percent of their sample were between the ages of 18 and 39.[6] Similarly, Halfon found that 58.7 percent of her sample fell into this age category, that is, between 18 and 39.[7] In like manner Choldin and Trout found that half (47%) of their respondents were between the ages of 20 and 29 years of age.[8] And an earlier study conducted in Kern County (California) found that "Almost one-third were under 25 years old and over half were under 35."[9] The state legislative report, The California Farm Labor Force, made the general observation that "The average Mexican farm worker is somewhat younger than the average worker in the entire California labor force."[10] Likewise, a study conducted by the U.S. Department of Agriculture in 1973 found that 59.6 percent of the 203,000 agricultural workers surveyed were between 18 and 44 years of age.[11] In his study of Mexican agricultural workers in Yolo and Solano counties (California) Haller also found that "The largest number of farm workers in the sample fell in the middle age group of 22-39 years."[12]

One of the most important reasons why agricultural workers are so young, besides the fact that Mexican Americans are younger as a population group in general, is that most only remain in the industry as long as they have to—they gleefully abandon this type of work at the very first opportunity. For example, the results of one longitudinal study found that of all the individuals who began working in the industry, over half were no longer in the agricultural labor force by the age of 25.[13] Clearly, younger workers view their tenure in the agricultural labor force as a temporary state of affairs. Consequently, this has a depressive effect on the mean age of agricultural workers in general. In addition, most studies include a substantial proportion of seasonal and migrant laborers, who historically are rather young.

The second-most important reason for the relatively young age of agricultural workers is that only a few are employed in the industry beyond the age of 55. For example, the results of the state legislative report indicate that

"About 10 percent of Mexican farm workers are 55 years of age or older compared to 17 percent of the total California farm labor force."[14]   This percentage would be even greater if we compared this small group of older Mexican agricultural workers with the percentage of workers who are active in other industries at this age.   However, the main reason for this sociological phenomenon is that agricultural workers generally expire at a relatively young age.   This situation is not difficult to comprehend when we consider that the average life expectancy of agricultural workers is only 49 years.[15]

While it is generally true that agricultural workers will leave for more auspicious job opportunities, as soon as such propitious circumstances present themselves, it is also true that those who opt to remain in this industry represent a very stable population.   Hence the "professional" farm worker will remain with one employer, over a period of years, if given favorable working conditions and opportunities.   For example, our respondents averaged four years with the same employer, which is a very high average among agricultural workers, while three respondents had worked for the same employer for 13, 15, and 18 years, respectively.   Obviously, the "professional" farm worker will remain on the job as long as he is needed and as long as the working conditions do not become excessively oppressive or the wage scale pitifully low.

In an effort to determine why agricultural workers change jobs from time to time, we asked those respondents who had changed jobs in the past five years why they had done so.   We found that half (47.3%) had located a "better job," while one-third (33%) said that they had been laid off.   Only six respondents had abandoned their jobs because of a "bad boss," while an equal number had quit their jobs as a result of a move.   Of the remaining respondents two had been fired, one quit because he could not get along with his fellow workers, and one did not like the working conditions at his place of employment.

Overall, it appears that most quit their jobs in an effort to improve their own personal situation.   However, most did not abandon their agricultural work for nonagricultural jobs, but rather they sought more lucrative positions within the agricultural industry.   This assumption is supported by the fact that nonagricultural work experience among our respondents was not very extensive.   In an effort to clarify this issue our respondents were asked, "How many different jobs do you think that you have had in your lifetime?" It was made clear that we wanted to know of any nonagricultural jobs that they may have held in the past. Our results reveal that two out of five respondents (38.5%) had worked in one other job outside of agriculture and one-third (31.9%) had worked at two jobs outside of agriculture, while one out of six (17.6%) had done so and only eleven respondents had worked at four or more nonagricultural jobs. Further investigation revealed that the majority of these nonagricultural jobs were only temporary positions and all of them returned to their agricultural work after a brief absence. In his study Metzler also found that "Less than half of the Spanish-American and Mexican workers had any non-farm experience."[16]

Following this mode of inquiry each respondent was asked if he or she had ever given consideration to a job change in the near future; in other words, had the individual thought of finding a job outside of the agricultural industry? To our surprise just over half of our respondents (54.9%) said that they were considering a job change in the near future. On the other hand, two out of five (44%) said that they were not considering a change in the future. Those who had said that they were interested in finding a new job were asked what type of work they would prefer if they had the opportunity. While their responses are difficult to present statistically (as their preferences covered the whole panoply of occupational categories), nonetheless their job aspirations were very realistic in view of their current job situation, that is, they only selected those blue-collar occupations which covered certain skilled, semi-skilled, and operative positions. Therefore, their selections were limited to those nonagricultural jobs that were similar, in many respects, to the type of work with which they were already familiar, making such a transition less difficult.

Of all the respondents only 15 were vague in their responses, with nine stating that they would like "just any job outside of agriculture" and six others saying that they were willing to take "any job." Five admitted that they just "didn't know" what type of job they would like to secure outside of agricultural work. However, when those respondents who said that they had an interest in working in some other industry were asked for whom they would work, we encountered a great deal of ambiguity in their responses. Therefore, while half of our respondents had an idea that they would like to make a transition to some nonagricultural job, we found that their responses regarding for whom they would work were very vague and amorphous.

In view of the "professional" character of our respondents it should come as no surprise to discover that only a small proportion has ever worked as migratory farm workers. Our results reveal that only two out of five (38.5%) had ever worked as migrant agricultural workers. However, the greater proportion (61.5%) said that they had never done so. Of those who had worked as migratory farm workers, we found that they had only done so as young men, particularly those who had worked under the Bracero Program. It seems to be a common pattern that once they accept family responsibilities they manage to develop methods by which they are able to locate work in one specific agricultural area and, as a result, soon become experts in one or two local crops. In this manner they establish themselves in one location, thereby eliminating the need to migrate with their families in tow. Lending further support to this image of a non-migratory lifestyle is the discovery that three out of four (75.8%) have not worked in any state other than California. Furthermore, four out of five (82.4%) indicated that they do not generally work for labor contractors. When asked if they had ever worked for farm labor contractors one out of three (36.3%) said that they had never done so. Of course, this indicates that the majority prefer to work directly for the grower or farm manager, rather than working for a labor contractor. When asked how they felt about farm labor contractors in general, three out of four (75.8%) reported that they were strongly opposed to their use and viewed them with repugnance and felt that they were "exploiters" of their people.

OCCUPATIONAL HISTORY OF AGRICULTURAL WORKERS

In view of the plethora of data collected by social scientists concerning the lives of peasants in agricultural communities in various parts of the world, it should come as no surprise to discover that our respondents began their occupational careers at a very early age. This observation is particularly true, "In a society where agriculture is carried out primarily at a subsistence level, [where] there is little distinction between household duties

and farm activities."[17]   The majority of our respondents
were introduced as children into the drudgeries of agricultural life by performing a variety of "light-duty" tasks.
Most recalled such personal experiences as having to feed
the chickens, take care of the goats, carry water, pull
weeds, and so on.   In most cases these were chores that
were performed before they started out for school, and
naturally these job assignments were waiting for them
when they returned home.   In some cases they would miss
a good deal of school, or were forced to terminate their
education altogether as a result of these domestic chores.
     When asked, we found that better than four out of
five (85.7%) of our respondents had worked as children.
In posing this question each respondent was told to consider any work that they were required to do, either
around the house or in their community, on a regular
basis before their eighteenth birthday.   Our results reveal
that the average age of first employment for our respondents as a group was 12.2 years; with a range of six to
31 years.   The extreme high reading was obtained from a
female respondent who said that she did not have to work
until after she was married.   Overall, these results are in
concord with the findings of other social scientists.   For
example, in their study Choldin and Trout found that "Over
38 percent of the Mexican-American migrant workers had
begun farm work by the age of 14. . . ."[18]   In a comparative study of first and second generation Mexican-
American agricultural workers Goldner also found that
"Most respondents went to work at an early age.   Members
of both generations began working at an average age of
twelve; the youngest members of each generation beginning
at the age of six."[19]
     Given the multifarious demographic characteristics
of our sample it seems appropriate that the majority of our
respondents began their occupational careers as agricultural workers.   When asked what kind of work they did as
children, 94.9 percent indicated that they were employed
in agriculture.   Similarly, Sultan and Enos asked their
sample of 600 agricultural workers, "what was the first
full time job you had?" and they found that three out of
five (61.5%) had worked in agriculture.[20]   However, we
can safely assume that their results would have been
higher if they had asked their respondents what kind of
work they did as children, and if they had included temporary and part-time work.

Obviously, the high percentage of respondents in our study who had their first work experience in agriculture stems from the fact that they were reared in an agricultural environment. Our findings reveal that 85.7 percent said that their fathers' principal occupation, when they were children, was in agriculture. The others said that their fathers were engaged in various blue-collar occupations, such as truck drivers, welders, carpenters, and so on. However, it was generally the case that even these blue-collar workers operated small farms in their spare time; which is frequently the case in the rural areas of Mexico. These observations would certainly account for the overall propensity for their first work experience to occur in the agricultural industry. When our respondents were asked for their fathers' highest occupational position, four out of five (78%) said that their fathers had remained in agriculture all of their lives. Consequently, the majority of our respondents were reared in families with a long tradition of agricultural employment. These findings are in accord with the results of a recent California study in which half (55.5%) of the Mexican and Mexican-American agricultural laborers could trace their families' involvement in agronomy back three or more generations.[21]

OCCUPATIONAL SKILLS OF AGRICULTURAL WORKERS

While it is true that the major work experience of our respondents was restricted to the agricultural industry, it is also true that from time to time most agricultural workers find it necessary to seek out nonagricultural job opportunities. In fact, these respites from their agricultural travails provide agriculturists with an opportunity to learn new job skills. In many cases these newly acquired skills prove to be most useful within their own agronomical environment. Therefore, on the surface it seems that these grangers really do possess a reservoir of "hidden skills."

While it is difficult to measure the skill level of most occupational groups, it is a particularly onerous undertaking to attempt to determine the skill level of agricultural workers. This is particularly true since the typical farm worker is required to perform a variety of jobs within a single day. Overall their skill levels can be bifurcated into those tasks that require learned skills and those that require mechanical aptitude.

Additionally, agricultural tasks that require skill must be learned over a substantial period of time and therefore are the direct result of continuous practice. In effect, the development of skills requires a good deal of practical experience. Consequently, a skill cannot be acquired in a matter of days or weeks but must be practiced and acquired over a period of months, or even years. For example, skill is demonstrated at the rudimentary level when an agricultural worker develops the ability to pick a certain type of fruit with great dexterity and at a very rapid pace. An intermediate level of skill level is exhibited by the agricultural worker who is known for his expertise as an irrigator. An even higher level of skill is found among those individuals who graft young vines in the vineyards.

On the other hand, mechanical aptitude is found among those who are able to make repairs and perform the necessary maintenance on various pieces of agricultural equipment and machinery. In this sense certain individuals have a penchant for working with machinery, while others do not, for a whole host of reasons. For example, an agricultural worker with mechanical aptitude would be able to transfer his propaedeutic knowledge of auto mechanics to the maintenance and repair of sophisticated pieces of agricultural equipment. This then would certainly be recognized as a very valuable skill.

For analytical purposes our survey results were classified as either exhibiting a skill or a specific mechanical aptitude. Over half of our respondents (56%) indicated that they had "general agricultural skills," and the remainder (41.8%) said that they were "machine operators." According to our schema we interpreted "general agricultural skills" as learned skills and that of "machine operators" as mechanical aptitude. In actual practice, "general agricultural skills" require laborers to harvest certain crops, tend to young plants, irrigate the fields, and other duties, all of which would be classified as skills. By the same token, "machine operators" would perform such tasks as operating tractors, combines, and other pieces of agricultural equipment. In addition, the operators' duties would probably include the daily maintenance of and minor repair of such equipment. By comparison, Haller, in his study of Mexican agricultural workers, found that over

70 percent of his respondents indicated that they had previous experience in the operation of agricultural equipment.
He also found that 29.9 percent of his male respondents had
had previous experience repairing or maintaining farm
equipment.[22]

An effort was also made to identify the repertoire of
skills possessed by our respondents that could be readily
transferred to a more urban setting. This information
would then provide an index of the human potential that
is currently available in the campestral labor force.
Therefore, each respondent was asked if he or she had
any additional job skills outside of those required in the
present position. Their responses dichotomized our sample,
inasmuch as 49.5 percent indicated that they did have job
skills that could be useful in an urban-industrial environment. Concomitantly, the other half (50.5%) said that they
did not have any job skills that they felt would be useful
in a nonagricultural environment. Our findings seem to
complement those of other researchers; for example, in their
study of agricultural workers Choldin and Trout found that
the tasks that their respondents were able to perform were
"numerous and extraordinarily varied."[23] Consequently,
agricultural workers do possess a variety of untapped and
yet dormant skills that could be easily transferred to an
industrial milieu. In the conclusion to his study, Grafton
Trout was prompted to point out that "One misconception
commonly held concerning Mexican-American migrant farm
workers is that they have a low level of mechanical aptitude. Our survey data indicated that this is not the case;
many of the respondents indicated that they have mechanical skills which they do not use in their current jobs."[24]

Of those respondents who indicated that they did
have industrial job skills, one-third (31.1%) reported having skills as auto mechanics, one-fourth as carpenters
(24.4%), one out of five (17.8%) as plumbers, one out of
eight (13.3%) as cement workers, and one out of ten (11.1%)
as machine operators in industrial plants. Once again
these results are congruent with the findings of other investigators. For example, Choldin and Trout found that
"The most often-mentioned skills in order of frequency were
carpenter, mechanic, house painter, plumber, welder, cook,
truck driver, brick layer or mason or cement worker, elec-
trician, radio and TV repair, sewing, musician and barber."[25] Even a cursory perusal of this smorgasbord of
job skills reveals that the skills most frequently mentioned

are those that are essential to the home construction industry. This reflects the fact that building a house in
Mexico, particularly among low-income groups, is still a
family affair, and very often a community project. Therefore, those born and reared in Mexico, particularly the
young men, would have at least a rudimentary knowledge
of the skills associated with the home construction industry. Likewise many of the other skills are really service-
related skills, such as auto mechanic, cook, musician, and
barber. Obviously, these are the very skills that provide
them with some independence and allow them to "moonlight"
and thereby secure additional income for the family.

Closely related to these untapped reservoirs of occupational skills, is the desire for opportunities such as
access to job-training programs, their past experience in
job-training programs, and their personal preference for
job-training programs. Consequently they were asked if
they would be interested in participating in a job-training
program. While the majority said that they would be most
interested, only one in four (25.3%) said that they would
not be interested. In comparison to the results obtained
in other studies our respondents appear to be a very ambitious group. For example, Sultan and Enos found that
only half (50.6%) of their 600 respondents were interested
in participating in a job training program if it were made
available.[26] In his study Haller found that half (56.2%)
of his respondents said that they "might be interested,"
while only a third (31.2%) said that they "would be" interested.[27] In their study Choldin and Trout formulated a
question with a good deal of incentive, for they asked each
of their respondents, "If you had the chance, would you
be willing to enroll in a six-month training program, with
pay, in order to get into a better line of work?" Even
so, they found that only two-thirds of their sample (64%)
indicated that they would be interested, while one out of
four (27%) stated that they would definitely not be interested.[28] Perhaps the high level of interest found among
our respondents can be related to the fact that our survey
group consisted of mature, married individuals with families to support. Therefore, it would seem that they would
be interested in any program that would offer them the
opportunity to improve their present lot in life.

Furthermore, our findings reveal that three out of
five (60.6%) respondents had previous experience in a job-
training program. Once again this high level of partici-

pation is congruent with their general maturity, stability, and years of work experience. However, other studies have not found such high levels of participation. For example, Choldin and Trout found that only 42 percent of their respondents had received any form of job training.[29] Even less comforting is the fact that only 7.7 percent of Halfon's sample of 584 Mexican and Mexican-American agricultural workers indicated that they had ever had any experience in a job-training program. Only one out of ten of her respondents had ever been referred to a job-training program.[30]

Of our respondents who said that they would be interested in participating in a job-training program, that is, 74.7 percent of our sample, one in four were interested in receiving auto mechanic training, and one out of six (17.6%) wanted to enroll in an ESL (English as a second language) class. The others demonstrated a kaleidoscopic repertory of interests and therefore their responses could not be properly categorized. For example, they were interested in such job-training programs as construction, welding, carpentry, plumbing, and others. In comparison, Choldin and Trout found that of their respondents who had received adult education instruction, over half (58%) had participated in ESL classes.[31] In contrast Haller found that only one in four (28.8%) of his sample of 263 Mexican and Mexican-American agricultural workers had enrolled in an ESL class.[32]

Those respondents who indicated that they would not be interested in receiving any form of job training, that is, 25.3 percent of our sample, were asked why they were not interested. Half of them (47.8%) felt that they were too old to participate in a job-training program. The second largest group (17.4%) said that they could not participate because they could not afford to leave their present job. Similarly, Haller found that three out of five (60.6%) of her respondents would only participate in a job-training program if they could receive a stipend or some other form of economic support during their period of training.[33]

Given these findings, and those obtained by other researchers, we have to wonder about the nature of the variables that influence this kind of decision, that is, whether they should or should not participate in a job-training program. Our results reveal that age and maturity are very important factors. In fact, there is a

direct relationship between age and maturity, and a positive response to the idea of participating in a job-training
program.

Overall, most agricultural workers view job training
as an opportunity to learn a skill that would qualify them
for a more lucrative position in the future. Therefore,
they view job training as a means by which they can re-
lieve themselves of the drudgery of agricultural work. In
addition, those with previous experience in job-training
programs would naturally be more amenable to the idea of
matriculating into a new program to improve old skills or
to learn new skills. In like manner, enthusiasm and interest would be high among those agriculturists who have
had previous work experience in some other industry. This
favorable attitude results from the fact that they have had
an opportunity to observe skilled craftsmen at work and
can appreciate the many advantages that are available to
the individual who has mastered a trade.

ATTITUDES TOWARD WORK AND JOB SATISFACTION

In recent years a good deal of controversy has developed among social scientists and laymen alike concerning the general feelings or attitudes that agricultural
workers have toward their work. In effect, the question
at hand is, How does the Mexican agricultural worker feel
about himself and his job, that is, is he satisfied with
his work and with his lifestyle? In order to investigate
this issue of job satisfaction a number of key questions
were asked of our respondents in regard to their personal
feelings about their role in the agricultural industry and
their level of satisfaction with their occupational position.

When asked, the vast majority of our respondents
(86.8%) said that they liked their present job, a rather
surprising result. However, in a second test question the
results remained virtually the same, as 87.9 percent said
that they liked their work in agriculture. Therefore, given
this level of consistency, we can say that the majority of
our respondents are satisfied with their work in the agricultural industry. Similarly, a study of agricultural
workers conducted in Kern County (California) found that
two-thirds of the Mexican respondents "preferred to stay in
farm work. . . ."34

However, upon further investigation it appears that these sanguine results are rather tenuous at best, and can be somewhat misleading at worst. While initially 86.8 percent of our respondents said that they were satisfied with their present jobs, we also found that four out of five (80.2%) were very willing to engage in some other type of work if they only had the opportunity. Consequently, there is a significant difference between their promulgated level of job satisfaction and their desire to abandon their present occupation for some other type of work. This rather amorphous situation seems to indicate that while they are satisfied with their current job situation, they would certainly take advantage of any propitious opportunity to enter a nonagricultural work environment. On the other hand, their apparent complacency may simply reflect the acceptance of their "fate" in the economic structure and therefore they feel somewhat powerless to make any constructive changes in their current situation. In effect, the fact that they say that they like their work in agriculture may only mean that they have accepted their situation in life and are simply trying to make the best of it. At the same time this would account for their overwhelming interest in doing some other type of work.

In fact, our results are not anomalous on this issue. For example, while four out of five (80.2%) of our respondents said that they would be willing to do some other type of work, Halfon found that a similar proportion (i.e., 82%) of her respondents said that they would like to pursue nonagricultural jobs.[35] The congruency of our results is rather striking. On the other hand, in his Kern County (California) study Metzler found that "40 percent of the Spanish Americans expressed a definite preference for some type of nonfarm employment."[36] By the same token, in his study of Mexican agricultural workers in Yolo and Solano counties (California) Haller found that half (51.4%) of his respondents said that they would prefer industrial employment to agricultural work.[37] Initially, Haller found that only one in four (27%) of his respondents preferred agricultural work over nonagricultural work. But then, he asked a very interesting question: "Would you still prefer agricultural work if you were able to receive all of the benefits available to individuals in non-agricultural work?" Given this most important stipulation, the preference for agricultural work among his respondents increased from 27 percent to 40.8 percent, with only 16.9 percent undecided.[38]

Similarly, Halfon asked her sample of 584 Mexican agricultural workers if they would prefer agricultural employment to nonagricultural employment, if conditions improved. She found that half (52.9%) of her respondents preferred to remain in agricultural employment if the working conditions would only improve.[39] This represents a 29.1 percent increase above the 13.8 percent of her respondents who originally indicated that they did not want to remain in agricultural work. Conversely these findings reveal that almost one-third more of the agriculturists in her study would prefer to remain in the industry if working conditions were only meliorated. The obvious implication is that if working conditions ameliorated in the agricultural industry, this then would result in the development of a more permanent labor force, which in turn would lead to greater stability within agri-business in general.

Naturally, these findings impel us to posit the query: What are some of the things that agricultural workers like and dislike about their work? But when asked this question one in four of our respondents (23.1%) simply said that they "just like the work." Perhaps it is significant that their most frequent response to this question was a rather ambiguous retort. The second largest response category (15.4%) revealed that they liked agricultural work because they were most familiar with this type of work and consequently felt most comfortable working in agriculture. A few (12.1%) said that they were satisfied with their work because of the level of remuneration. Another small group said that they enjoyed the great variety of tasks that their work in agriculture required them to perform. Others enjoyed their work because it allowed them the freedom to move about in the "out of doors," while another group said that they enjoyed the personal autonomy on the job, that is, they liked the idea of knowing what had to be done and then going out and doing the work without the need for direct supervision. Others gave a variety of reasons for being satisfied with their work, such as the fresh air, the working conditions, the joy of operating farm equipment, "just satisfied with this type of work," and so on.

While it is difficult to pinpoint exactly why an individual enjoys his or her work, particularly when it is so physically demanding, others have obtained results that are very similar to our own. For example, Haller found that 60 percent of his respondents said that they liked their work because they were very familiar with this type of work. He also found that 27.7 percent of his respondents "just liked farm work."[40] This last figure coincides very closely with our 23.1 percent response from our respondents to a similar question. In like manner Sultan and Enos found that 11.3 percent of their 600 respondents indicated that they liked agricultural work because of the money; this corresponds to our figure of 12.1 percent. However, their largest single response category (21.8%) revealed that they did not like anything about their work in agriculture. Another 16.4 percent stated that they just enjoy working out of doors.[41]

In sum, the majority of Mexican agricultural workers, in our study and in others, who say that they like their work seem to like it only because they are familiar with it. In effect, they like their work because they are inured to it and have developed a whole lifestyle around it.

Logically, our next objective was to determine those idiosyncrasies that they dislike about their work. Surprisingly, three out of ten (28.6%) said that they did not like anything about their work in agriculture. So it must be the case that some agricultural workers are only in the industry because they cannot find anything better to do. In effect a rather significant group of agricultural workers are simply caught in an inextricable situation. The second largest response from our respondents (13.2%) indicated that they did not like the work because it was "muy pesado" (very heavy). Others voiced dissatisfaction with such things as the dirty and dusty working conditions (12.1%), their low rate of pay (12.1%), the health hazards involved in agricultural work (9.9%), and even the maltreatment they received from their supervisors (8.8%).

Others have found that the major complaint among agricultural workers is simply that they feel they are underpaid for the type of work they do. For example, Sultan and Enos found that two out of five (43.6%) of their respondents said that they did not like the "low wages" paid in agricultural work.[42] Similarly, Haller also found that two out of five (44.4%) of his respondents objected most vigorously to their low rate of pay.[43] But on the contrary, only a few (12.1%) of our respondents were dissatisfied with their rate of pay. However, this may reflect the fact that the majority of our workers were rather

well paid, that is, in comparison to the wages commonly
paid in agricultural work.

Their second most serious complaint was related to
the difficulty and drudgery of their work. Other researchers have also made this observation, for example, Sulton
and Enos found that one in four (23.8%) of their respondents felt that their work was "hard and heavy."[44] Likewise, Haller found that three out of ten of his respondents
(28.6%) felt that their work was very difficult.[45] In
view of the consistency of these results, it is safe to conclude that next to their low rate of pay their major complaint is that their work is too physically demanding.
However, the reason so few (i.e., 13.2%) of our respondents
felt that their work was both difficult and heavy, in comparison to the results obtained in other studies, may simply
derive from the fact that "professional" farm workers do
not have to contend with the day-to-day drudgery of agricultural work as it is experienced by seasonal and migrant
farm workers. This results from the fact that, as in other
industries, the less physically demanding jobs are allo-
cated to those who have been working in the industry for
a longer period of time. In reality, the greater the
length of time on the job, the greater the development of
job skills; and consequently, the higher the skill level of
the worker, the less physically demanding the work.
Therefore, the disparity between our findings and those of
other researchers is closely related to the skill level of
the individuals surveyed and the differential degrees of
physical drudgery experienced by workers who operate at
these different levels.

In addition to these two major complaints, that is,
the low rate of pay and the difficulty of their work, agricultural workers frequently object to such things as the
long hours of work, seasonal nature of the work, lack of
year-round employment, lack of job security, lack of job
benefits, the health hazards on the job, safety hazards on
the job, the boss, and dirty working conditions. Therefore, as a group they would experience higher levels of
job satisfaction if their wages were higher, the work were
not so heavy, they could work regular hours, they could
work for the entire year, among other reasons. If these
conditions were met, then this would provide them with
the job security they all desire. In addition, they would
like to receive the job benefits that are automatically
given to laborers employed in other industries. They

would also like to be assured of a healthy and safe working environment.   In effect, they only desire to obtain the
same benefits, and be allowed to work under the same conditions, that are guaranteed to employees in other industries.   Therefore, they do not seek special privileges or
special treatment, but only want to be guaranteed the
humane and safe working conditions that are offered to
every other employee, in every other major industry as a
matter of course.

Having made a number of inquiries of our respondents regarding their job preferences, we then proceeded
to determine what they would consider the "ideal job."
For this reason they were asked to select the type of job
that they would consider as the ideal job, if they had the
opportunity to make such a selection.   At the outset this
appeared to be a rather enigmatic question for our respondents since the concept of an ideal job gave them a good
deal of difficulty.   In the majority of cases an explanation was required.   However, Zarrugh had a very similar
experience when she discovered that her respondents found
"it difficult to imagine themselves in other occupations.
Asked what sort of careers they would prefer if they could
do anything, some are unable to respond. . . ."[46]

While a potpourri of responses was offered as to
their "ideal job" a number of logical categories revealed
themselves.   For example, the largest single group said
that they wanted to be carpenters (13.2%).   Others wanted
to be auto mechanics (11%), while a similar number said
that they "did not know" what they would consider as an
"ideal job."   The remainder of our respondents provided
an assortment of miscellaneous answers, such as welder,
plumber, brickmason, construction laborer, truck driver,
machinist, and so on.   It is interesting to note that they
invariably selected jobs within the blue-collar world, but
at the upper skill levels.   It is also important to note
that the majority of these "ideal jobs" fall outside of the
agricultural industry.   These results conform closely to
those of Sultan and Enos, who observed that their "most
unanticipated finding was that the Mexican-Americans have
negligible interest or attraction for farm labor.   They
much prefer industrial employment."[47]   Invariably, the
main attraction of these nonagricultural jobs was the
higher rate of pay that they offered (47.3%).   In addition,
they were also interested in the various benefits that they
would secure in these nonagricultural jobs.   In their

study, Choldin and Trout also found that half (48%) of their respondents mentioned the rate of pay as the most important attraction of nonagricultural employment. Similarly, they also found that their respondents were attracted by the job security available in nonagricultural employment (12%), the "intrinsic satisfaction in the work (11%), working conditions (10%), the relative ease compared with farm work (8%), the social relations on the job (6%), and the status or responsibility conferred on the job (5%)."[48]

NOTES

1. Historically, it has been the case that these four states in Mexico have always provided a large proportion of the immigrants to this country. In his 1930 study the famous Mexican sociologist Manuel Gamio felt that the reason for this high rate of immigration from these states was directly related to "the fact that conditions there for agriculture are difficult, the land having always been in the hands of a small number of big proprietors. For this reason, the excess population of the prolific 'peon' class has been obliged to emigrate periodically." See Manuel Gamio, Mexican Immigration to the United States: A Study of Human Migration and Adjustment (Chicago: University of Chicago Press, 1930), pp. 22–23.

2. Vernon M. Briggs, Jr., Chicanos and Rural Poverty (Baltimore: Johns Hopkins University Press, 1973), p. 21.

3. Walter Fogel, Mexican-Americans in the Southwest Labor Markets, Mexican-American Study Project, Report #10, Graduate School of Business Administration, University of California, Los Angeles, 1967, pp. 14–15.

4. David Lillesand, L. Kravitz, and J. McClellan, An Estimate of the Number of Migrant and Seasonal Farm Workers in the United States and the Commonwealth of Puerto Rico, A Report Prepared for the Legal Services Corporation, 1977, pp. 76–77.

5. Paul Sultan and Darryl D. Enos, Farming and Farm Labor: A Study in California, A Report Prepared by the Center for Urban and Regional Studies of Claremont Graduate School, National Technical Information Service, Springfield, Illinois, 1974, p. 136.

6. Ibid., p. 172.

7. Susana Halfon, Campesinas: Women Farmworkers in the California Agricultural Force (Sacramento, Calif.: The California Commission on the Status of Women, 1978), p. A-5.

8. Harvey M. Choldin and Grafton D. Trout, Mexican Americans in Transition: Migration and Employment in Michigan Cities, Michigan State University, Department of Sociology, East Lansing, Michigan, 1969, p. 91.

9. William H. Metzler, The Farm Worker in a Changing Agriculture, Giannini Foundation Report No. 277, University of California, Berkeley, 1964, p. 29.

10. California Assembly Legislative Committee on Agriculture, The California Farm Labor Force: A Profile, Sacramento, 1969, p. 58.

11. Lillesand et al., An Estimate of the Number of Migrant and Seasonal Farm Workers, p. 80-81.

12. Tom Haller, A Study of the Employment and Training Needs and Interests of Farm Workers in Yolo and Solano Counties, A Preliminary Report to the Interagency Coordinating Committee, Davis, California, Rural Economics Institute, 1979, p. 9.

13. Jorge Balan, H. L. Browning, and E. Jelin, Men in a Developing Society (Austin: University of Texas Press, 1973), p. 138.

14. California Assembly Legislative Committee on Agriculture, The California Farm Labor Force, p. 58.

15. Lillesand et al., An Estimate of the Number of Migrant and Seasonal Farm Workers, p. 80.

16. Metzler, The Farm Worker in a Changing Agriculture, p. 73.

17. Balan et al., Men in a Developing Society, p. 115.

18. Choldin and Trout, Mexican Americans in Transition, p. 224.

19. Norman Goldner, "The Mexican in the Northern Urban Area: A Comparison of Two Generations," Ph.D. dissertation, Michigan State University, East Lansing, 1963, p. 42.

20. Sultan and Enos, Farming and Farm Labor, p. 144.

21. Halfon, Campesinas, p. A-15.

22. Haller, A Study of the Employment and Training Needs and Interests of Farm Workers, p. 14.

23. Choldin and Trout, Mexican Americans in Transition, p. 222.

24. Grafton Trout, "Mexican Americans in Transition in the Midwest," In part 7B, Hearings before the Subcommittee on Migratory Labor of the Committee on Labor and Public Welfare, Migrant and Seasonal Farm-Worker Powerlessness, U.S. Senate, 91st Congress, 1970, Part 7B, p. 4543.

25. Choldin and Trout, Mexican Americans in Transition, p. 222.

26. Sultan and Enos, Farming and Farm Labor, p. 165.

27. Haller, A Study of the Employment and Training Needs and Interests of Farm Workers, p. 30.

28. Choldin and Trout, Mexican Americans in Transition, p. 167.

29. Ibid., p. 165.

30. Halfon, Campesinas, p. A-24.

31. Choldin and Trout, Mexican Americans in Transition, p. 166.

32. Haller, A Study of the Employment and Training Needs and Interests of Farm Workers, p. 16.

33. Ibid., p. 32.

34. Metzler, The Farm Worker in a Changing Agriculture, p. 69.

35. Halfon, Campesinas, p. A-24.

36. Metzler, The Farm Worker in a Changing Agriculture, p. 69.

37. Haller, A Study of the Employment and Training Needs and Interests of Farm Workers, p. 27.

38. Ibid.

39. Halfon, Campesinas, p. A-25.

40. Haller, A Study of the Employment and Training Needs and Interests of Farm Workers, p. 24.

41. Sultan and Enos, Farming and Farm Labor, p. 146.

42. Ibid., p. 155.

43. Haller, A Study of the Employment and Training Needs and Interests of Farm Workers, p. 26.

44. Sultan and Enos, Farming and Farm Labor, p. 155.

45. Haller, A Study of the Employment and Training Needs and Interests of Farm Workers, p. 26.

46. Laura H. Zarrugh, "Gente De Mi Tierra: Mexican Village Migrants in a California Community," Ph.D. dissertation, Department of Anthropology, University of California, Berkeley, 1974, p. 45.

47.   Sultan and Enos, Farming and Farm Labor, pp. 49–50.

48.   Choldin and Trout, Mexican Americans in Transition, p. 245.

5

Making a Living: Wages, Economic Conditions, and Unemployment

SUBSISTENCE WAGES

Even a cursory review of the available data reveals that there are two major stumbling blocks that are encountered in any attempt to determine the annual income of agricultural workers--that their rate of pay is variable over a given period of time and, secondly, there is always fluctuation in their overall period of employment. Consequently, agricultural workers are forced to sell their labor on the open market at constantly changing rates of pay during the year depending upon such factors as the season, whims of the employer, the place, the type of crop, the general availability of agricultural workers, and so on. The result is a very unstable situation in which manpower needs, job performance, and skill requirements will vary with the maturation of certain agricultural products. Therefore, their hourly rate of pay will fluctuate depending on whether, for example, they are required to operate a tractor, irrigate the fields, pick fruit, prune trees, graft vines, or whatever. In effect, the maturation and fruition of certain crops determine the great variety of tasks that must be performed and this in turn has a direct impact on their rate of pay, as these various tasks require different skills and abilities and therefore call for differential rates of pay.

From the outset a number of basic observations were made concerning pay scales in general, that is, their annual rate of pay is strongly influenced by a set of four interrelated variables: place, type of crop, employer, and general availability of agricultural workers. These variables are interrelated in the sense that place (i.e., geographic location) very often determines the type of crops that are suitable to a particular climate, topographical conditions, and environment. By the same token place will also influence the general availability of agricultural workers, that is, with reference to its distance from certain key population centers. Therefore, if we can agree that place determines the type of crops that will be most productive in a particular climate, then we can anticipate that the type of crop will determine the rate of pay that is offered in a particular climate. Consequently, the type of crop will determine the rate of pay that an agricultural worker can expect to earn in a particular geographic location. The result is that agricultural workers can earn more money by working certain crops than they can by working others, depending on the season of the year, of course.

In reality, every agricultural product has an established rate of pay for its general cultivation and harvest. In this manner, over a given period of time, a recognized wage scale is established for each and every crop that is cultivated in the vast cornucopia of agricultural products.[1] For example, an agricultural worker can earn more money by working in fruit and nut trees than by working in vegetable and row crops. However, this disparity in the rate of pay is strongly related to the period of time agricultural workers are needed to care for and harvest a particular crop. In the case of fruits and nuts a small but specialized labor force is required for extended periods during the year, as these trees require a good deal of care and attention throughout the year. On the other hand, vegetables and row crops require a large, unskilled labor force for a relatively short period of time, that is, during the harvest season. Consequently, row crops can only support a large labor force for a short period of time. The result is that wages, and therefore annual income, are subject to radical fluctuations depending on the type of crop worked and the season of the year. By contrast, fruit and nut trees provide a more reliable source of income during the year. Therefore, we would expect that the annual income of agricultural workers who specialize in fruit and nut trees will be higher as a direct result of the higher skill levels that are required, the greater duration of the work period, and the inherent stability of these particular agricultural products.

Obviously, "place" and "type of crop" are two variables that are strongly related to the annual income of agricultural workers. However, place is also closely related to the general availability of agricultural workers, which in turn has a significant impact on wages. A basic principle in agricultural economics holds that the rate of pay of agricultural workers will fluctuate with the distance of certain crops from known population centers, which in turn is simply an index of the general availability of laborers who are willing to work in agriculture. This observation simply reflects the well-known economic axiom that the greater the surplus of laborers, the lower the prevailing rate of pay, and conversely a shortage of laborers will often result in a higher wage scale. For example, note the wages that are offered in agricultural counties located adjacent to the Mexican border, as compared with the wages that are paid in northern counties for similar agricultural work.[2]

Given the four variables of place, crop, season, and general availability of agricultural workers, it is a simple matter to develop a composite picture of the type of agricultural worker whom we would expect to have a relatively high and dependable income. For example, we would expect that agricultural workers who specialize in fruit and nuts in the northern counties of California would have the highest rates of pay. According to our data this assumption is supported.

In view of the complexity and insurmountable difficulties that one encounters in any attempt to obtain accurate information concerning the annual income of agricultural workers, it was decided early on to approach this issue from a number of methodological perspectives. Therefore, rather than adopt the orthodox methods of survey research and ask each respondent for an estimate of his or her annual income, it was decided to utilize a set of more specific questions to arrive at a very close estimate of the annual income of each respondent. While the orthodox methods of survey research may work well with industrial or professional workers, it would be most inappropriate to ask agricultural workers for their yearly income in such a direct manner. With industrial or professional workers the direct approach is very effective in view of the fact that they have job security and can count on a set salary or wage and therefore can estimate, with a good deal of accuracy, their yearly income. But when one approaches an agricultural worker with this question, it is easy to appreciate the complexity and difficulties involved. Indeed most agricultural workers do not really know how much they earn in any given year. Therefore, it would be both inefficacious and nugatory to attempt to approach this issue in such a direct manner, particularly when field experience has revealed that such an approach is fraught with pitfalls.

The method utilized in this study encompassed a number of indirect but closely related questions. We began by asking each respondent how many months out of the year they were generally employed in agriculture. In this manner we were able to determine that our respondents worked a minimum of three months and a maximum of 12, with an average of 9.6 months for the total sample. We then asked how many days a week they generally worked and found that they worked an average of 6.1 days per week. From our field observations we had anticipated that they worked almost every day of the week, that is, so long as the opportunity existed. In the following question we asked each respondent how many hours a day he or she worked. The results indicate that they worked an average of 10.1 hours per day while they were gainfully employed. While these hours of continuous labor may seem rather high—and, in fact, they are—we should recall that the typical agricultural worker begins his/her day at four or five and often will work until eight or nine in the evening. It is also true that during the harvest season the typical laborer works 12 hours a day, seven days a week. What we have then is a composite picture of an agricultural worker who typically works ten hours a day, six days a week, for nine months out of the year. However, most of our respondents are "professional" agricultural workers and therefore must spend the major portion of their time on the job.

Obviously, the objective of this line of questioning was to gain a close approximation to the total number of hours worked per year. But our ultimate objective was to calculate the total number of hours worked per year and then multiply this figure by their hourly rate of pay. Therefore, each respondent was asked how much he or she was generally paid per hour and our results yielded an overall average of $3.78 per hour.[3] Given this information, we were able to multiply the number of hours that each respondent worked per year by the mean hourly wage and thus arrived at an average income for the total sample. For this procedure, the following calculations were observed:

$$10.1 \text{ hours worked per day}$$
$$\underline{\text{X } 6.1} \text{ days worked per week}$$

$$61.61 \text{ hours worked per week}$$
$$\underline{\text{X } 38.4} \text{ weeks worked per year, i.e., 9.6 months}$$

$$2,365.824 \text{ hours worked per year}$$
$$\text{X } 3.78 \text{ average wage paid per hour}$$

$$\$8,942.82 \text{ average yearly income for total sample}$$

By this circuitous method we were able to obtain an average yearly income of $8,942.82.[4]

However, one of the most significant social and economic characteristics revealed by these calculations is the enormous amount of time that agricultural workers must devote to their jobs in order to maintain themselves. For example, the point can be made that when we compare the time that they spend on the job to the amount of time that the average worker spends on the job, we observe that during the 9.6 months of employment they actually spend enough time on the job to account for 14.79 months of labor.[5] This figure is arrived at in the following manner: We gave consideration to the fact that the average worker spends 40 hours a week on the job, giving a total of 160 hours of labor per month. Then we divided the total number of hours (worked per year by the average agricultural worker in our study) by 160 hours, that is, a month's labor. Besides the fact that they are seriously overworked, it is also true that our sample of agricultural workers only made $600 a month (before taxes and deductions). Again this figure is obtained by dividing 14.79 months into their average yearly income of $8,942.82, and we discover that they really only earn $604.65 per month. What is worse is that this amounts to less than $100 per month per capita, when we consider that each respondent has an average of 4.5 children. Of course, if their average yearly income of $8,942.82 is divided by the typical

12 months of employment, then they only earn an average of $745.24 per month (before taxes and deductions).

A very significant sociological observation that can be extrapolated from these calculations is that while our respondents only work 9.6 months out of the year, they nonetheless accumulate enough hours during this period of time to provide them with more than a full year of regular employment, or 14.79 months. Therefore, in a strictly economic sense, these agricultural workers are not chronically underemployed. Perhaps this observation sheds light on one of their major complaints, which is that they are dissatisfied with their low rate of pay. In effect, they only want better wages and regular working hours during the entire year, so that they do not have to overwork themselves for eight or nine months and still have to struggle to make ends meet.

FACTORS AFFECTING DURATION OF EMPLOYMENT

In our previous discussion it was aptly demonstrated that a direct relationship exists between annual income and duration of employment of agricultural workers. Succinctly stated, the hourly rate of pay and the number of weeks in a given year will determine the income-earning potential of agricultural workers. Theefore, it is important to isolate and examine the factors that influence the ability of agricultural workers to maintain a steady source of employment. In this sense an analysis of key personal factors that influence their duration of employment is essential. However, the rate of pay is in the hands of the employer and therefore falls outside of the sphere of control of the typical agricultural worker. Rather, our focus will be on the significant personal factors that can serve to extend their period of annual employment.

For comparative purposes the number of weeks worked during a given year will serve as our point of reference, that is, the number of weeks worked will serve as our dependent variable and in turn the independent variables will consist of those factors whose occurrence or change will affect the number of weeks worked during a given year. This analytical approach will help us obtain a clear understanding of the social and economic factors that can strongly influence the rates of employment and unemployment among agriculturalists in general.

Given the general demographic characteristics of the agricultural labor force in this state it would appear that age would have a significant impact on the duration of employment. Therefore, as a hypothetical statement we can say that there is a direct relationship between the number of weeks worked per year and age; that is, with each increment in age we can expect an increase in the number of weeks worked during a given year.

A brief review of our survey results indicates strong support for this hypothetical statement inasmuch as in case after case, when analyzed on a comparative basis, the number of weeks of employment increased with each increment in age for the respondents in our study. This relationship does not appear to be anomalous as other researchers have made very similar observations. The basic reason for this relationship is that typically the younger agricultural workers tend to only work on an ad interim basis. For example, most high school and college students only work during the harvest season. As one study found, "The youngest workers, those under twenty, had the least attachment to the labor force. This is understandable, since 71 percent of these young workers were students not seeking full employment for the entire year."[6] Therefore, younger workers have a strong propensity to view agricultural work as a temporary source of employment, suitable to their lifestyle and economic needs.

By the same token, age is also strongly related to a number of intervening variables. For example, age is strongly related to skill level, and skill level in turn will influence the number of weeks worked during a given year. As a rule, skill level will increase in direct proportion to the number of years of experience. Therefore, the greater the experience, the higher the occupational skills. And similarly the higher the skill level, the greater the period of annual employment.

For all practical purposes skill level is a given in this economic equation inasmuch as the individual who has more skills to offer is more flexible and therefore experiences longer periods of employment. In labor economics it is an axiomatic observation that the greater the skill level of an employee, the greater the probability of obtaining continuous employment in a particular field. Therefore, given the historic labor trends and the periodic cycles of employment and unemployment in the agricultural industry, we would expect to find that those who have the

most to offer in terms of job skills would also be the ones
who would have the longest period of continuous employment, and vice versa.   In the final analysis, higher skill
levels, job experience, and flexibility result in longer
periods of employment and ultimately higher income levels.
        By the same token, the development and acquisition
of certain "talents" is strongly related to the time spent
on the job, that is, to experience.   This is true in the
sense that talent is something that cannot be acquired in
a matter of weeks, but rather is something that must be
developed over a period of years.   But in fact experience
and duration of employment act and react upon one another
in a cyclical fashion.   Therefore, the more experience,
the greater the length of employment, and the greater the
length of employment, the greater the level of experience.
And so the process seems to feed upon itself.   Consequently, greater experience results in more work and
eventually in higher income levels.
        When reference is made to "tenure" we simply mean
to indicate the period of time that an individual has lived
in a particular agricultural area, and subsequently serves
as an indication of residential stability.   In a hypothetical sense the higher the tenure, then the greater the number of weeks of employment, that is, if all other "ad rem"
variables are held constant.   The upshot is that greater
geographical stability results in more weeks of full employment in any given year, and vice versa.   In a very real
sense the key distinction here is between migrant and
nonmigrant agricultural workers and their abilities to pro-
cure a regular source of employment during the year.
Simply stated, our hypothesis holds that nonmigratory
workers experience higher levels of employment than migratory agricultural workers.
        There are a number of important social and economic
reasons why nonmigratory workers, that is, local agricultural workers, report higher levels of employment than
migratory workers.   One of the most frequently made observations is that by their very nature migratory agricultural workers must transmigrate in an effort to secure as
regular a source of employment as possible.   But in their
interminable peregrinations they sacrifice a great deal of
time searching for another job.   Consequently, they suffer
from high rates of unemployment and meager annual incomes.   As a result, they must move continuously from one
place to another and canvass as many potential employers

as possible. However, in the process they forfeit several
weeks or months out of each year just looking for work,
during which time they could, of course, be more productive. While, on the other hand, nonmigratory agricultural
workers are in a most favorable position insofar as they
are familiar with the local job market and therefore know
where to look for work when unemployed. For example,
nonmigratory agricultural workers are able to solicit work
from former employers who are in most cases familiar with
the quality of their work. In effect, they have had time
to build a reputation in the local agricultural labor market
and can use this reputaton to their best advantage when
seeking employment.

In addition, nonmigratory agricultural workers can
utilize the services of both public and private agencies
when unemployed. Furthermore, many are qualified in
terms of residency and certain other requirements for such
benefits as unemployment insurance and various welfare
services if needed. In comparison, migratory agricultural
workers are often not qualified for, or are not even aware
of, the general availability of social services in the various communities in which they are only employed on a
temporary basis. Consequently, the absence of such aid
and services as are frequently offered by both public and
private agencies in various communities places an additional burden on the meager resources of migratory agricultural workers. In sum, nonmigratory agricultural
workers can draw upon a number of benefits and services
that are not generally available to migratory agricultural
workers, all of which serve to provide "locals" with a
greater period of employment in any given year, and in
the end with higher annual incomes.

While "attachment to the agricultural labor force"
may at first appear as a rather amorphous concept to be
given serious consideration in our analysis of personal
factors that affect the duration of employment, we shall
demonstrate that it can have a very significant impact on
the unemployment rate among agricultural workers in general. In brief, attachment to the agricultural labor force
is simply an indication of the personal commitment of agricultural workers to their work. Here we make reference
to the personal dedication of the individual to his/her work
assignment. Therefore, in a hypothetical sense, an increase in the level of dedication will result in an increase

in the period of employment for any given year. Simply
stated, dedication is a crude index of the need to work.

From an operationalized perspective it is clear that
older individuals will be more dedicated to their work than
younger individuals; therefore, the more mature agricultural workers will experience higher levels of employment
than younger workers. This observation is true in light
of the evidence provided in our previous discussion. However, concealed behind the variables of dedication and age
are the significant factors of desire, motivation, and the
need to work. Therefore, age and dedication are simply
reflections of the additional duties and responsibilities
that are assumed during the normal course of the life
cycle. Consequently, we observe an increase in the attachment to the agricultural labor force among those who have
taken on the responsibilities of supporting a family.

In light of these syllogisms, the statement can be
made that those who are young and single will have the
least amount of attachment to the agricultural labor force;
and concomitantly those who are married and have families
to support will demonstrate the greatest degree of dedication. For example, one researcher has observed that "Men
who are married generally earn more than those who are
not, particularly in comparison with younger men who
have never been married."[7] By the same token, the observation can be made that men, as a group, probably
have a greater degree of attachment to their work than
women. This observation is true in view of the traditional
role of men as family providers, particularly among Mexican males, in view of their socialization and attendant
cultural expectations. However, upon closer examination of
the available data we observe that the critical difference
is really whether the person is the head of household or
not. Therefore, married middle-aged men with families to
support are simply more attached, or dedicated, to their
work because they are heads of households and by cultural
fiat must provide for the needs of their families.

Given this observation, we would expect to find that
women who are the heads of households would also be more
dedicated to their work, as opposed to those women who
are not, or as compared to single males. In fact, a number of studies have obtained results that support this
hypothesis.[8] In conclusion, the need and the desire to
work are strongly related to the duties and responsibilities

of supporting a family; in other words, attachment to the agricultural labor force is strongly related to age and family responsibilities.

Closely related to our variable of dedication is the distinction that can be made in terms of the differential rates of participation of males and females in the agricultural labor force. In a hypothetical sense the statement can be made that male workers will be employed for longer periods during any given year--as opposed to female agricultural workers. Again this differential attachment to the labor force is generally the result of cultural expectations that adhere to the male and female roles within the social and cultural milieu of Mexican agricultural workers. Specifically, the cultural expectation is that the male will provide the major support, and often the only source of support, for his family; however, the female will work, when necessary, in order to supplement the family's income.

A review of the available data supports our original assumption inasmuch as males do work, on the average, more weeks out of the year than female agricultural workers. In a similar analysis, the California Farm Labor Force researchers found that while 16.2 percent of the males in their sample reported working 50 to 52 weeks during the year, only 5.4 percent of the females responded in like manner. Therefore, three times as many males as females reported that they were employed for the whole year.[9] In addition, almost two-thirds (63.5%) of the women in their sample reported working under 15 weeks per year, while only one-third (34.3%) of the men fell into this category. In a more recent study Halfon notes that "Most of the women reported themselves as the most fully employed during the summer season. . . ."[10] In addition, Haller found that, while 9.3 percent of the Mexican agricultural workers in his sample reported working in agriculture on a full-time basis, none of the women in his sample were thus employed.[11]

From our general observations of employment practices and wages paid to agricultural workers, it appears that the legal status of the individual is a most important consideration for analysis. Given these observations a hypothetical statement can be made, that is, the greater the degree of legitimacy then the greater the period of employment during any given year. Therefore, the general expectation is that the legal agricultural worker will experience higher levels of employment than the undocumented worker, with a resulting higher income.[12] One of the important reasons for this difference is that undocumented workers constitute a large proportion of the migratory labor force and therefore only work in California agriculture for a few months out of each year and then return to Mexico. This truncated period of employment also stems from the ever-present threat of detection and subsequent deportation by the authorities.

The second-most important reason for this income gap is that undocumented workers are often paid less for their labor. Therefore, while the undocumented worker presents a very attractive economic proposition to employers as they will work for less pay, it is also the case that their annual income is far less than we would normally expect. The upshot is that they are typically employed for fewer weeks during the year and will also be paid less for the work that they perform. The overall result is that the mean income of agriculturalists in general is depressed by the participation of undocumented workers in the labor force; which means that local documented workers will continue to suffer from this general depression of wages.

Our field observations also reveal that the number of weeks worked per year is a function of the type of crop or crops in which a laborer had had an opportunity to work. As a general statement it can be pointed out that the greater the degree of crop specialization, the greater the period of employment and the greater the yearly income. Concomitantly, the lower the level of specialization, the higher the unemployment rate and the lower their annual income. Of course, the economic impact of crop specialization is strongly associated with the type of crops selected. For example, there is a considerable difference between the number of weeks worked and the annual income of agricultural workers who specialize in tomatoes and those who specialize in grapes. The critical difference is the requisite talent and skill level required to insure the propagation of these crops, for example, certain aspects of the cultivation of grapes require a great deal of talent, which takes years to develop. On the other hand, the cultivation and harvest of tomatoes is highly mechanized and repetitive, and therefore requires little talent and very few skills. The expectation, of course, is that agricultural workers involved in the cultivation of grapes would be paid more for their labor, in view of their need for

greater talent and higher skill levels. In fact, this is
the case.

The second-most important aspect of specialization
stems from the fact that certain crops need continuous care
for greater periods of time than other crops. For example,
tomatoes require a very large unskilled labor force during
a key period of the year, that is, the harvest season, but
otherwise only require the assiduous labor of a handful of
individuals during the remainder of the agricultural season. Consequently, their term of employment is relatively
short and likewise their annual income is drastically low.
In comparison the production of grapes requires a relatively stable and skilled labor force for a much longer
period of time. Consequently, agricultural workers who
specialize in grapes will experience a greater degree of
stability, a longer period of employment, and a higher
annual income than those who concentrate their efforts on
a strictly seasonal crop like tomatoes.

THE CROSS-CULTURAL PERSPECTIVE

From the cross-cultural perspective we can compare
the differential level of participation among the various
ethnic groups currently employed in agriculture in terms of
the number of weeks per year in which they are gainfully
employed. For our purposes ethnicity can be viewed as an
independent variable and in this manner a comparison can
be made between the level of participation of Mexican and
Anglo agricultural workers in the labor force for any given
year. Therefore, we would expect that Anglo agricultural
workers will experience more weeks of employment during
the year than Mexican agricultural workers, that is, if all
of the other variables are held constant.

While there are a whole host of reasons why ethnicity would make a significant difference in the number
of weeks worked per year, one of the major reasons for
this discrepancy—the difference between the length of employment for Mexican and Anglo agricultural workers—is
that full-time Anglo workers are often employed in positions that offer greater job security, for example, in su-
pervisory positions. Very often Anglo agricultural workers
have more skills to offer, or are employed in agriculture
as family members and this virtually guarantees them job
security. It is also true that as a group the Anglo

agricultural labor force contains a large proportion of short-term student workers, which in the final analysis would make the difference between these two groups even greater.

From this brief review of the most significant variables affecting the duration of employment among agricultural workers, it is easy to appreciate the complexity of social and economic factors that can play a very significant role in the determination of the yearly income of agricultural workers. Consequently, any analysis of the wage structure of the Mexican-American agricultural labor force should take into account such factors as age, skill level, tenure, sex, migrancy, ethnicity, experience, dedication, attachment, marital status, legal status, and crop specialization.

The situation is made more difficult when we consider that a change in any one of these variables will result in the variation or change of some other variable or set of variables, which will have a direct impact on the number of weeks of gainful employment, which in turn will affect their annual income. While sex and ethnicity are ascribed statuses, and therefore cannot be changed, and age is a characteristic that will change without any particular effort, it is true that all of the other variables that have been reviewed can be changed or modified in some constructive way as a result of an individual's effort to do so. Therefore, agricultural workers can improve their skill level, reduce their migrancy and thereby increase their tenure, gain more experience over a given period of time, alter their marital status, increase their level of dedication, work to improve their legal status, and finally, develop some form of specialization in the more lucrative crops. All of these steps can serve to increase their level of gainful employment and at the same time will serve to increase their annual income.

WOMEN AND FAMILY INCOME

The traditional cultural expectation for the woman in the Mexican-American family is that she will devote all of her time to her household duties and care for the children. Indeed, a cultural stereotype has developed over the years in which the Mexican woman is viewed as a docile and devoted homemaker and the Mexican male, on the other hand, is viewed as the authoritarian provider for his wife and children. However, the available demographic data and a number of research studies have shattered this traditional stereotypic view of the Mexican woman's role in the family. In fact, Mexican-American women in an agricultural setting are more likely to work and provide additional income for their families than not. In addition, research results reveal that Mexican-American women participate in the labor force almost as often as Anglo women. For example, a review of the census data (1970) reveals that the labor force participation rate for Mexican and Anglo women is very similar. If the participation rate of women with children is compared we find that Anglo women with children under the age of six have a participation rate of 28.4 percent, while the women of Spanish heritage, in the five southwestern states (i.e., Chicanas) have a participation rate of 29.8 percent. For Anglo women with no children under 18 years of age, 41.5 percent were working, while 40.1 percent of the Mexican women were employed. The overall results indicate that 39.6 percent of the Anglo women were involved in the labor force as compared with 37.7 percent of the Mexican women.[13]

In effect, there is less than a 2 percent difference between the number of Anglo and Mexican-American women who were active in the labor force. These statistical results, and others, certainly bring the validity of the hackneyed stereotypes concerning the role of Chicanas in the family into serious question. Indeed our observations reveal that the Mexican-American woman is an active participant in the agricultural labor force and that her income contributes to the sustenance of the family.

Given certain demographic and social trends, it seems safe to say that the percentage of Chicanas who are active in the labor force at the present time is somewhat higher than two out of five. In addition, given the traditional undercount of the Spanish-speaking population, we would expect that the percentages given by the census bureau are on the conservative side. It is also the case that the labor force participation rate is always higher among Chicanas in rural environments, as opposed to Chicanas who live in more urban settings. When asked if their spouses were working at the time of the interview, almost two-thirds (63.7%) of our respondents indicated that their wives were employed. The majority of studies seem to support our observations. For example, Metzler found that "Mexican households averaged 2.4 workers per household. . . ."[14] In a more recent study of Mexican agricultural workers, Haller found that the average number of workers per family was 2.0.[15] In a more extensive state-sponsored study it was discovered that almost half (47.7%) of the Mexican agricultural families had two wage earners.[16]

In view of these findings it does appear that better than half of all Mexican agricultural families rely on two wage earners for support. It was also our experience that, in almost every case, the second wage earner was invariably the respondent's wife. Other studies have confirmed this observation in that any time two wage earners are reported, it almost always means that the wife is gainfully employed. It is also the case that when three or more individuals are counted as family wage earners, these others are simply the older children in the family.

When our respondents were asked for their major sources of income, 98.9 percent said that their agricultural employment was their primary source. The second-most significant response revealed that their wives were major contributors to the family's annual income (64.8%). We then asked our respondents, "How much do you think that your family contributes to your total family income?" The results reveal an average of $3,687 per year, with a minimum of $1,008 and a maximum of $9,840. Consequently, the working woman in the Mexican agricultural family does play a very significant role in the economic survival of the family.

Additional survey results reveal that the working wives in our sample have been active in the agricultural labor force for an average of five years, and a maximum of 29 years. In the majority of cases these women will work when the opportunity presents itself. But on the other hand, the demands of child rearing can act as a major obstacle to continuous full-time employment. As a general rule the more children that a woman has, the lower her level of participation in the labor force. Conversely, childless women always have the highest level of participation, while those with four or more children reveal the lowest levels of participation.

Another handicap that working women must deal with is the fact that they "are overwhelmingly employed in the low-status and low-paying tasks of weeding, thinning, and hoeing, with some harvesting work."[17] But what is

important is that these working women are working for the
basic support of their families and are not out working
for "extra" money. Therefore, they constitute a very significant part of the Mexican-American agricultural labor
force.

Of those respondents who indicated that their spouses
were working, 71.4 percent were employed in the agricultural industry. However, the majority were only occupied
on a full-time basis during the harvest season; consequently, their term of employment was usually restricted
to three or four months out of the year. This observation
would serve as a partial explanation for the low annual
income ($3,687) found among our sample of working women.
Most said that they were willing to work for longer periods
if the work were available.

The results obtained in our study reveal that the
mean family income was only $11,353 per year,[18] as op-
posed to the individual mean income of $8,773. Of course,
it is important to observe the difference between the average family income and the per capita income. When consideration is given to the per capita income it becomes
apparent that these agricultural families have very little
money to go around. Naturally, this produces an additional hardship since the Mexican-American family is
larger than the average family.

ADDITIONAL SOURCES OF INCOME

Thus far our focus has been on the necessity for
two wage-earners in the Mexican-American agricultural
family. However, it is also important to take account of
the innumerable methods by which these families augment
their income. While our intent is not to cast aspersions
on the dignity of these sedulous agricultural workers,
rather we simply wish to outline some of the more common
methods by which they are able to make the very best of
their unfortunate economic conditions. In most cases
these are methods that often fall outside of the traditional
sphere of labor economics and therefore are not usually
given consideration.

One of the most common methods of augmenting one's
income is to secure part-time or temporary employment.
For the most part the acceptance of temporary, full-time

employment has become very acceptable among agricultural workers, particularly in view of its seasonal nature. In many cases just finding a temporary job is a requisite for economic survival among agricultural workers in general. Most often they will work as truck drivers, common laborers, construction workers, warehousemen, factory workers, gardeners, and so on. Depending on the employer and the work situation, their income may be reported in the prescribed manner, or they may simply be paid in cash on a daily basis. Most cash transactions take place in situations where the services of the worker will only be required for a few days at a time. By this means the employer avoids all of the paperwork that is normally involved in hiring new employees, but more importantly the employer can save money in the form of unpaid taxes and employee benefits. In most cases temporary workers are satisfied with this arrangement, primarily because they know exactly how much they will take home at the end of each day, without having to give up a portion of their pay in taxes. While this additional income is not reported, it does in fact increase the annual income of the worker.

Another opportunity to earn extra income occurs when an agricultural worker possesses special talents or refined skills. In most cases he will present himself as an "independent contractor," in that he provides a particular service or performs a specific task for a set salary or bid. For example, the agricultural worker may have an extracurricular talent as a cook, a barber, or a musician. In the case of the barber and the musician it is common knowledge that they are paid in cash and that this source of extra income is seldom, if ever, reported. Most barbers and musicians do not have any difficulty in earning an extra $40 or $80 a week. Once again, this additional income serves to increase their actual or real annual income. Even those who do not possess any particular skill can, if nothing else, provide transportation to those who are in need of it. Providing transportation services can be a very lucrative business if it can be provided on a regular basis and for long distances.

The point of this discussion, of course, is to indicate that a whole host of methods exist whereby the more ambitious individuals can supplement their annual incomes, while the actual means and methods that are utilized simply depend on the talents and the resources of the individuals involved; but the most important consideration, for our purposes, is that these additional sources of income are rarely ever reported and consequently are seldom taken into account in the evaluation of the annual income of agricultural workers.

Undoubtedly, unreported income does play a very significant role in the overall economic panorama of the agricultural worker. In reality these individual adaptations are very effective methods by which they attempt to compensate for their low wages and the frequent, and often long, periods of unemployment. In some situations unreported income becomes an institutionalized portion of their regular employment in agriculture. For example, according to several of our key informants, it is a common practice among certain growers to pay their permanent employees their standard 40 hours a week and any additional hours are remunerated in cash. Naturally, the employer and his employees are both satisfied with this arrangement inasmuch as they both stand to reap certain economic gains.

In many family situations it is not uncommon for wives and daughters to work at a variety of odd jobs, which can add substantially to the family's annual income. Generally, they are employed in businesses where it is a common practice to pay employees in cash, for example, housekeeping, domestic cooking, providing child care, ironing clothes, catering meals, and so on. Essentially, these are situations where they are employed by a private party and wages are customarily paid in cash, generally on a weekly basis or on a contractual basis. While this additional source of income is not substantial, in view of the amount of time and labor involved, nonetheless it is an additional source of income for the family.

Just a few short years ago the state of California, in its infinite wisdom, extended unemployment insurance benefits to agricultural workers. As a result, those who are employed for the required period of time are now eligible for benefits. Even though these benefits may only amount to $60 or $70 per week, this will certainly help with the family's grocery bill. [19] In addition, unemployment benefits are frequently a source of unreported income for the agricultural worker, that is, these benefits are generally not taken into account in estimating their annual income.

Another source of extra money is often available during the harvest season and is obtained via the piece rate method of remuneration. During the harvest season

an agricultural worker can often earn twice as much
money in a single day than he would normally expect to
earn at the established hourly rate of pay. For example,
if the hourly rate of pay for cultivating grapes is $4.00
per hour, then the laborer can expect to earn $32 a day.
By working at the piece rate during the harvest season he
can expect to earn $80 to $100 a day. Once again this
will make a significant difference in annual income.
Therefore, it would not be difficult for an ambitious and
talented worker to earn up to three times his regular income. The point, of course, is that consideration must be
given to any extreme fluctuation in the established rate of
pay for agricultural workers.

The more fortunate agricultural workers are lucky
enough to work for an employer who provides them with
housing facilities and other amenities. Therefore, if housing is provided, at no additional cost, then this must be
considered as an additional source of income, which would
certainly make a significant difference in their overall
annual income. If housing is provided this could mean a
difference, indeed, an increase in their annual income of
anywhere from $2,000 to $4,000, depending, of course, on
the type of housing that is offered and the price of rentals
in the immediate area. In most cases all of the standard
utilities are included. In the long run they can channel
their resources into other more productive areas.

In some cases Mexican agricultural workers are
known to be owners of private property and agricultural
land in Mexico. During the three to five months that they
are unemployed each year they return to Mexico and supervise the harvest of their own crops. In these situations
their sedate efforts can produce a very significant increase
in their annual income. Other agricultural workers will
save their money and establish a small business in Mexico
and commission a responsible relative to operate the business in their absence. In this manner they add substantially to their annual income.

From this summary it becomes obvious that there are
a number of methods by which agricultural workers can
supplement their annual income. However, this is not to
imply that all agricultural workers are able to take advantage of these various methods of undocumented income
maintenance; for there are many who, for whatever reason,
are not able to take advantage of these opportunities. On
the other hand, there are always those ambitious and

resourceful individuals who manage to take advantage of
every opportunity to increase their incomes. Naturally,
these individuals are held up as the models of success in
their own communities.

COPING WITH CHRONIC UNEMPLOYMENT

Agricultural workers become inured to the seasonal
aspects of their work and the concomitant fluctuation in
the source of family income at a very young age. In
most cases they are reared in households that are beset
with financial difficulties and therefore learn, at an early
age, to cope with the difficulties of periodic unemployment.
Most can recall the social and economic impact that this
chronic cycle of unemployment had on their own families.
As a result, most are accustomed to the perpetual cycle of
employment and unemployment, that is, of periods when the
family can experience a sense of stability and security,
and other times when things are not so ruddy.

As adults, agricultural workers quickly develop
their own modes of adaptation to this annual cycle of employment and unemployment. Those with foresight and a
good deal of discipline manage to set aside a few dollars
each week and thereby garner a savings account, however
paltry, from which they can draw during times of unemployment. But those who have not saved for the winter
unemployment period or who have depleted their "nest egg"
will have to rely on close friends and relatives for support. It is during these hard times that the agricultural
worker will call upon his kinsmen for support and assistance.

On the other hand some have become so accustomed
to these annual economic fluctuations that they look forward
to the yearly respite from their arduous work. As one
researcher has pointed out, "Seasonal workers frequently
regard no work during the winter months as part of their
annual life pattern."[20] Our findings were similar as
over one-third (37.4%) of our respondents stated that they
just "sat around the house" when asked what they did
while unemployed. One in four (27.5%) indicated that he
or she did not have any problem with unemployment, which
meant that the individual was fortunate enough to secure
year-round employment. Eleven percent said that they
spent their period of unemployment visiting friends and

relatives in Mexico. Others said that they collected unemployment benefits, repaired their homes, and did various odd jobs.

Overall there appears to be a healthy pattern of adaptation to the annual period of unemployment. In most cases the first few weeks are spent organizing things around the house and making needed home and automobile repairs. During this early period of unemployment they also pay visits to friends and relatives whom they have not had time to see during the regular agricultural season. In a reciprocal manner they also invite guests over to their homes. After an initial two or three weeks of unemployment, most will begin in earnest on their job search, whether temporary or part-time. Those with special talents and skills sell their services, while others go out to the various farms and contract for pruning and clean-up jobs. These odd jobs generally occupy from four to five days out of the week, for six to eight hours a day, as the hours of daylight are rather short during the winter months. For the typical agricultural worker these truncated hours represent a half day's work. In addition, these periods of unemployment are frequently interrupted by inclement weather.

Besides relaxing, visiting, taking care of the house, auto repairs, and accepting odd jobs, some will make extensive preparations for their annual visit to friends and relatives in Mexico for the holiday season. Their sojourn to the old country will generally last about a month. Many indicated that they would like to extend their vacations to Mexico but are compelled to return as their children must return to school. Upon their return they ferret out odd jobs, at least until the regular agricultural season begins. By late February or March the more fortunate, that is, those with permanent jobs, are recalled, while the less fortunate continue to look for a permanent source of employment for the coming year.

While they find a variety of constructive things to do with their time, it is also true that most are available for agricultural work if the opportunity should present itself. In this regard our respondents were asked what they considered to be the major obstacles to finding work when unemployed. Of those who suffered from chronic unemployment, half (52.6%) felt that the lack of jobs in agriculture was the major obstacle. From their perspective, all they wanted was to work, but they simply could not find a job within their immediate area and therefore felt that the major problem was the basic lack of job opportunities. However, one in four (27.6%) felt that their inability to speak English was a very serious handicap. They felt that while this incumbrance did not necessarily deprive them of job opportunities within the agricultural labor market, it did restrict their job search activities to this industry, which they already knew offered very few job opportunities. In their opinion English-speaking ability would allow them to look for job opportunities outside of agriculture, where they felt more opportunities existed. Yet others (9.2%) felt that their inability to read English was a serious obstacle. Lack of transportation was viewed as a major obstacle in one out of ten (10.5%) cases. Consequently, many felt rather isolated from most job opportunities, even if they should become available.

During the study period a determination was also made to see if our respondents would be willing to move to some other area within the state, or even to another state, if they were offered a permanent job with all of the standard amenities. Surprisingly, two out of three (69.2%) said that they would definitely consider such a move. Of those who said they would not consider moving, one in three (33.3%) said that they would not sell the house that they were buying and another third (33.3%) said that they "just like it here" and had no desire to move from the area. One in five (19.6%) said that they would not move because their children liked it where they were living. In effect, half of these respondents (50.9%) said that they would not move because they liked where they were living. This simply indicated that many have established strong ties in their communities and prefer to find work within their communities rather than having to move to a new area and have to start fresh. Others (15.7%) felt that they were too old to move and therefore would not give any serious consideration to the idea. Overall, the majority of respondents (69.2%) were willing to consider a move if it meant an improvement in employment opportunities and economic conditions. Our results are high when we consider that in her study Halfon found that only a third (33.3%) of her sample expressed a willingness to move and almost half (46.9%) indicated that they were not interested in such a prospect.[21]

JOB SEARCH TECHNIQUES

Inasmuch as these extended periods of unemployment are accepted as a way of life by most agricultural workers, it is essential that we take a closer look at their job search techniques. The objective then, is to determine the methods that have proven to be the most successful for the majority of agricultural workers and discover why certain methods are more successful than others.

When asked what they did to find work when unemployed, better than half (58.2%) of our respondents said that they went directly to potential employers. This meant that they would canvass the various individual growers in the immediate area and ask if they had any need for their services. Our results would have been much higher except that one in five of our respondents (20.9%) indicated that they never had any reason to look for work, that is, they were fortunate enough to have agricultural jobs that provided them with year-round employment. Our original assumption is confirmed by our findings and those of others who have addressed themselves to this particular question--in study after study the principal method of job search among unemployed agricultural workers is to go directly to the employer.

Following this direct approach, the second most important method of job search among unemployed agricultural workers is to rely on friends and relatives for aid in securing employment. Generally, when they are laid off they will notify close friends and relatives immediately, so that they will be on the alert for any job prospects in the area. In effect, unemployed agricultural workers galvanize an extensive network of concerned individuals who will help them find a job. While this social network is very informal, it can be, and very often is, a most effective job search technique.

The question then occurs: Which of these two sources of job information and referral, that is, friends or relatives, is more important to agricultural workers in their job search efforts? The findings of Choldin and Trout and other researchers seem to indicate that of the two sources, friends and relatives, friends were useful in 20 percent of the cases, whereas relatives were only 2 percent effective.[22] In the final analysis friends are more important than relatives in job search efforts because of the more extensive social networks that exist among friends in any given location. In addition, friends have a greater variety of work experiences and more extensive social contacts from which they can draw.

It is important to point out that this strong reliance upon the aid of friends and relatives in their job search efforts is strongly rooted in the cultural expectations that exist in every Mexican-American community, in other words, the cultural expectation that close friends and relatives will do their very best to help them find work. For example, in his study of peasants making the transition from their rural communities to Mexico City, Kemper found that most migrants found their first jobs in the city with the aid of friends and relatives.[23] In fact, the very process of finding a job for a friend or relative simply means that existing relationships will be crystallized and permanently solidified. Indeed, this fundamental service is very important to the formation and maintenance of social networks in the Mexican-American community.

In sum, it appears that the key factor is really the individual initiative of the agricultural worker who is willing to go out and make direct contact with a prospective employer. The second most important job search technique centers around the unemployed worker's entrée to the existing network of friends and relatives, who are in a position to gather, collate, and disseminate any available information concerning potential job opportunities. While it is true that the combined efforts of both friends and relatives are very important, our observations tend to confirm the findings of other researchers, which are that friends are more important than relatives when looking for a job. Therefore, it should come as no surprise to discover that agricultural workers are more likely to rely on the informal methods of job search that are readily available in every Mexican-American community rather than on the more traditional, formal channels of job search techniques. Our observations are confirmed by the results of a recent study that concluded that Mexican Americans "made less use of the state employment services than did other workers, that they more frequently applied directly to employers, and that they were more apt than other workers to rely on friends and relatives for their employment. Direct application to employers was by far the most common method of job seeking."[24]

In fact, Mexican-American agricultural workers, as a matter of common practice, make very little use of the more formal job search techniques and state services that are currently available. In our study only 8.8 percent of our respondents utilized the services of the state employment office. Other researchers have made similar observations. For example, Choldin and Trout found that only 9 percent of their sample made use of the services offered by the state employment office.[25] In a more recent study, Halfon found that only 15 percent of her sample of Mexican-American agricultural workers indicated that they had obtained a job through the state employment department.[26] Similarly, Friedland and Nelkin observed that "Practically no migrants use such formal government agencies . . . recruitment is highly casual and fortuitous."[27]

In addition to these job search techniques, there are a number of additional methods that are utilized by a small percentage of agricultural workers. For example, some growers will do their best to locate new sources of employment for their permanent workers when it becomes necessary to discharge them for short periods of time. Several respondents indicated that they always had enough work because their employer made arrangements with other growers to provide his permanent employees with a steady source of employment. Naturally, such "kid-glove" treatment is only given to those key employees who are viewed with special favor by their permanent employers.

In some communities the local social service agencies play an important role in finding jobs for unemployed agricultural workers. Sometimes they even manage to locate jobs in nonagricultural industries. Unfortunately, these agencies can only provide services to a relatively small proportion of the total unemployed population. Basically, these agencies are formal organizations that provide informal services, that is, informal in the sense that they provide an atmosphere in which agricultural workers feel comfortable. This congenial atmosphere derives from the personnel employed by such agencies as they are usually people drawn from the community who are not only bilingual but who also understand and can identify with their personal situation and needs.

Perhaps the preceding obsevations concerning the effectiveness of community-based social service agencies can provide some insight into their overall success in providing services to agricultural workers, as opposed to the apparent dereliction of the more formal state agencies.

State employment agencies have failed in the sense that the types of services that they offer are rarely used by the members of the agricultural labor force. This in part is a reflection of the formality of the services that they provide and also relates to the inability of state personnel to appreciate or understand the problem of agricultural workers. Specifically, state employment agencies are generally beset with files of red tape and rarely hire bilingual/bicultural personnel who can communicate with local agricultural workers. On the other hand, their lack of success may also be a direct result of the proven effectiveness of the less formal means of job search with which every agricultural worker is intimately familiar. This simply means that agricultural workers prefer to restrict their job search activities to the tried and proven methods with which they are most familiar and tend to view any other methods as futile. Perhaps these are some of the reasons why 90 percent of unemployed agricultural workers rely solely on the informal means of job search: direct application, and an informal appeal to close friends and relatives.

NOTES

1. Schwartz points out that as early as 1892 about 200 raisin growers met in Fresno County to set the wage scale for the coming grape harvest. See Harry Schwartz, Seasonal Farm Labor in the United States (New York: Columbia University Press, 1945), p. 70. Also refer to the documentation provided in Lloyd H. Fisher, The Harvest Labor Market in California (Cambridge: Harvard University Press, 1953), p. 97; and Clark A. Chambers, California Farm Organization (Berkeley: University of California Press, 1952), p. 31.

2. In study after study the conclusion seems to be the same--the presence of illegal Mexican laborers has a tendency to depress wages in those areas where they represent a significant portion of the population. For an economic analysis, see the results obtained by David North and Marion F. Houstoun in The Characteristics and Role of Illegal Aliens in the U.S. Labor Market (Washington, D.C.: Linton & Co., Inc., 1976), particularly p. 124; and

Vernon M. Briggs, Jr., "Labor Market Aspects of Mexican Migration to the United States in the 1970s," in Views Across the Border, ed. Stanley R. Ross (Albuquerque: University of New Mexico Press, 1978), pp. 183–203.

3. It is a general historical tendency that agricultural workers are only paid about half of what the average production worker is paid for his labor. For example, see the historical comparison of wage scales conducted by Richard Fineberg, in "Green Card Workers in Farm Labor Disputes," Ph.D. dissertation, Claremont Graduate School, 1970, p. 26. In fact, we note that the union pay scale for a common laborer in 1977 was $8.03 per hour. This means that our respondents, as a group, only earn 47.1 percent (at $3.78 per hour) of what is currently being paid to common laborers in other industries.

4. For ethical purposes, we should consider that if agricultural workers were paid a just wage they would have a much higher standard of living. For example, if we consider that the union pay scale for a common laborer in 1977 was $8.03 per hour and multiply this wage by the 2,365.824 hours worked per year, as an average, by our sample of agricultural workers, we arrive at an annual income of $18,997.57. This means that our respondents should be earning $10,054.75 more per year than their current level of remuneration indicates. What is worse is that the growers are, in effect, able to realize a profit of $10,000 per year for each agricultural worker that they employ.

5. In his study Belshaw found that his sample of Mexican agricultural workers worked an average of 2,487 hours per year, which converts to 15.54 months per year. Michael H. Belshaw, A Village Economy (New York: Columbia University Press, 1967), p. 150.

6. California Assembly Legislative Committee on Agriculture, The California Farm Labor Force (Sacramento, 1969), p. 28.

7. George Wilber, Minorities in the Labor Market, Vol. 1 (Lexington: Social Welfare Research Institute, University of Kentucky, 1975), p. 190.

8. For example, see the study by William H. Metzler, The Farm Worker in a Changing Agriculture, Pt I, Giannini Foundation Research Report No. 277, U. C. Berkeley, 1964, particularly pp. 46–47; and also California Assembly Legislative Committee on Agriculture, The California Farm Labor Force, p. 32.

9. California Assembly Legislative Committee on Agriculture, The California Farm Labor Force, p. 135.

10. Susana Halfon, Campesinas: Women Farm Workers in the California Agricultural Labor Force (Sacramento: The California Commission on the Status of Women, 1978), p. 8.

11. Tom Haller, A Study of the Employment and Training Needs and Interests of Farm Workers in Yolo and Solano Counties (Davis, California: Rural Economics Institute, 1979), p. 11.

12. For example, Wilber found that "Native born Mexican men earn more than other Mexican men, particularly aliens." Wilber, Minorities in the Labor Market, p. 200.

13. For documentation see, Fred E. Romero, Chicano Workers, Monograph No. 8, Chicano Studies Center Publication, Los Angeles, University of California, 1979, in particular p. 88.

14. Metzler, The Farm Worker in a Changing Agriculture, p. 25.

15. Haller, A Study of the Employment and Training Needs and Interests of Farm Workers, p. 9.

16. Halfon, Campesinas, p. A-11.

17. Ibid., p. 1.

18. Our mean family income figure of $11,353 per year compares with $16,009 per year for the country as a whole, a difference of $4,656.

19. The average unemployment benefits paid out in California during 1978 were $75.28 per week. The legal minimum at that time was $30.00 and the legal maximum $104 per week.

20. Metzler, The Farm Worker in a Changing Agriculture, p. 51.

21. Halfon, Campesinas, p. 33.

22. Harvey M. Choldin and Grafton D. Trout, Mexican Americans in Transition, Michigan State University, Department of Sociology, 1969, p. 118.

23. Robert Van Kemper, "Migration and Adaptation of Tzintzuntzan Peasants in Mexico City," Ph.D. dissertation, Department of Anthropology, U.C. Berkeley, 1971, pp. 116-21.

24. Vernon M. Briggs, Jr., W. Fogel, and F. Schmidt, The Chicano Worker (Austin: University of Texas Press, 1977), p. 40.

25. Choldin and Trout, Mexican Americans in Transition, p. 123.

26. Halfon, Campesinas, p. A-31.

27. William H. Friedland and Dorothy Nelkin, Migrant (New York: Holt, Rinehart & Winston, 1971), p. 19.

6

Adaptation to American Society: Family Life, Social Relations, and Education

MARITAL STATUS OF AGRICULTURAL WORKERS

The family as a social institution has long been characterized as a very strong and cohesive unit among Mexican Americans, and this was certainly true in this study. In fact, one of the most salient characteristics of our respondents was their high level of marital stability: 96.7 percent were married, only one respondent was single, one was separated, and another was divorced. Overall, 98.8 percent were either married at the time of the interview or had been married in the recent past.[1] This very high level of commitment to the connubial lifestyle probably results, in part, from the selection process, as our respondents were 23 years of age or older. Therefore, if consideration were only given to the age of our respondents, an average of 41 years, we would expect the majority to be married.[2]

Furthermore, these marital relationships are not only stable, but also reveal a deep commitment to the conjugal state, as the couples were married an average of 16.3 years. Given an average age of 41 years, their average age at the time of marriage was 25 years.[3] Similarly, their spouses married at a mean age of 20 years.[4] If allowance is made for a variance of plus or minus three years at the time of marriage, we can estimate that the men in our study married between the ages of 22 and 28, while their spouses married between the ages of 17 and 23.

124

The overall impression of family life among our respondents appears to be one of stability and permanence. This stability provides a most favorable atmosphere for the rearing of children.[5] While the Spanish-speaking population of the Southwest is not only younger than the population in general, their family size is also larger. For example, the average family size in California was 3.5 in 1960, but among the Spanish surname population it was 4.29. In 1970 the figures were 3.47 and 4.20 respectively. However, those of Spanish heritage living in the Southwest had an average family size of 4.4.

According to the findings of this study, the average number of children per family was 4.5, resulting in an average family size of 6.5. The largest family in the study had 13 children. However, the average number of children per family would have been slightly higher but that five respondents were childless, and one single. When compared to the findings of other researchers, our findings are rather typical. For example, Choldin and Trout found that the median number of children per household in their study was 4.5. In addition, they point out that, "About one-third of the households have seven or more persons in them."[6] In his study, Haller found an average family size of 5.4.[7] A safe conclusion is that the average family size of Mexican-American agricultural workers in the Southwest is probably between five and seven. For comparative purposes our respondents were asked how many children their parents had and they averaged 8.1 children, with a minimum of two and a maximum of 19. The average family size among Mexican agricultural workers has decreased considerably within one generation. Of course, this rapid decrease in family size, within one generation, is associated with a number of sociological variables; therefore, the obviousness of this relationship may not be as clear as it appears.[8]

SOCIAL RELATIONS AMONG AGRICULTURAL WORKERS

Given our field observations, it was anticipated that many of the respondents had established strong community ties. The first substantive clue was the fact that many of the respondents were born and reared in the same states in Mexico. For example, 22 percent were from Michocan, 20.9 percent were from Jalisco, 13.2 percent were from Guanajuato,

and 8.8 percent were from Zacatecas. Of course, these results simply reflect the dynamics involved in the migration
process. Historically the majority of Mexican immigrants
came from certain states within Mexico. In addition, once
the migration process is set in motion, it has a tendency
to perpetuate itself and attract people from similar locations. In the majority of cases, their migration to this
country can be viewed as a chain migration process: migrants will almost always attract their family members and
close friends. Consequently, extensive social networks are
frequently established between immigrants from Mexico living in this country and those who happen to be from the
same state or from the same village.[9] In most cases, the
neophytes are introduced to an existing system of social
networks that are already in effect when they arrive. It
is these informal institutions of indoctrination that provide
the immigrants with social, economic, and emotional support
once they arrive in the community.

In an effort to gain a better understanding of these
social networks, each respondent was asked if he had any
relatives living in close proximity at the time of the interview. We found that three out of four (73.6%) had relatives living close to them. A relative was defined as anyone within the second degree relationship, such as first
cousins or closer. Information obtained from the key informants also revealed a very close-knit pattern of family
relationships. In those cases where the members of two
families had intermarried, the most extensive family networks revealed themselves. Those respondents who did have
relatives living within an acceptable propinquity were
asked to identify them. The largest single response was
brothers at 38.5 percent of the cases, while sisters were
only mentioned in 4.4 percent of the cases. The real sociological significance of these observations lies in the fact
that the male members of a family determine if, when, and
where each family will migrate and live.[10] This interpretation would certainly coincide with the patriarchal view of
the Mexican family. The second-largest response category
was parents, who accounted for 7 percent of the cases. It
appears that the majority of these parents were the pioneers
in the immigration process who in their old age simply decided to remain near their adult children. While other
categories were mentioned, they were not statistically significant. Overall, in the majority of communities studied,
strong family ties did predominate, within which each fam-

ily member could expect to find security and emotional support.

Similarly, 91.2 percent of our respondents had close relatives living in Mexico. This finding confirms our assumption that Mexican agricultural workers have strong family connections with relatives in Mexico. When their kinsmen were identified, the sibling relationship was the most prevalent. Half (48.4%) said that they had brothers and/or sisters living in Mexico at the time of the interview. The second most common relationship was that between sons and daughters living here and parents living in Mexico; one-third (36.3%) gave this response.[11]

In addition to gaining an understanding of family relationships and network patterns, friendship patterns were also investigated. When asked if they had any friends living close by, 90.1 percent said that they did. This simply means that they have lived in an area long enough to establish close relationships with individuals outside of their immediate family. When asked, 92.3 percent said that they got along well with their neighbors. Indeed, during the course of these field observations it was noted that neighbors would very often rely on each other for various household and food products, baby-sitting services, and so on. Consequently, there was a good deal of reciprocal exchange of goods and services between neighbors, and most were very responsive to each other's needs.

One of the most significant relationships that can be established between close friends in the Mexican culture is that which is created between compadres (godparents). The relationship that is established between baptismal godparents is the most meaningful and strongest, and therefore the most honored and respected. When someone is asked to baptise a child, this means that he is held in the highest esteem, as this sacrosanct relationship represents the most cherished relationship that can be consummated outside of the bond of consanguinity. The existence and extent of such relationships should serve as a barometer of the development of close-knit social networks.[12] When asked, over half (58.2%) of the respondents said that they had compadres living in their community. Most said that they did spend time with their compadres when the opportunity presented itself. But overall, it does appear that the ties of consanguinity are more meaningful than the relationships that are established between close friends.

PARTICIPATION IN VOLUNTARY ORGANIZATIONS

In addition to learning about the depth and extent of their social networks, this study revealed more about the participants' roles in voluntary organizations. The sociological literature on this subject has long held that active participation in voluntary organizations is basically a middle-class phenomenon and that members of the working class do not have the interest or the time to become active in such organizations. In short, the assumption is that working-class people are not "joiners." In addition, a whole body of sociological literature exists that holds that there is a strong cultural bias against any participation in voluntary organizations by Mexican Americans in general. However, these views result from biased stereotypes and are not necessarily based on facts that apply to specific situations.[13]

An effort was made to study this matter more closely and each respondent was asked to provide a list of the organizations or clubs in which he was an active member. Just over half (56%) said that they had no associations, but the others (44%) said that they were active members in a local organization. About half of these (55%) said that they were members of one of the local Mexican-American community organizations. Most of these voluntary organizations serve as "mutual benefit associations" or attract a membership from among those who share a common interest, such as a soccer team, horseman's club, car club, or whatever. Of the active respondents, one in four (27.5%) said that they were union members, while others (12.5%) said they were active in their church and belonged to one or more of the church organizations that cater to the needs of church members. Only two respondents were active in local civic organizations that did not have any affiliation with the Mexican-American community.

Obviously, nominal membership in an organization does not reveal anything about the quality or level of participation in that organization. However, 85 percent of the active respondents indicated that they did attend the regularly scheduled meetings and functions of their organizations. It is also curious to note that the well-known middle-class "joiners syndrome" surfaced, that is, certain individuals were always active in various community organizations, always served on boards and committees, and were always recognized as representatives of their communities.

EDUCATIONAL ACHIEVEMENT AMONG
AGRICULTURAL WORKERS

Educational achievement among agricultural workers is a most important consideration; but on the other hand, their educational achievement is not very important. That is to say, it is not important in the sense that educational achievement does not generally make a significant difference in their working conditions and their rate of pay. While it is true that educational achievement can be seen as their key to social and economic improvement, it can also be viewed as one of their major stumbling blocks.

After reviewing the available data and consulting our findings, two conclusions seem noteworthy: first, that their level of educational achievement does not make any significant difference in their rate of pay, working conditions, or opportunities for upward social mobility; and, second, that their level of educational achievement is excessively low. One of the most significant findings of the California Legislative Committee study was that educational achievement among agricultural workers does not have any significant impact on their earning potential or annual income. As the authors of this state study note, "neither educational attainment nor literacy in English has any important bearing on medial earnings. This can be explained by the fact that most Mexican workers are field workers performing jobs where skills acquired in school are not important."[14] Similarly, in their study of Mexican laborers in Michigan, Choldin and Trout arrived at the conclusion that in "job markets at the lower skill levels, education does not have a particularly significant effect on the pay and occupational status of the job. . . ."[15]

The ineluctable conclusion is that academic knowledge, that is, educational achievement, does not make any difference in the rate of pay or the working conditions of agricultural laborers. In every case, the required tasks remain the same and are not affected by the educational accomplishments of the laborers. Indeed, some authorities have postulated that an increase in the level of education can only result in profound dissatisfaction with the monotonous and dirty tasks that are inherent to the agricultural industry.

The second-most important observation that can be made concerning their educational achievement is that when compared to laborers in all other industries, they are at the nadir of educational preparation. Even when compared with other laborers within the agricultural industry, the level of educational achievement among Mexican agricultural workers is among the lowest. For example, the California state study found that, "About 80 percent of the farm workers with no formal education are Mexican."[16]

These observations are particularly significant when we consider that the majority of our respondents were educated in Mexico (82.4%) and only one out of six (17.6%) received their formal education in this country. In her study, Halfon found that half (54.5%) of her respondents were educated in Mexico, while two out of five (40.2%) were educated in this country.[17] The higher percentage of her respondents who were educated in this country probably results from the fact that her respondents were younger. Many of our respondents were born and raised in Mexico and migrated to this country as young adults; therefore our respondents constitute the pioneering first generation of Mexican immigrants.

In the final analysis, the findings reveal that the average level of formal educational achievement for our respondents was 5.7 years. However, 11 indicated that they never had an opportunity to receive a formal education; six said that they were only literate in Spanish; while the others were illiterate. Overall, two-thirds (65.9%) of our respondents had seven years of education or less. Nonetheless, these findings are congruent with the results obtained by other researchers. In her study, Halfon found that two-thirds (67%) of her respondents had eight years of education or less, while half (48.4%) had seven years or less.[18] Again the higher levels of achievement obtained in her study can be attributed to the inclusion of second- and third-generation adults who received their educations in this country. Similarly, Sultan and Enos found that almost half (47.6%) of their respondents had achieved only eight years of education or less. However, one in eight (12.8%) had graduated from high school, while only 3.3 percent of our sample had done so.[19] The findings of Sultan and Enos compare very closely with those of Halfon, who found that 11.8 percent of her sample had graduated from high school.[20] In their Michigan study, Choldin and Trout found that the average level of educational attainment for their sample was six years; and only one in eight household heads had ever attended school. However, one out of seven had finished high school or had gone

further.[21]   Therefore, we can conclude that the average
level of formal educational achievement among Mexican
agricultural workers is somewhere between six and seven
years.

In addition to questions dealing with their formal
education, our respondents were also asked if they had
ever taken any classes or enrolled in school since the
termination of their formal education.   Half (48.4%) said
that they had taken classes or enrolled in school as adults.
Of this group, seven out of ten had taken ESL (English as
a second language) classes.   One out of nine had taken
classes at a community college, and one out of ten had
participated in an adult education program.   Only 7 percent said that they had enrolled in a trade school.   In
their study, Choldin and Trout found that over half (58%)
of their respondents had taken ESL classes, as opposed to
seven out of ten in this study.[22]

As a general rule, our respondents exhibited a most
favorable attitude toward education and viewed it as a
means of improving their present social and economic condition.   In fact, most viewed education as a means of securing a better job outside of the agricultural industry. When
asked, 97.8 percent felt that more education would help
them find a better job, and they viewed this deficiency as
a serious handicap to improving their present economic condition.

During the course of these field investigations, information was also obtained regarding parental educational
achievement.   This was done in order to provide a comparison between the educational levels of the respondents and
their parents.   Perhaps the most striking result was the
high levels of illiteracy found among the parents of the
participants.   Almost two out of three (63.8%) of the parents had not received a formal education, and, of this
group, only half were able to read and write, while the
others were profoundly illiterate.   The very best estimate
for the average number of years of formal education for
their parents was 4.1 years; this compares with an average
5.7 years for the sample as a whole.   This indicates that
there was a slight increase in education between the two
generations.

The high levels of illiteracy and the low levels of
educational achievement found among the parents of the respondents can be attributed to the general lack of educational opportunities in Mexico a generation ago.   In addi-

tion, there was very little time for children to attend
school, even if they had the opportunity, as they were required to help their parents in the fields. For example,
one source commented that, "Forty or fifty years ago . . .
the majority of school age population in the country (Mexico)
did not have an opportunity even to enter school. Educational facilities were clearly insufficient, and they were
almost totally absent in rural areas."[23] Similarly, Zarrugh
found that "Illiteracy is the norm among Jacalans over 40,
and it is not uncommon among people, especially women, in
their 20s who were raised in the ranchos where school was
considered a luxury."[24] Furthermore, many respondents
said that their parents could not afford to send them to
school, or that they were needed at home, and many parents did not see any advantage in sending their children
to school. Fortunately, this negative orientation toward
schools and education in general is changing rapidly with
the introduction of more educational facilities and the
greater availability of teachers, particularly in the rural
areas of Mexico.

Similarly, in their study of Mexican-American laborers in Michigan, Choldin and Trout compared the educational
achievements of fathers and sons and found that "Nearly
half (47%) of the respondents' fathers had no formal education at all but only 13 percent of their sons are this disadvantaged."[25] Given all of the available sources of information, it appears that the level of education has increased substantially over the span of one generation.

LANGUAGE USE AND ABILITY

Those who are most concerned with the social and
economic melioration of Mexican-American agricultural workers are quick to point to the urgent need for English as a
second language (ESL) classes, the impetus being that facility in English would increase the number of job opportunities available to them, particularly nonagricultural jobs,
with a concomitant improvement in their social and economic
conditions. In short, this view holds that an improvement
in English communication skills will result in a gradual
improvement in their social and economic conditions.

The results of our study reveal that three-fourths
(73.6%) of the respondents were monolingual in Spanish,
while only two were monolingual in English, and one out

of four (24.2%) were bilingual. However, while some individuals may say that they cannot speak English, this does not necessarily mean that they do not understand what is said to them in English. During field observations, it was discovered that Anglo foremen and Mexican agricultural workers can communicate with one another, inasmuch as many Mexican farm workers understand enough English to get the job done, and Anglo foremen usually speak enough Spanish to make their wishes known. In these situations, Mexican laborers and their Anglo bosses are able to compensate for each other's English/Spanish speaking abilities and disabilities. The point is, that even though three-fourths of the respondents claim to be monolingual in Spanish, this does not necessarily mean that they are unable to communicate with an English-speaking person.

In order to gain a better understanding of their total language environment, each participant was asked to indicate the principal language used in his home. While most (84.6%) indicated that Spanish was the predominant language spoken in the home, one out of eight (12.1%) said that both Spanish and English were used. In bilingual home environments the parents usually speak Spanish, while their children will rely on English. However, the children generally restrict their use of English to siblings and peer group members, and always address their parents and elders in Spanish. This observation serves to explain why many of our respondents understood some English, as they must be familiar with the language in order to understand what their children are up to. In only three cases was English the principal language used at home, but then this does not necessarily mean that Spanish was not also used, only that English predominated.

The fact that Spanish is used so extensively at home explains the tenacity of, and their continued dependence on, the Spanish language. These households and communities are cultural islands that have evolved throughout the Southwest where they can live out their entire lives without ever having to master the English language, as there is little need or incentive to do so. In the majority of cases, Mexican agricultural workers use Spanish exclusively in their homes, communities, and at work. Should the need arise for English-speaking ability, they can simply call on the assistance of one of their bilingual children and the problem is solved.

Upon further investigation, it was determined that three out of four respondents (76.9%) were able to read Spanish, 16.5 percent were bilingual, 2.2 percent could read only English, and 4.4 percent were illiterate. In an effort to ascertain their reading ability, each respondent was asked if he or she could read the newspaper or follow instructions at work in the language selected. If the answer was affirmative, then it was assumed that the individual was able to read in the language or languages indicated. Overall, one out of five respondents (18.7%) read English. In comparison, Halfon found that half (53.2%) of her subjects read Spanish, one-third (32%) were bilingual, and one in ten (11.1%) read English.[26] Her results compare with this study's finding of one out of five (18.7%) who could read English. However, this difference can be attributed to the greater number of young people in her sample of agricultural workers.

One curious fact about the ability to read a particular language is that it is often possible to read, that is, to decipher, a particular language and at the same time not have the ability to write in that language. This proved to be the case in this study as 84.6 percent wrote in Spanish but only 3.3 percent could write in English. In addition, 7.7 percent were bilingual, and four respondents could not write at all. While 15 respondents were able to read English, only seven were able to write in English. However, almost an equal number were able to read in Spanish (93.4%) and also write in Spanish (92.3%). One in five (18.7%) were able to read in English, and only one in ten (11%) could write in English. In comparison, Halfon found that half (54.9%) of her sample wrote in Spanish, one in six (15.7%) wrote in English, one in four (24.8%) were bilingual, and 3.9 percent could not write at all.[27]

In view of these results, and those obtained by other researchers, it is clear that there are a number of key sociological variables that can affect the English-speaking ability of Mexican agricultural workers in general. One rudimentary observation holds that language ability will vary inversely with age. The older the Spanish-speaking person, the less likely he will be able to speak, read, or write English, and conversely, the younger the Spanish-speaking person, the greater the likelihood that he will be able to speak, read, and write English.[28] For example, the youth of Halfon's respondents is the principal reason that she found a higher percentage of persons with the ability to speak, read, and write English, as compared with the findings of this study.

Another significant variable closely associated with age is that of generation level. Generation level is important because it can serve as an index of the degree of assimilation into American society. Therefore we would expect language ability to vary directly with generation level, that is, the higher the generation level, the greater the English-speaking ability. For example, recent immigrants would be classified as first generation and therefore their English-speaking ability would, at best, be minimal. However, their children, the second generation, would demonstrate a greater facility with the English language. Logically one would expect to find greater English proficiency among the children of second-generation Mexican Americans, that is, the third generation.

Language ability will also vary directly with the level of education; the greater the educational achievement, the greater the English language ability. This observation would certainly apply to our respondents as agricultural workers in general have low levels of educational achievement and also contain a very high percentage of individuals who cannot speak, read, or write English. But more important, the majority of Mexican agricultural workers live and work in a socio-cultural environment that is strongly orientated to the use of Spanish; therefore no premium is placed on English-speaking ability.[29]

ASPIRATIONS FOR THEIR CHILDREN

To gain an unlderstanding of their views regarding the importance of an education, particularly the relationship between education and job opportunities, the respondents were asked a number of questions concerning the educational and occupational aspirations that they had for their children. Three out of four (75.8%) were very sanguine about their children's occupational prospects as they felt that they would do well in their jobs and careers. However, one in five (19.8%) did not know how their children would do. Of course, the expectation is that most parents would hope, and even believe, that their children would do well in the future; after all, most parents live and sacrifice so that they can provide a better life for their children.[30]

When asked more specific questions about the future of their children in the job market, a degree of ambiguity appeared in their responses. Three out of four (74.7%) gave very equivocal answers when asked directly about specific jobs that they would like their children to hold in the future. One in four (26.4%) said that any job would be good for their children, and one in five said that any profession would be good enough. Others (14.3%) simply stated that they did not know what sort of job they would like their children to have. A handful (12.1%) said that any job outside of agriculture would be just fine. Of those who gave definite answers (25.2% of the sample), half said that they would like their children to be doctors or lawyers. It seems that even their most definite response was an idealized reaction to the question. This is true inasmuch as an answer of this type is closely associated with what might be termed "wishful thinking." This conclusion carries a certain amount of weight in view of the current social and economic situation of most agricultural workers and the life chances that confront their children. The probability of their children ever fulfilling their expectations is rather remote. When Zarrugh asked her respondents about their children's future, she also noticed that "most parents show neither strong feelings nor much concrete knowledge about possible alternatives to their own way of living."[31]

When asked how much education they would like to see their children receive, three out of five (59.3%) were rather ambiguous in their responses, as they only wanted their children to receive as much education as they could get. The single most definite response was given by one out of ten (11%), who wanted their children to go to college. An additional 10 percent said that they did not know. One of the major reasons for this equivocation is that they are not cognizant of the various requirements for obtaining a higher education, as they only know that their children should go to school while they are still living at home and not working full-time. The problem in many cases is that they are not aware of the important relationship between their children's regular attendance at school or academic preparation, and the probability of their offspring entering some technical or professional career. Metzler also found that his respondents demonstrated a "lack of understanding that education is a necessary part of preparation for life. Almost half, and possibly more, of the parents have not caught the generally accepted belief that education now is a necessity."[32]

When asked directly if they wished to see their children finish college, the vast majority (91.2%) answered in the affirmative. Similarly, Choldin and Trout found that "almost 90 percent indicated a desire for their sons to go to college."[33] In their study, Balan, Browning, and Jelin found that "education is the item most frequently chosen by the respondents among the qualities or characteristics a young man should have in order to get ahead in life."[34] In response to a very similar question, eight out of ten of the respondents (79.1%) said that a good education was most important. The second most frequently mentioned characteristic was a good job (13.2%). When education is viewed in the concrete "goal oriented" sense of obtaining a college education, it appears that this most desirable goal is something that all individuals can recognize and identify as a most worthy objective.

NOTES

1. In comparison only 67.2 percent of the household heads were married in the general population of the United States in 1978, a difference of almost 30 percent. Similarly, while only 1.1 percent of the sample were single, 11 percent of the household heads were single throughout the country in 1978. In addition, 8.7 percent of the household heads were divorced in 1978 as compared to our study's 1.1 percent divorce rate.

2. In comparison, Halfon found that out of 583 respondents, 73.8 percent were married; 4.7 percent were divorced; 3 percent were separated; 3.4 percent were widowed; and 13.6 percent were single. See: Susana Halfon, Campesinas (Sacramento: The California Commission on the Status of Women, 1978), pp. 2-6. In a similar manner, Choldin and Trout found that "Almost all the male heads of household (95%) were married at the time of the interview. Less than 2 percent were single, one percent were divorced or separated and 2 percent were widowers." See: Harvey M. Cholden and Grafton D. Trout, Mexican Americans in Transition (Department of Sociology, Michigan State University, 1969), p. 37.

3. The median age at the time of first marriage for the typical American male was 24.0 years in 1977 as

compared to the estimated age of 25.1 years for the members of our sample in 1978.

4. The median age at the time of first marriage for the typical American female was 21.6 years in 1977 as compared to the estimated age of 20 years for the spouses of the members of our sample.

5. It is the case that rural Mexican Americans not only have the lowest educational and income levels but also the highest rates of marital stability. For example, see the study by Peter Uhlenberg, "Marital Instability Among Mexican-Americans: Following the Patterns of Blacks?" Social Problems 20(1) (Summer 1972):49-56.

6. Choldin and Trout, Mexican Americans in Transition, p. 44.

7. Tom Haller, A Study of the Employment and Training Needs and Interests of Farm Workers in Yolo and Solano Counties (Davis, Calif.: Rural Economics Institute, 1979), p. 8.

8. The infant mortality rate was much higher in rural Mexico a generation ago and so the number of children that survived until adulthood was actually less than the number of children born to a given woman. It may also be the case that those who immigrate to this country just have smaller families, when compared to the nonmigrants. This is usually the case when fertility rates among migrants and nonmigrants are compared. For example, see the study by G. C. Myers and E. W. Morris, "Migration and Fertility in Puerto Rico," Population Studies 20 (July 1966).

9. A number of researchers have commented on and described this process of chain migration and resulting social networks that are established in various communities. For example, see the following studies: Wayne A. Cornelius, Building the Cactus Curtain (Berkeley: University of California Press, 1980); Michael Kearney, "Migration from the Mixteca of Oaxaca to the Californias: A Case Study" (Department of Anthropology, University of California, Riverside, 1978); Larissa A. Lomnitz, Networks and Marginality (New York: Academic Press, 1977); Richard Mines, "The Workers of Las Animas: A Case Study of Village Migration to California" (Department of Agricultural Economics, University of California, Berkeley, 1978); Laura H. Zarrugh, "Home Away from Home: The Jacalan Community in the San Francisco Bay Area," in The Chicano Experience, ed. Stanley West and June MacKlin (Boulder, Colo.: Westview Press, 1979), pp. 145-63.

10. In her study of 162 families that migrated from rural villages to Mexico City, Professor Lomnitz made a very similar observation. See Lomnitz, Networks and Marginality, p. 119.

11. These extensive ties with relatives living in Mexico result, primarily, from the fact that most agricultural workers in the Southwest are first-generation immigrants. For an in-depth analysis of familial relationships among recent immigrants to Sacramento, California, see the study by Vieno Lindstrom, "An Analysis of Relationships in a Network of Mexican-Americans United by Kinship," M.A. thesis, Department of Anthropology, California State University, Sacramento, 1966.

12. For a classic anthropological description and analysis of compadrazgo, see the article by Robert Ravicz, "Compadrinazgo," in Handbook of Middle American Indians, ed. Robert Wauchope and Manning Nash (Austin: University of Texas Press, 1967).

13. For a criticism of the popular Anglo view that Mexican Americans cannot organize themselves, see the in-depth study by Ralph C. Guzman, "The Political Socialization of the Mexican American People," Ph.D. dissertation, University of California, Los Angeles, 1970 (reprint ed., Arno Press, 1976). For a case study of Chicano political action, see the book by John S. Schockley, Chicano Revolt in a Texas Town (Notre Dame, Ind.: University of Notre Dame, 1974).

14. California Assembly Legislative Committee on Agriculture, The California Farm Labor Force (Sacramento, 1969), p. 57.

15. Choldin and Trout, Mexican Americans in Transition, p. 241.

16. The California Farm Labor Force, op. cit., p. 70.

17. Halfon, Campesinas, p. A-8.

18. Ibid., p. A-7.

19. Paul Sultan and Darryl D. Enos, Farming and Farm Labor, A Report Prepared by the Center for Urban and Regional Studies of Claremont Graduate School, National Technical Information Service, Springfield, Illinois, 1974, p. 174.

20. Halfon, Campesinas, p. A-7.

21. Choldin and Trout, Mexican Americans in Transition, pp. 47-48.

22. Ibid., p. 166.

23. Jorge Balan, H. L. Browning, and E. Jelin, Men in a Developing Society (Austin: University of Texas Press, 1973), p. 88.

24. Laura H. Zarrugh, "Gente De Mi Tierra: Mexican Village Migrants in a California Community," Ph.D. dissertation, Department of Anthropology, University of California, Berkeley, 1974, p. 89.

25. Choldin and Trout, Mexican Americans in Transition, p. 267.

26. Halfon, Campesinas, p. A-7.

27. Ibid.

28. For a more detailed discussion of the relationship between age and English-language ability, see the results obtained in Fred E. Romero, Chicano Workers, Monograph Number 8, Chicano Studies Center Publications, University of California, Los Angeles, 1979, in particular, p. 101.

29. In their study of the "Tenacity of Ethnic Culture," Grebler, Moore, and Guzman have observed that "An extensive study of 'language loyalty' among ethnic groups in the United States shows conclusively that Spanish is the most persistent of all foreign languages, and the one with the greatest prospects of survival." Leo Grebler, Joan Moore, and Ralph Guzman, The Mexican-American People (New York: The Free Press, 1970), p. 423.

30. For an in-depth treatment of the job aspirations of Mexican-American adolescents, and the aspirations of their parents, see the study by Terry Cole, "The Chicano in the Anglo World, Factors Affecting Job Choice," Ph.D. dissertation, Department of Sociology, Colorado State University, 1972. Or see the more accessible source by Celia S. Heller, New Converts to the American Dream? Mobility Aspirations of Young Mexican-Americans (New Haven, Conn.: College and University Press, 1971).

31. Zarrugh, "Gente De Mi Tierra," p. 47.

32. William H. Metzler, The Farm Worker in a Changing Agriculture, Giannini Foundation Research Report no. 277, University of California, Berkeley, 1964, p. 75.

33. Choldin and Trout, Mexican Americans in Transition, p. 67.

34. Balan et al., Men in a Developing Society, p. 258.

7

Perception of Social Class Differences among Mexican-American Agricultural Workers

In view of the fact that most people perceive their opportunities for social improvement in terms of their own evaluation of their current position within the existing social structure, it is imperative that we arrive at a clear understanding of the complex web of social relations that exist within the Mexican-American community. Therefore, once a basic understanding of the system of social stratification is obtained, as it currently exists within the Mexican-American community, then we can begin to understand the social position and the role that our respondents play within this socio-cultural complex and begin to evaluate not only their position as it relates to the other members of society but also, and perhaps more important, we can gain some appreciation of the position that they do occupy.

THE DETERMINATION OF SOCIAL CLASS DIFFERENCES

A review of the cross-cultural aspects of social stratification will reveal a number of key sociological variables that can always serve as rigid indicators of the position held by an individual with reference to the allocation and distribution of power, wealth, prestige, and privileges. These variables can either be viewed as being "ascribed" or "achieved" by an individual. The ascribed variables include those characteristics that are obtained as a result of birth; consequently "accident of birth" determines the ascribed characteristics that an individual assumes and maintains throughout life. The three most important ascribed characteristics bestowed at the moment of birth are family background, sex, and age.

Family background is the most important of the ascribed characteristics inasmuch as it determines the "life chances" of an individual. In effect, everyone is born into a social position as the family of orientation always provides a ready-made social position within the community. Consequently, some are fortunate and are born into families with high socio-economic positions, while most are born into families with a common background.

The second most important ascribed characteristic is sex. Gender is important in the sense that, within certain cultural environments, whether a person is male or female has a most significant impact on the final determination of his or her position within the existing social structure. For the most part, the designation of social position and social role is culturally determined. In sum, an individual's position within any system of social stratification is strongly affected by the biological accident of being born either male or female; but the ultimate effect and the intensity of this distinction are socially and culturally determined. Historically, women have not had an equal opportunity to participate in the system of social stratification; therefore, as a group, women have been deprived of many benefits commonly made available to the male members of society. This observation, of course, is particularly true of women in the Mexican and Mexican-American culture.[1]

A person's age is important to any system of social stratification to the extent that individuals who have arrived at ·culturally recognized periods in their life cycle receive a certain amount of deference from the members of their community for having attained a particular age. Generally, age is given more respect in traditional cultures and receives less deference in the more modern egalitarian societies. Therefore, the older an individual and the more traditional the culture, the greater the respect bestowed on that person. For example, age as an ascribed characteristic is very significant within the Mexican cultural tradition and therefore guarantees respect within the Mexican-American community.[2]

While the number of ascribed characteristics that affect the social status of an individual within a given

socio-cultural environment are rather limited, there nonetheless exist a whole host of sociological variables that
can come into play when consideration is given to the
panoply of factors that can interact, often in a synergistic fashion, to determine the social class position of a
member of society. These characteristics are most commonly
referred to as "achieved status" variables. Achieved status
includes all of those characteristics that are acquired
through personal efforts and accomplishments, which often
require the use of special abilities, skills, or acquired
knowledge. In the world of occupations and professions
an example of achieved status would be that of a barber
or doctor, for in each case the individual achieves the
particular status by assiduous effort and dedication.

In terms of the determination of achieved status, a
number of studies have revealed that within the Mexican-
American culture three key variables play a significant
role in the determination of social class position: income,
occupation, and education.[3] Of these three variables, income is the most important in the determination of social
class position within the Mexican-American community. For
example, Peñalosa found that his Mexican-American respondents named the following six variables, in order of significance, as being the most important for the determination of social class position: economic position, occupation,
mobility orientation, education, way of life (personal conduct and dress), and sociability (i.e., participation in
civic events and social activities).[4] In her study of the
behavior of middle-class women in Michoacan (Mexico),
Hubbell also found that her respondents felt that "money"
was the most important consideration in the determination
of social class position, followed closely by education, occupation, age, "culture," social connections, and the possession of consumer goods (e.g., household furnishings,
cars, servants, etc.).[5] In a similar manner, Tumin and
Feldman, in their study of social stratification in Puerto
Rico, also found that the determination of social class "is
primarily and dominantly a matter of differences in wealth
and standard of living; in comfort and luxury."[6] Consequently, the evidence is rather convincing that income
(i.e., wealth) is the most important consideration in the
final determination of social class position among Mexicans
and Mexican-Americans in general.[7] Indeed, when asked,
our respondents felt that the most important characteristic
that could serve to differentiate social classes was income
(40.7%).

The available research studies all concur that occupation is the second-most important variable in the determination of social class position within the Mexican-American community. Of course, the statistical propinquity between income and occupation results from the fact that these two variables are closely associated in the economic marketplace, in other words, the type of employment generally determines the annual income of an individual. It is also recognized that various occupations carry a certain amount of social status in and of themselves, regardless of the income that is generated. In this regard our data reveal that the second-most important response given by our participants was that the type of job was most important (20.9%) in the determination of a person's social position. Therefore, a person's occupational position is of utmost importance and plays a very significant role in the development of self-esteem and close identification with certain segments of society.

Education was found to be the third-most important variable in the determination of social class position, that is, the higher the education level, the higher the person's position in society. The majority of studies support our observations on this point. However, our results do reveal that occupation (20.9%) and education (19.8%) are equally important in the final determination of social class position. Educational achievement is culturally significant in the Mexican-American community inasmuch as a good deal of respect is granted those who have worked to secure a good education. In this sense educational achievement serves to enhance the social standing of the individual who has earned a college degree, for example.

It should be clear, however, that the achieved characteristics, that is, income, occupation, and education, do not exist in isolation, rather they are closely related to other variables that are also based on individual achievement. For example, a cursory inventory of the ascribed characteristics, that is, family background, sex, and age, discussed thus far are most closely associated with the personality of the individual (i.e., ego). (See Figure 2.) Next in order of significance are the "achieved" characteristics of income, occupation, and education, and are most significant in terms of their relationship to the individual and his/her position in the system of social stratification, particularly as it has developed within the Mexican-American community. This preliminary discussion

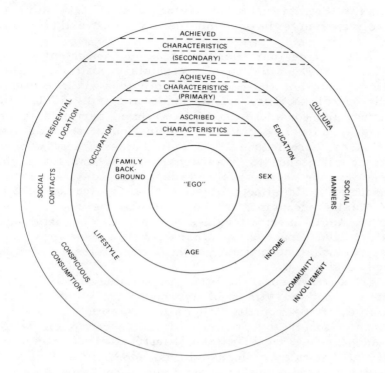

FIGURE 2   Variables Affecting the Determination of Social
Class Position in the Mexican-American Community

results in a discussion of other sociological variables that
also deserve our consideration, but fall into a secondary
level of analysis.

        In his in-depth study of social stratification among
Mexican-Americans, Peñalosa found that in addition to income, occupation, and education, other sociological variables play an important part in the determination of social
class position. For example, he found that "mobility orientation" was very important in the final evaluation of an
individual's social standing in the community.[8] His concept of mobility orientation simply makes reference to the
disposition and orientation of the individual who "wants
to get ahead." The implication, of course, is that those
who possess this mobility orientation are what sociologists
refer to as "social climbers," that is, individuals who

invariably orientate their behavior so as to take advantage of their current situation and thereby improve their lot in life.

It is true that lifestyle is a very important consideration in any evaluation of social class position. Lifestyle is important inasmuch as it provides an indication of the overall mobility orientation of the individual. In addition, the consideration of lifestyle is particularly important in any cross-cultural examination of social stratification as there is usually a split between those who hold a strong allegiance to "traditional values" and those who seek to change their ways and adopt the lifestyle of American society. In effect, lifestyle is an indication of an individual's acceptance of the values of the core society, that is, Anglo-American values and goals.[9] Lifestyle generally includes such social characteristics as manner of dress, personal deportment, speech, use of the English language, and so on.

Generally speaking, the "assimilated lifestyle" is closely associated with mobility orientation of the individual; therefore, if the mobility orientation is directed toward economic and social advancement within the core society, then the adoption of the assimilated lifestyle will surely follow. However, Mexican Americans who do adopt the assimilated lifestyle are sometimes referred to in such derogatory terms as agringados, vendidos, Tio Tacos, and others by those who have chosen to follow the more traditional lifestyle. These derogatory terms are most often used as epithets by the members of the Mexican-American community who still respect and adhere to the values of the traditional Mexican culture. Similarly, assimilated Mexican Americans also have a repertoire of derogatory terms from which they can draw to characterize those who continue to adhere to the old traditional values. Assimilated Mexican Americans are those who rely almost exclusively on English in all of their conversations, and only rarely speak Spanish or perhaps do not speak Spanish at all. In addition, most of their friends are Anglos and they show disdain and have little knowledge of and respect for Mexican cultural values and traditions. Indeed, many prefer to think of themselves as Anglo Americans. Consequently, mobility orientation and lifestyle are very important considerations in any evaluation of the system of social stratification within the Mexican-American community.

While it is true that a certain amount of prestige is gained by those who have committed themselves to the assimilated lifestyle, it is also true that social status within the Mexican-American community can be enhanced by those who have chosen to retain the traditions and values of the Mexican culture. Anthropologists and others refer to this characteristic as cultura (i.e., the possession of cultural characteristics and values).[10] A person of culture (i.e., una persona de cultura) would be a person who has a great deal of respect for and knowledge of the traditions and values of the Mexican culture and who orientates his/her lifestyle with a view toward these values and beliefs. Therefore, la persona de cultura would be one who has considerable knowledge and expertise in Mexican art, literature, language, folklore, history, and so on. In most cases only those who are beyond middle age are designated as gente de cultura (i.e., people of culture) and receive a good deal of deference from the members of the community. However, a person must earn the respect of his/her peers in the community in order to be designated as a persona de cultura, as they can never make this claim for themselves. Very often individuals who epitomize the values and traditions of the Mexican culture are rewarded by the appellation of ultimate respect: viz. Don or Doña.[11]

The social status of an individual is also affected by his or her level of participation in community activities, which is recognized as a form of community involvement and social recognition. Generally, people who are active in the Mexican-American community are recognized for their participation in local events and are identified as community leaders. These community leaders are generally drawn from the middle levels of society and their involvement in the community has a very beneficial effect on their overall social standing. Closely associated with a person's active participation in community events is the recognition and evaluation of the social caliber of friends and associates that a person attracts. Therefore, if an individual has friends and associates who have achieved a social standing in the community, then chances are good that they will also derive a certain amount of social prestige from their association with certain "important" people in the community. This is an excellent example of the "halo effect" in the determination of social status and prestige. For example, Mexican folklore holds that "If you tell me who your friends are, I will tell you who you are."

In addition to these strictly social characteristics, it is also true that the possession of certain material objects serves to differentiate one individual from another. In the day-to-day world the ownership and display of certain possessions serve as a convenient indication of an individual's position within the social hierarchy and these objects in turn are readily recognized as status symbols. When asked, our respondents provided the following examples of status symbols: nice clothes, automobiles, type of home, location of home, type of household furnishings, and so on. These examples are congruent with the results obtained by other researchers.[12] But when asked if they could determine a person's social class position by merely talking with them, half of our respondents said that they could (51.6%) and conversely an almost equal number (46.2%) felt that they could not do so. Subsequently, they were asked if they could determine a person's social class position by merely looking at them. These results reveal a greater degree of unanimity inasmuch as seven out of ten (71.4%) felt that they were not able to do so, while only one in four (27.5%) felt that they could.[13]

In sum, the determination and delineation of social class position by our respondents are congruent with the results obtained by other researchers and reveal that, in addition to the basic ascribed characteristics, there are other important considerations based on personal achievement and success in the day-to-day world that must be taken into account. Therefore, in addition to certain status indicators, such as income, occupation, and education, there are also certain recognized social relations and status symbols that can place one individual at a certain level in the social hierarchy within the Mexican-American community and another individual at a different level. What we have then is the interaction of the basic ascribed characteristics of social status with the primary and secondary characteristics of achieved status, both material and social in character. It is the synergistic interaction of these three sociological categories that can provide an indication of the social class position of any individual within the sociocultural milieu of the Mexican-American community. (See Figure 2.)

PERCEPTION OF SOCIAL CLASSES

It has become commonplace and very acceptable for
sociologists to outline three basic social class categories
in society: the upper class, the middle class, and the
lower class.   In most instances they subdivide each of
these major categories into two or three subgroups and arrive at a total of six or nine distinct groups for their
analysis of social classes in American society.   These for-
malities allow sociologists to spout such shibboleths as
"lower-middle class" or the "upper-lower class," and so on,
and in the process allow for a set of social and economic
characteristics that are peculiar to these social categories
as they appear in American society.

However, any consideration of social stratification,
particularly from the cross-cultural perspective, must also
take into account the unique cultural characteristics and
social values of the members of the society under investigation.   Therefore, the active members of the existing social system must be viewed as representatives of distinct
social categories operating within that particular system
of social stratification, and sociologists and anthropologists should not arrive on the scene with prefabricated
models of what the system of social stratification should
look like.   Consequently, in order to obtain even a rudimentary understanding of the system of social stratification,
particularly as it occurs in the Mexican-American community, we must consult those studies that have been conducted in specific communities and consider their findings
in the light of current theories of social stratification.

Much time and effort has been expended in the detailed examination of the social conditions that existed in
prerevolutionary Mexico by a whole host of investigators,
mostly sociologists, anthropologists, and historians, who
have focused on the system of social stratification that
has existed for hundreds of years.   While it is certainly
true that the study of the development of social classes in
prerevolutionary Mexico is essential for even an elementary
understanding of the contemporary relationships that exist
among social classes in Mexico, such an exposition would
clearly take us beyond the scope of the present study.[14]
Suffice it to say that our purpose here is quite modest and
we shall simply state that the contemporary system of social relations in Mexico is tinged with the patina of prerevolutionary contacts between an elite group of feudal

landlords and the great mass of landless economically dependent peasants.[15] In effect, an elite landed aristoc-
racy held the vast majority of the indigenous populations
of Mexico in the grips of debt peonage, that is, in virtual
slavery. In their didactic publication "Stratification Since
the Revolution," Stern and Kahl have observed that "The
rural structure was dominated by the hacendados or large
landowners, who constituted less than one percent of the
rural population; there was a group of small landowners
that added up to another 7 percent; about 3 percent were
artisans; about 9 percent were traders or village service
workers; and the remaining 80 percent were landless peasants."[16]

In their detailed studies of various Mexican and
Mexican-American communities social scientists have developed, over the years, a number of classification systems
in an effort to better understand the system of social stratification as it exists in these various communities. For example, in her pioneering study of the origins and development of a Mexican community in San Bernardino (California),
Ruth Tuck simply divided the members of the Mexican community into high class and low class groups, that is, the
representatives of the rich and the poor.[17] In a very
similar manner, Lasswell[18] and Clark[19] bifurcated the social classes in the Mexican-American communities that they
studied.

On the other hand, in his study of the Mexican-
American community in Tucson, the anthropologist George
Barker arrived at a much more sophisticated evaluation of
social classes. From his field observations he developed a
schema based on five distinct strata: (1) an "upper class"
which was composed of the wealthy old families, (2) a
"lower-upper class" which was a young but well established social class, (3) a "middle class" composed of small
shopkeepers, clerks, and skilled workers, (4) an "upper-
lower class" which included all of those individuals who
were steadily employed and who were semi-skilled and unskilled workers, and lastly, a (5) "lower class" which he
designated as a group of unskilled migrant workers.[20]

In an in-depth study of a small village in the
western part of Michoacan (Mexico) anthropologist John
Armstrong formulated three basic categories for his analysis of relations between social classes. At the apex of the
social hierarchy he designated a "Rico Class," that is, the
very rich. At the fulcrum of his system of stratification

was the "middle class" which included "small businessmen
of the towns. . . ." And at the nadir of the social hierarchy was the "campesino class" or the agricultural class.[21]
To his credit Armstrong was astute enough to recognize differences within the campesino class as he described four
types of agricultural workers, namely, (1) those who own
their own land, (2) those who rent their land, (3) those
who work as sharecroppers, and (4) those who possess an
"ejido parcel."[22]

In her study of middle-class women in Michoacan
(Mexico), Hubbell allowed her subjects to formulate their
own social demarcations, as they perceived them, and in
the process they described five distinct social class categories. Her subjects referred to the upper class as the
"Clase Rica" (the wealthy class) and two subcategories of
"Clase Rica Vieja" (the old wealthy class) and the "Clase
Rica Nueva" (the new wealthy class). Next in order of
succession was the "Clase Media" or the middle class,
which they divided into the "Clase Media Superior" (upper-
middle class) and the "Clase Media Baja" (lower-middle
class). Just below this middle class her respondents designated a class of "ejidatarios" composed of low-ranking employees, day-laborers, some factory workers, and agricultural workers. Following these three general categories
they also designated a "Clase de los Pobres" (the poor
class) and a "Clase de Gente Humilde" (the class of humble
people), whom they felt were represented by the local market vendors. Their final social class category was reserved for those "De a Mero Abajo" (those at the very bottom) which would encompass all of those who lived from
day to day at the verge of subsistence.[23]

In his study of social classes and social change in
Zamora (Mexico), Pi-Sunyer likewise found that his respondents recognized three general classes: "Los Ricos" (the
wealthy); a middle class composed of small landowners,
professionals, shopkeepers, and so on; and a lower class
composed of five distinct groups. The "Peones" were considered to be the humble members of society, and a second
group "La Miseria," those who survive from day to day. A
third group or "Campesino" class was composed of landless
farmers and a group of "Cargadores" or day laborers. The
final category he designated as the "Ejidatarios," a group
composed of skilled workers and small subsistence farmers.[24]

In her study of Jacala, Zarrugh developed four
basic social class divisions: a "Clase de Alta Socieded"

or the class of high society; a class of "Los Bien Acomodados" or the comfortable ones, composed of large landowners, cattle ranchers, and proprietors of small businesses; a third category of "Humildes," or the humble ones, whom we would normally consider as the working class of the community and which would include both the skilled and the semi-skilled; and at the lowest rung of the social hierarchy were "Los Pobres" or the poor ones--the landless peasants who survive at the subsistence level of existence.[25]

This brief review of the available research allows us to make some very useful insights into the nature of social stratification within the Mexican-American community. Indeed, the results obtained by these researchers were frequently confirmed by our own investigations. The introductory query made of our respondents was: "Do you think that there are differences in the social classes among Mexican people?" This is probably the only question, in the entire survey, to which we received unanimous agreement: all of our respondents agreed that basic social class differences do exist among Mexican people. Then they were asked, "How many social classes exist in society?" The number of social classes went from two to a high of four, and the majority seemed to agree that there were either two or three major social classes in society, as we arrived at a mean of 2.7. Peñalosa's findings coincide with our own as he found that "The number of social classes perceived by respondents varied from 1 to 4, with a mode of 2, a mean of 2.3 and a median of 2.6."[26]

The nomenclature used by our respondents to make various distinctions among social class categories were also very similar to the findings of other researchers. For example, our respondents spoke of "los Ricos, los de Medio, y los Pobres," (i.e., the rich, those in the middle, and the poor). A few referred to certain members of the lower class as "la Gente Humilde," or the humble people, and also "los de mero abajo," or those at the very bottom. Therefore, certain names or labels are applied to each of the social classes that normally appear within their lexicon of social differentiation. Furthermore, their perception of social class differences was very consistent within each of the stipulated categories and as a result their operational definitions of these differences were generally congruent with one another.

SOCIAL STRATIFICATION IN THE
MEXICAN-AMERICAN COMMUNITY

Given the significance of our survey results we can suggest a more refined paradigm of social stratification as it currently exists within the Mexican-American community. Therefore, while we shall utilize the standard sociological terminology in the delineation of social classes, special attention will be given to the unique socio-cultural variations that are such an important part of the Mexican cultural tradition. This simply means that the idiosyncrasies of stratification within the Mexican-American community must be taken into account, that is, full consideration must be given to the cross-cultural differences that do occur among Mexican Americans. The upshot, of course, is that the values that account for status and prestige in middle-class American society may not be the same values as those that are attached to the evaluation of middle-class status within the Mexican-American culture. Consequently, what may be considered middle class among Mexican Americans may not coincide with the accepted concept of middle-class standing within the general culture of American society. These basic differences in the evaluation of social class standing were indubitably demonstrated in our discussion of the key variables that account for social class differences within the Mexican-American community. Therefore, we shall discuss and evaluate the cross-cultural differences that are important in the determination of social class differences within the scope of the various beliefs and traditions as they occur in the Mexican-American community.

Our description and analysis of social stratification among Mexican Americans will begin with the recognition of three major groupings: the lower class, the middle class, and the upper class. In addition, several subdivisions will be made within these three major groupings; specifically the lower class will be divided into three groups: the lower-lower class, the middle-lower class, and the upper-lower class. The middle class will be divided into two groups: the blue-collar middle class and the white-collar middle class. In like manner the upper class can be divided into three subcategories: the lower-upper class, the middle-upper class, and the upper-upper class. Each social class category will be discussed in full detail, with examples of each, beginning with the lower-lower class and concluding with the upper-upper class. However, before we begin our prolegomenon on social stratification in the Mexican-American community it will be necessary to provide a succinct discussion of some of the more important independent variables that can affect the characteristics commonly associated with social class categories.

Independent variables are consequential to our analysis since the appearance of one variable, the independent variable, can result in the occurrence of change in another variable, the dependent variable. For example, if consideration is given to the effects of the split labor market on the determination of social status we observe that the position occupied within the split labor market will have a profound influence on the social status of the individual, particularly in terms of economic remuneration and job security.[27] A split labor market situation exists when we have "at least two groups of workers whose price of labor differs for the same work, or would differ if they did the same work."[28] Therefore, a split labor market situation exists when two individuals or two groups of individuals are doing similar work, but are being paid at different rates.[29] This economic paradigm is germane to our analysis inasmuch as it can help us to understand the income differentials that do exist between Mexican-American and Anglo-American laborers who are engaged in the same type of work but are remunerated according to very different pay scales and receive very different employee benefits.

The level of assimilation is also an important intervening variable that must be taken into consideration in any cross-cultural analysis of social stratification, particularly when we are concerned with the interaction of ethnic groups in a pluralistic social milieu, and specifically when dominant-subordinate relations between these groups are based on a prolonged historical experience. By level of assimilation we simply mean the degree of acceptance of Anglo-American ways by individual Mexican-Americans. In practice the systematic evaluation of the degree of assimilation can serve as an index of the level of integration or absorption of the members of an ethnic group into the cultural influences of the dominant society. Therefore, a number of social indicators could be collated into an index of assimilation that would serve as a sociological weather vane, and in this manner determine the level of absorption of specific ethnic groups into the dominant American cultural pattern. For example, consideration could be given to such cultural patterns as manner of dress, facility with the English language, spending and consumption patterns, value orientation, and so on. Once the basic cultural differences have been observed and documented, note can be taken of their impact on the system of social stratification as it functions in the Mexican-American community. In most cases the higher the level of assimilation, the higher the level of social standing within the Mexican-American community, that is, from the Anglo-American perspective. In sociological parlance there is a direct relationship between a person's position in the system of social stratification and his or her level of assimilation. Consequently, the higher a person is within the social hierarchy, the greater the degree of assimilation. Conversely, the lower a person's position in the social hierarchy, the lower his or her level of assimilation.

Closely associated with the degree of assimilation is the generation level of individuals. Generation level can serve as an index of an ethnic group's commitment to the "American way" in that the most recent immigrants to this country, that is, the first generation, are the least likely to fully accept the values of the core society. However, we would expect to see a greater degree of acceptance of the American way with each accretion in the generation level. And in view of the historical trends in social mobility, as documented among the various immigrant groups in this country, it can be hypothesized that with each increase in generation level, we can expect a concomitant increase in the social mobility among the members of these groups. In theory the expectation is that the second generation will be more advanced than the first generation and the third more advanced than the second, that is, with specific reference to the social stratification system of the core society. Given these sociological trends, we would expect to find the high achievers within the higher generation levels.[30] Consequently, a prediction can be made that the middle-class Mexican American is probably a member of the second or third generation and is also relatively well assimilated. In sum, there is a direct relationship between generation level and the position that a person occupies within the social hierarchy, that is, the higher their position, the higher the generation level.

THE DISTRIBUTION OF SOCIAL CLASSES IN
THE MEXICAN-AMERICAN COMMUNITY

We shall initiate our discussion and analysis with
an elaboration of the chief characteristics of the members
of the Mexican-American lower class and its three subcategories: the lower-lower class, the middle-lower class, and
the upper-lower class. The lower-lower class was often
referred to by our respondents as "la gente humilde."

The Gente Humilde manage to survive at the subsistence level of existence, that is, they live from one day to
the next and never know for sure where they will obtain
their next meal or their next dollar. In urban areas they
work as street vendors, beggars, and day laborers. In
rural areas they are referred to as "peones" or landless
peasants who hire themselves out on a daily basis, migrant
farm laborers, or illegal agricultural workers. The Gente
Humilde are the most abused and exploited of all of the
members of the Mexican-American community in that they
are employed on the fringes of the labor market, and in
many cases work at the very bottom of the secondary labor
market within the split labor market system. In brief, the
secondary labor market consists of those jobs that offer
the lowest wages and the least security and benefits to
the worker. In almost all cases the members of the lower-
lower class are relegated to jobs within the extractive industries.

CHART 1   Characteristics of the Lower-Lower Class

1. Spanish nomenclature: Gente Humilde

2. English nomenclature: "The Downtrodden"

3. Examples of: Street vendors, beggars, and day laborers

4. Segment of the labor market: Secondary

5. Level of assimilation: Not assimilated

6. Generation level: First

7. Income level: Subsistence

8. Education level: Little formal education or none at all

According to the information presented in Chart 1, the Gente Humilde, that is, the lower-lower class, are not well assimilated and in fact consider themselves, in most cases, Mexican citizens with very strong ties to Mexican cultural traditions. From their perspective, American society is a system within which they must live ephemerally and therefore many view their present situation as only a temporary inconvenience. The upshot is that they have very little or no investment in the American system and have no intentions of becoming American citizens. Invariably they are first-generation immigrants from Mexico, and the majority have no intention of remaining in this country permanently. While their income remains at the subsistence level, when compared to American economic standards, it is nonetheless true that this income is more than they could expect to earn in their own country. In addition, they have little or no formal education and consequently there is little hope of improving their current situation and little or no opportunity for upward social mobility.

In Mexico, and in most Mexican-American communities, the members of the middle-lower class are referred to as the Ejidatarios or as "La Clase Popular" (the popular class) when they are located in a strictly urban environment. The middle-lower class, according to our schema, is generally made up of unskilled factory workers, unskilled assembly line workers, unskilled operatives, common laborers, and general agricultural laborers. The members of the middle-lower class are also relegated to the secondary labor market and as a result they are rarely represented by a union, they are paid at the minimum wage, and sometimes below the minimum wage. They are often found in small job shops and in what may best be described as sweatshops, where the major emphasis is on speed and the mass production of consumer goods (see Chart 2). An excellent example of the working conditions found in this particular job market is exemplified by the working conditions that are commonplace in the garment industries of Los Angeles and El Paso.

In the agricultural setting the Ejidatarios are most often found working as temporary and/or seasonal agricultural workers. In addition to being paid at or below the minimum wage, they are often in the United States illegally and therefore are always from the first generation. The most important difference between the middle-lower class and the lower-lower class is that the former has a greater

---

CHART 2   Characteristics of the Middle-Lower Class

1. Spanish nomenclature: Los Ejidatarios or La Clase Popular

2. English nomenclature: "The Working Poor"

3. Examples of: Unskilled factory workers, common laborers

4. Segment of the labor market: Secondary

5. Level of assimilation: Not assimilated

6. Generation level: First

7. Income level: Poverty level

8. Education level: Elementary (1–5 years)

---

degree of job security and is employed more days of the year, whereas those in the latter group work for a variety of employers during the year and often work as day laborers. It is also true that the members of the middle-lower class subsist at a more comfortable level, primarily because they experience longer periods of full employment. An additional advantage is that each family may have two or three full-time workers; consequently, they are able to pool their meager resources.

In contrast to the Ejidatarios, the members of the upper-lower class are in a much more advantageous position even though, in many instances, they may be employed in very similar industries and often find themselves doing the same type of work. In his meticulous analysis of social classes in Mexico, José Iturriaga referred to the members of this social class as Los Jornaleros Industriales (the industrial laborers).[31] For the most part the upper-lower class is composed of unskilled and semi-skilled factory workers who typically are employed as factory operatives, assembly line workers, warehousemen, truck drivers, semi-skilled maintenance men, semi-skilled mechanics, and so on. The reason they are members of the upper-lower class is that they have managed to locate employment within the primary labor market (see Chart 3). This is the critical difference that separates them from the members of the middle-lower class, who very often perform similar tasks

CHART 3   Characteristics of the Upper-Lower Class

1. Spanish nomenclature: Los Jornaleros Industriales

2. English nomenclature: "Industrial Laborers"

3. Examples of: Semi-skilled factory workers, truck drivers

4. Segment of the labor market: Primary

5. Level of assimilation: Assimilated

6. Generation level: First and second

7. Income level: Union scale

8. Education level: Majority are high school graduates

---

as the members of this class but do not have the job benefits nor receive the wages that they receive. The critical
difference is that their rate of pay is very often regulated
by a union contract; consequently, this insures that an
equitable wage scale and lucrative employee benefits will
be bestowed. Therefore, while they may be engaged in the
same type of physical labor as those in the middle-lower
class, they are often paid twice as much, if not more, for
the same type of work. In addition, they have the full advantages of union sponsorship and protection.

For example, take the case of the middle-lower
class truck driver who is employed by a small company in
the secondary labor market and is paid at just above the
minimum wage scale, probably $3.50 an hour, while on the
other hand, someone else is driving a similar truck for an
employer in the primary labor market and therefore is receiving the union pay scale of $9.00 to $12.00 an hour. In
actual fact these two laborers are doing similar work, but
with the critical difference that the person in the primary
labor market is being paid from three to four times as
much for his labor.

This additional income earning potential of upper-
lower class members means that their lifestyle is much improved. Another crucial difference is that employment in
the primary labor market guarantees the workers' job security. Consequently, they can count on a regular source of

income and this allows them to plan for the future and set certain goals for themselves and their families.

Overall, upper-lower class members are well assimilated and are usually second- or third-generation citizens. Generally, they are the sons and daughters of immigrants from the lower-lower class or the middle-lower class and their parents were fortunate enough to be able to provide their children with certain opportunities, which in turn allowed them to find employment in the primary labor market. Most are high school graduates, as the jobs in the primary labor market typically require a high school education.

Given our findings, and those of other researchers, it seems safe to conclude that these subcategories are representative of the lower socio-economic classes as they are currently found within the social hierarchy of the Mexican-American community.

However, some may question our creation of a middle-class category that includes a stratum of what are essentially blue-collar workers. In the development of a representative group that could be designated as members of the middle class, within the Mexican-American community, we realized that our inclusion of a basically blue-collar segment would be considered sacrilegious by certain members of the profession. However, while our approach is rather unorthodox, our intent is not to be iconoclastic simply for the sake of being different; rather full account must be taken of the perception of what constitutes a "middle class" within the confines of and the cultural expectations that exist within the Mexican-American community. Hence, what may be considered as middle class among Anglo-Americans may not necessarily apply to the evaluation of middle-class characteristics within the Mexican-American community.

The essential characteristics of middle-class status within the Mexican-American community requires that a person have a respectable position in the labor force, earn a wage that allows his family to live in relative comfort, and provide an environment where family members live in freedom from need or want. Therefore, the essential difference between middle-class status in the Mexican-American community and middle-class status in the core society is simply a matter of degree, that is, along the continuum of middle-class characteristics we can move from a modestly secure lifestyle to a lifestyle of conspicuous consumption

and lavish living. According to our schema, the majority
of middle-class Mexican Americans would fall into that segment of the continuum where we would find those who lead
a modest but secure lifestyle. For purposes of analysis,
we have divided the Mexican-American middle class into
two distinct segments: the blue-collar middle class and
the white-collar middle class.

The members of the blue-collar middle class are
sometimes referred to as "Los Artesanos" (literally "the
artisans"). Los Artesanos have learned a valuable skill
or trade within one of the more lucrative industries, hence,
they are recognized as craftsmen who are employed as
plumbers, carpenters, welders, machinists, mechanics, elec-
tricians, and so on. In every case, Los Artesanos have
been officially certified as craftsmen within their trade and
most have obtained their apprenticeship training under the
auspices of one of the local trade unions (see Chart 4).
Consequently, they not only have their official credentials
but also receive all of the benefits of union protection and
union pay scales. Therefore, they are employed in the
primary labor market and earn a very respectable income
and thereby provide their families with a rather comfortable
lifestyle.

CHART 4   Characteristics of the Blue-Collar
Middle Class

1. Spanish nomenclature: Los Artesanos

2. English nomenclature: "The Artisans"

3. Examples of: Plumbers, carpenters, welders

4. Segment of the labor market: Primary

5. Level of assimilation: Well assimilated

6. Generation level: Second and third

7. Income level: Union scale

8. Education level: High school, trade school, some
college

An important distinction that must be made clear is that the members of the blue-collar middle class, within the Mexican-American community, are well assimilated and are from the second or third generation. Therefore, they are American citizens by birth and consider themselves as much Americans as the next person. In fact, "the middle class Mexican tends to emphasize, and to display, certain behavior patterns and aspirations which are generally considered characteristic of middle class America. They include self-reliance, ambition, industriousness, and thrift, all of them patterns commonly associated with 'getting ahead'. . . ."32

Indeed, members of the blue-collar middle class are filled with aspirations for self-improvement and upward social mobility, not only for themselves but, more importantly, for their children. This constant drive for success probably derives from their own personal experiences; as they had to work hard to get to where they are, they want their children to do even better than they have done. This means that they want their children to attend college and, it is hoped, obtain a lucrative white-collar position.

The white-collar middle class, within the Mexican-American community, can be divided into two groups: the clerical middle class and semi-professional middle class. While it is true that the clerical middle class is numerically larger than the semi-professional middle class, it is also true that they do not rate as high as the semi-professional middle class in terms of prestige and social standing within the community. In this sense we can think of the clerical segment as a lower-middle class group, and the semi-professionals as an upper-middle class group.

The most significant distinction between the white-collar middle class and the blue-collar middle class is that the blue-collar workers work with their hands and white-collar workers work with their minds. This critical distinction is demonstrated, for example, in the way that the members of these two groups dress for work, that is, the blue-collar group will always wear work clothes and the white-collar group will always wear dress clothes. This example serves to demonstrate that both the manner of dress and the place of employment are very important considerations in terms of the prestige and social position held within the Mexican-American community. However, while the pay scale of the blue-collar middle class and the semi-professional white-collar group is often comparable, the pay scale of the clerical middle class is generally substantially lower than both. In his study of social classes in a medium-size city in Mexico, Whiteford has referred to this middle-class group as "La Clase Media sin Dinero" (the middle class without money).[33] Therefore, the clerical group constitutes a "social amphibian" inasmuch as it has the social standing and the social manners of the middle class, but does not have the income of the middle class. In fact, the income is generally on par with that of the "upper-lower class" group (see Chart 5).

CHART 5   Characteristics of the Clerical Middle Class

1. Spanish nomenclature: La Clase Media sin Dinero

2. English nomenclature: "The Clerical Middle Class"

3. Examples of: Secretarial and clerical workers

4. Segment of the labor market: Primary

5. Level of assimilation: Well assimilated

6. Generation level: Second, third, etc.

7. Income level: Modest

8. Education level: High school, some college classes

The members of the clerical middle class are most often employed in the primary sector of the economy, where they work for large businesses and government agencies in a variety of secretarial and clerical positions. A large proportion of the clerical middle class is made up of Mexican-American women, both single and married. While some are bilingual and bicultural, the majority are well assimilated and are mostly drawn from the second and third generations. As a job requirement, the majority are high school graduates and most are the daughters and wives of middle-lower class and upper-lower class blue-collar workers.

The members of the semi-professional middle class are generally employed as medical technicians, licensed vocational nurses, junior accountants, firemen, policemen, court reporters, store managers, small businessmen, junior executives, and so on. All of the members of this class are employed within the primary labor market and consequently receive all of the benefits and moderate salaries that are appropriate to this particular segment of society (see Chart 6). Within this social class, the salary range is quite variable in that the degree of education and training, job experience, and job responsibilities has a significant impact on their pay scale.

CHART 6   Characteristics of the Semi-Professional
Middle Class

1. Spanish nomenclature: La Clase Tecnica

2. English nomenclature: "The Semi-Professional Middle Class"

3. Examples of: Medical technicians, small businessmen, policemen

4. Segment of the labor market: Primary

5. Level of assimilation: Well assimilated

6. Generation level: Second, third, etc.

7. Income level: Moderate

8. Education level: Technical training, A.A. degree, B.A. degree

---

However, in each case they do provide a comfortable lifestyle for themselves and their families, that is, they live in a relatively new home located in a well-maintained neighborhood, take their scheduled vacations, and entertain guests in their homes occasionally. In sum, they have embraced the traditional American middle-class lifestyle with enthusiasm and also have high mobility aspirations for their children. In fact, all are at least high school graduates, some have two years of college or technical training, and some have college degrees--but in all cases they have earned the respect of their families and

of the community in general. Consequently they feel good
about themselves and are proud of their accomplishments.
For the most part they are sanguine about their own future
and the future of their children in American society.

The majority of those in the semi-professional middle
class have experienced a good deal of social mobility, as
many were reared in first- and second-generation middle-
lower and upper-lower class environments.[34] All have
worked hard for their success and therefore they are of the
opinion that anyone could do the same thing, if only they
apply themselves and strive to get ahead. While all are
well assimilated second- and third-generation Mexican Americans and adhere very strongly to what they consider to be
the middle-class expectations of American society, there are
some who have taken the "altruistic view" and feel that
they must do all they can to improve the social and economic conditions of their "brothers" who are not as fortunate
as themselves. In this regard they are very conscious of
their position within the Mexican-American community and
have a great sense of community responsibility. As a result,
they are very active in the community and often serve as
community spokesman.

The key characteristics of the upper class reveal
that they are strongly integrated into American society,
well educated, employed in the primary sector of the economy, and many hold positions as "free professionals." In
addition, they are primarily from the third or fourth generation and provide a very comfortable living for their
families. Obviously the members of the Mexican-American
upper class have a great deal in common; however, we
shall delineate some of the basic differences that do exist.

The members of the lower-upper class are well respected in their communities and are often recognized for
their leadership abilities. Lower-upper class members are
found in such professions as teaching, social work, administration in large private businesses or government bureaucracies, nursing, management, and so on. The members of
the lower-upper class are well educated, as most have a
minimum of a college education and some may even have a
year or two of graduate school (see Chart 7). As a result
of their professional positions and above average incomes,
even when judged by Anglo standards, they frequently purchase homes in middle-income Anglo neighborhoods. Their
general acceptance in Anglo neighborhoods is greatly facilitated by their total social and cultural integration into the

---

CHART 7   Characteristics of the Lower-Upper Class

1. Spanish nomenclature: La Alta Sociedad

2. English nomenclature: "The High Society"

3. Examples of: School teachers, social workers, nurses

4. Segment of the labor market: Primary

5. Level of assimilation: Well assimilated

6. Generation level: Second, third, etc.

7. Income level: Moderate to comfortable

8. Education level: B.A. degree, one or two years of graduate school

---

values of the core society. In most cases, both the husband and the wife are employed, and in some situations both are recognized as professional people in their own right. In addition, there is a high rate of intermarriage, most often with eligible Anglos. Indeed, this observation holds true for the members of the upper class in general. The parents in the upper class also expect, and indeed demand, that their children go to college and upon graduation expect that they will pursue a respectable career that will eventually allow them to partake of the many advantages of upper-class life.

The major distinction between those who are members of the middle-upper class and the upper-upper class has to do with generation level, family background, and family ties within the community. Hence, we can make a distinction between the old upper class and the new upper class. In our analysis, the old upper class is equated with the upper-upper class and the new upper class with the middle-upper class. In a similar manner, Whiteford found that "Some people referred to the 'Old Upper Class', a few referred to 'la aristocracia' or simply 'la alta sociedad'. The most incisive distinction was made by those who referred to the two sections as 'clase alta por abolengo', that is, Upper Class because of lineage, and 'clase alta por dinero', Upper Class because of money. It would not be too far amiss to call these Upper Upper Class and Lower Upper

Class respectively."[35]   Hence the members of the middle-upper class and the upper-upper class are similar in many ways, with the major exception of lineage (see Chart 8).

CHART 8   Characteristics of the Middle-Upper
and Upper-Upper Classes

1. Spanish nomenclature: La Aristocracia

2. English nomenclature: "The New or the Old Upper Class"

3. Examples of: Doctors, lawyers, leading politicians

4. Segment of the labor market: Primary

5. Level of assimilation: Very well assimilated

6. Generation level: Second, third, etc.

7. Income level: Comfortable to very comfortable

8. Education level: B.A., M.A., J.D., Ph.D., M.D.

The members of the new and the old upper classes are most often found within the "free professions," such as doctors, lawyers, architects, college and university professors, judges, successful attorneys, leading politicians, very successful businessmen, successful engineers, highly placed bureaucrats in private industries and in government bureaucracies, and so on.   Again it is a matter of degree of professional success and/or community recognition that would ultimately determine whether an individual in any one of these professions would be considered a member of the middle-upper or the upper-upper social class.[36]   For example, a neophyte attorney would probably rank in the middle-upper class, while an experienced attorney with community recognition and a successful practice would be relegated to the upper-upper class, particularly if his/her parents were already members of the upper-class structure.

Therefore, while most members of the upper class have earned a position in a recognized professional field, their eventual status or ranking in the social hierarchy will depend upon their recognition in the Mexican–American community as successful individuals who are aware of their responsibilities to the members of the community. For example, in his now classic field investigations in the cities of McAllen and San Antonio (Texas), Simmons found that "the most successful Mexican physician and the wealthiest businessmen were singled out for approbrium time and again by informants for the isolation they maintain from 'service' organizations and activities and their failure to contribute funds to community projects although well able to do so. Their notable achievements as physician and businessman are acknowledged, but they are accorded little respect or esteem apart from this."[37]

Given this review of the system of social stratification as it applies to the distribution of wealth, status, privilege, and power within the Mexican–American community, it appears that the entire system of stratification, within this cultural context, is skewed in a subordinate direction when compared to the system of social stratification as it is applied to the members of the core society. For example, in his cross–cultural study of social stratification among Black, Chicano, and Anglo groups, Ransford arrived at a very similar observation when he notes that even an upper–class Mexican American may only register as a middle–middle class Anglo.[38] This observation is often true in terms of the objective characteristics of social status among upper–class Mexican–Americans, that is, within the definitions of social class position as perceived and applied in the core society.

This simply means that if we take all of the objective criteria of occupation, education, and income, for example, of an upper–class Mexican American, as defined within the Mexican–American community, and compare these same objective indicators with those that are routinely applied to the members of the core society, the results would probably reveal that this upper–class Mexican American would only fall into the "middle class," that is, in accord with the Anglo–American core group's perception of middle-class status. In a sense this is an extreme case, in that the stratification gap becomes greater as one moves from a comparison of ethnic and core group members at the lower social and economic levels to the upper levels of the social hierarchy. Consequently, lower–class Mexican Americans have more in common with lower–class Anglo Americans. However, upper–class Mexican Americans will probably only fall into the Anglo middle class, that is, according to the definition applied by the core group. The graphic relationship between the two systems of stratification and the differential placement of individuals within the two systems is presented in Figure 3.

Closely related to the socio-economic differences between the system of social stratification among Mexican Americans and Anglo Americans is the observation that upper-class Mexican Americans identify more closely with the middle-class values of American society. Therefore they generally exhibit many of the same tastes, values, goals, and lifestyles that are strongly associated with the American middle class. This observation was made long ago by Milton Gordon in his classic work, Assimilation in American Life. He demonstrated that individuals from an ethnic background will often share certain "behavioral similarities" with members of the core group, that is, they will adopt similar lifestyles, but will not share a sense of "peoplehood" with them.[39] On the other hand, their lifestyle will probably be different from the majority of the members of their own ethnic group; however, they will share a sense of peoplehood with them, in other words, they will share a sense of ethnic identity, or, in the words of Franklin H. Giddings, a "consciousness of kind." Gordon has referred to the relationship between social status and ethnic identification as an "Ethclass," which he has defined as "the subsociety created by the intersection of the vertical stratifications of ethnicity with the horizontal stratifications of social class. . . ."[40]

In an effort to simplify matters and demonstrate the relationships that do exist between the different strata within the Mexican-American system of social stratification, we have developed a graphic representation of this complex relationship (see Figure 4). Since we have discussed the chief characteristics of each of these social class categories, we shall not belabor the point, but will only point out that the graphic representation is significant in and of itself, inasmuch as it does serve to clarify the relationships that exist between the various social groups within this system of stratification.

The pyramid shape of the social hierarchy is indicative of the existing numerical relationship among social class groupings. In an effort to quantify these relationships, we have supplied a set of percentages that are fairly representative of the occupational distribution of

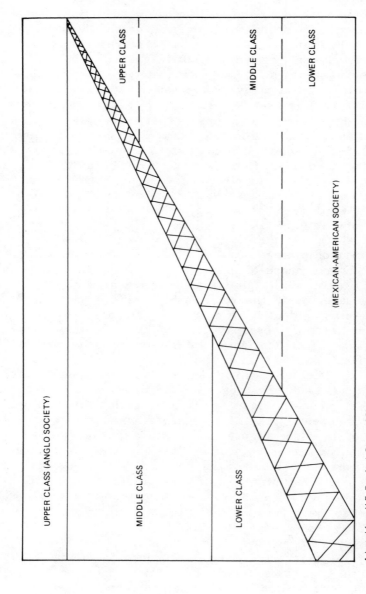

Adapted from H.E. Ransford, *Race and Class in American Society: Black, Chicano, Anglo*
(Cambridge: Schenkman Publishing Company, 1977)

FIGURE 3. Revised "Class Within Caste" Model of Stratification

each of the various social classes. Therefore, according to the 1970 census, 8.7 percent of those using the Spanish language or bearing a Spanish surname were found in the "Professional-technical" category, 4.8 percent were in the "Managers administrators" and so on down the list of occupations.[41] The figures that appear in parentheses indicate the relative concentration of Spanish-surname individuals within these broad occupational categories, which are similar to our social class categories. Consequently, while 8.7 percent of the Spanish-speaking or Spanish-surname fall into the upper class, the figure of relative concentration (.51) indicates that only half as many are in this social category as we would expect to find on a statistical basis alone.[42]

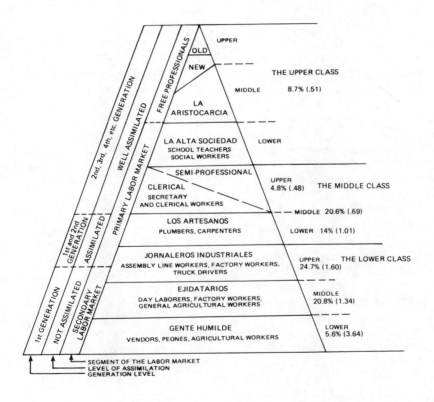

FIGURE 4   Social Stratification Among Mexican Americans

This simply means that instead of the 8.7 percent, we would expect to find at least 17.4 percent within this upper-class category. In a similar manner, 5.6 percent are working as farm laborers. But the most revealing figure is the index of "relative concentration," as this figure reveals that there are over three and one-half times as many Spanish-surname individuals working in agriculture as we would normally expect to find (i.e., 3.64). Overall, these figures indicate that the Spanish-surname population experience the highest level of representation among the lower socio-economic stratum, that is, among the agricultural workers, and the lowest level of representation among one of the highest socio-economic strata, that is, among the managers and proprietors.

NOTES

1. For a brief narrative of the cultural exploitations of women see Alfredo Mirande and Evangelina Enriquez, "The Socioeconomic Oppression of Chicanas," in La Chicana (Chicago: The University of Chicago Press, 1979), pp. 130-41.

2. For an account of the manner in which older Mexican Americans are treated in their communities, see Ben Crouch, "Age and Institutional Support: Perceptions of Older Mexican-Americans," Journal of Gerontology 27(4) (1972):524-29. Also see Billa Steinnagle, "Attitudes Toward the Status and Role of the Older Person in the Mexican-American Family," M.A. thesis, University of Arizona, 1967.

3. For example, see the following studies: Fernando Peñalosa, "Class Consciousness and Social Mobility in a Mexican-American Community," Ph.D. dissertation, University of California, 1963, p. 200; Linda J. Hubbell, "The Network of Kinship, Friendship, and Compadrazgo Among the Middle Class Women of Uruapan, Michoacan, Mexico," Ph.D. dissertation, Department of Anthropology, University of California, Berkeley, 1972, p. 44; Oriol Pi-Sunyer, Zamora: Change and Continuity in a Mexican Town (New York: Holt, Rinehart, and Winston, 1973), pp. 46-48; Margaret Clark, Health in the Mexican-American Culture (Berkeley: University of California Press, 1970), pp. 16-19; Frances J. Woods, "Mexican Ethnic Leadership in San Antonio, Texas," Ph.D. dissertation, Catholic University of America, Washington, D.C., 1949, pp. 80-84; John M.

Armstrong, Jr., "A Mexican Community: A Study of the Cultural Determinants of Migration," Ph.D. dissertation, Yale University, 1949, p. 292.

4. Peñalosa, "Class Consciousness and Social Mobility," p. 200.

5. Hubbell, "Network of Kinship," p. 44.

6. Melvin Tumin and A. S. Feldman, Social Class and Social Change in Puerto Rico (Princeton: Princeton University Press, Bobbs-Merrill Co., 1972), p. 153.

7. However, Simmons provides a word of caution and notes that during his investigations "Many informants would insist at first that money was the only determinant of status distinctions, but further conversation elicited qualifications that considerably reduced its importance." See Ozzie G. Simmons, "Anglo Americans and Mexican Americans in South Texas: A Study in Dominant-Subordinant Group Relations," Ph.D. dissertation, Department of Social Relations, Harvard University, 1952, p. 364.

8. Peñalosa, "Class Consciousness and Social Mobility."

9. In his book, Assimilation in American Life (New York: Oxford University Press, 1964), Milton Gordon has relied on the concept of a "core society" to demonstrate some of the basic differences that exist between members of the Anglo-Saxon "core group" and the various immigrant groups that attempt to assimilate into the values of the American culture.

10. For example, see the following sources: Clark, Health in the Mexican-American Culture; Peñalosa, "Class Consciousness and Social Mobility"; Pi-Sunyer, Zamora, pp. 46-48; Woods, "Mexican Ethnic Leadership," pp. 80-84.

11. For an excellent discussion of the cultural meaning of Don and Doña see "Donship in a Mexican-American Community in Texas," by Octavio I. Romano-V, American Anthropologist 62 (December 1960):966-76.

12. For example, see the findings of Peñalosa, "Class Consciousness and Social Mobility," p. 200; Clark, Health in the Mexican-American Culture, p. 19; Woods, "Mexican Ethnic Leadership," pp. 80-84; Hubbell, "Network of Kinship," p. 44; Pi-Sunyer, Zamora, pp. 46-48.

13. In his study of life in a Mexican village, Armstrong found that besides material possessions, economic standing and education, such personal characteristics as physical appearance, manner of speech, and social contacts were important determinants of social class position. See Armstrong, "A Mexican Community," p. 292.

14. For a general overview of land tenure and social relations in colonial Mexico and Latin America see Robert G. Keith, ed., Haciendas and Plantations in Latin American History (New York: Holmes & Meier, 1977); and also Rodolfo Stavenhagen, Agrarian Problems and Peasant Movements in Latin America (New York: Doubleday, 1970). For a specific view of conditions in Mexico, see François Chevalier's Land and Society in Colonial Mexico (Berkeley: University of California Press, 1963).

15. Most of the social philosophers who have written on this topic are of the opinion that the colonial experience was deleterious to the development of egalitarian relationships in modern times; for example, see the following works: Octavio Paz, The Labyrinth of Solitude (New York: Grove Press, 1961), in particular, pp. 65-116; Samuel Ramos, Profile of Man and Culture in Mexico (Austin: University of Texas Press, 1962); and the more recent work of Henry C. Schmidt, The Roots of Lo Mexicano: Self and Society in Mexican Thought, 1900-1934 (College Station: Texas A&M University Press, 1978), in particular, pp. 3-37.

16. See the work of Claudio Stern and Joseph Kahl, "Stratification Since the Revolution," in Comparative Perspectives on Stratification, ed. Joseph A. Kahl (Boston: Little, Brown, 1968), pp. 5-30.

17. See Ruth D. Tuck, Not with the Fist (New York: Harcourt, Brace, 1946), p. 113.

18. See Thomas E. Lasswell, "Status Stratification in a Selected Community," Ph.D. dissertation, University of Southern California, 1953, pp. 116-17.

19. Clark, Health in the Mexican-American Culture, pp. 16-19.

20. See George C. Barker, "Social Functions of Language in a Mexican-American Community," Ph.D. dissertation, Department of Anthropology, University of Chicago, 1947, pp. 189-92.

21. Armstrong, "A Mexican Community," p. 291.

22. Ibid.

23. Hubbell, "Network of Kinship," p. 43.

24. Pi-Sunyer, Zamora, pp. 39-48.

25. See Laura H. Zarrugh, "Gente De Mi Tierra: Mexican Village Migrants in a California Community," Ph.D. dissertation, Department of Anthropology, University of California, Berkeley, 1974, p. 66.

26. Peñalosa, "Class Consciousness and Social Mobility," p. 171.

27. For a review of a selection of articles that deal with the concept of the "split labor market," see Richard Edwards, M. Reich, and D. Gordon, eds., Labor Market Segmentation (Lexington Books, 1975).

28. Edna Bonacich, "A Theory of Ethnic Antagonism: The Split Labor Market," American Sociological Review 37(5) (1972):547-49.

29. According to Karl Marx and his disciples the major impact of a dual labor market situation is to (1) divide the members of the working class, particularly along racial lines, and (2) keep wages low, so as to give the greatest benefits of this situation to the capitalists. The upshot, of course, is that workers are divided against themselves and fail to recognize their mutual interests, that is, they suffer from "false consciousness" and the employer can maintain his wages at or close to the subsistence level of existence.

30. In his study, Teske found that "The greatest amount of initial upward mobility, . . . occurred among the third generation, forty-one percent, followed by the second generation, twenty-four percent. Sixty-five percent of initial upward mobility, then, had occurred by the third generation." In Raymond H. Teske, Jr., "An Analysis of Status Mobility Patterns Among Middle-Class Mexican Americans in Texas," Ph.D. dissertation, Department of Sociology, Texas A&M University, College Station, 1973, p. 103.

31. See José E. Iturriaga, La Estructura Social y Cultural de Mexico (Mexico, D.F.: Fondo de Cultural Economica, 1951), p. 41.

32. Simmons, "Anglo Americans and Mexican Americans," p. 370.

33. See Andrew H. Whiteford, Two Cities of Latin America: A Comparative Description of Social Classes (Garden City, N.Y.: Anchor Books, 1964), p. 104.

34. See Teske, "Analysis of Status Mobility Patterns," p. 65.

35. Whiteford, Two Cities of Latin America, p. 63.

36. For example, see the comments and observations made by Whiteford on this point; ibid., pp. 55, 61.

37. Simmons, "Anglo Americans and Mexican Americans, p. 363.

38. See Harry E. Ransford, Race and Class in American Society: Black, Chicano, Anglo (Cambridge: Schenkman Publishing Company, 1977), p. 52.

39. Gordon, Assimilation in American Life, p. 53.

40. Ibid., p. 51.

41. Ransford, Race and Class in American Society, p. 76.

42. For a complete review of these figures of "relative concentration" see Fred E. Romero, Chicano Workers: Their Utilization and Development, Monograph No. 8, Chicano Studies Center Publications, University of California, Los Angeles, 1979, in particular, p. 42.

8

Social Mobility among Mexican-American Agricultural Workers

PERCEPTION AND EVALUATION
OF SOCIAL MOBILITY

Upon due consideration and analysis our data reveal the presence of significant differences between individual perceptions of social class differences within the Mexican-American community. Furthermore, the members of the upper social classes were more sophisticated in their analysis and were able, in each instance, to outline in greater detail the complexity of the social class structure. Our findings confirm Peñalosa's, who observed that "Respondents who perceived class divisions in the Mexican community . . . had more schooling, had higher self-perception in the class structure, were younger, and a higher proportion of them were interviewed in English than was the case with those who perceived no class divisions."[1]

Overall, our respondents were very perspicacious in their ability to perceive social class differences within their own communities. Most placed themselves within the "lower class" (92.3%), and in fact this was a very valid assessment of their social standing. And it is interesting to note that only three indicated that they were members of the "middle class." Therefore, the vast majority correctly placed themselves within the social class structure, that is, as it existed within the Mexican-American community. The fact that almost all of our respondents were able to place themselves within the social class structure, as they perceived it, is rather significant when we consider

that Peñalosa found that fully 27.2 percent of his sample
"were unable or unwilling to categorize their own social
class membership."[2] The unanimous ability of our respondents to ascertain correctly their social status probably
results from the fact that as full-time agricultural workers
they are reminded, in a variety of ways, on a daily
basis that they are at the bottom of the economic heap.

When asked why social classes exist in society, one
in four (25.3%) simply said, "people are different" and
consequently there will always be different social classes
in society. An equal number (26.4%) said that social
class differences could be accounted for in terms of the
"income differences" that exist among people. Others
pointed to the "educational differences" (13.2%) found
among people, and some said that it was only "natural"
that there should be differences (13.2%) within social
classes, while others felt that "different jobs" within society (12.1%) served to account for the differences.

In retrospect, the most significant responses were
given in terms of differences in income, education, and
occupation. In comparison, Peñalosa found that two out
of five (41.5%) members of his sample "were either unable
to perceive important differences among the Mexican population of Pomona or unwilling to state their opinion with
regard to such differences."[3] The most significant hard
sociological indicator that was given as a response category was that of "educational differences."[4] In terms of
an overall comparison of our findings with those of
Peñalosa, it appears that, for whatever reason, our respondents were more sociologically aware of the key indicators that serve to account for social class differences.

Obviously, any attempt to measure the extent of
social mobility among Mexican agricultural workers in-
volves a number of perplexing methodological problems.
For example, one of the key sociological indicators of social mobility has traditionally been that of intergenerational occupation mobility. This approach compares the
occupational position of each respondent with the highest
occupational standing achieved by his or her father.
However, if this procedure is applied to our sample we
find that fully 85.7 percent of their fathers were agricultural laborers, while the others held occupations that would
fall into the lower-lower class category. If these findings
are accepted at face value, then we must conclude that very
few of our respondents have experienced any intergenera-

tional social mobility. However, in order to obtain a
meaningful evaluation of intergenerational mobility among
agricultural workers we must, of necessity, take other important socioeconomic factors into consideration.

As a matter of general procedure, it is acceptable
to consider such characteristics as lifestyle, type of home,
residential location, accumulation of consumer goods, and
so on, in an effort to arrive at a complete evaluation of
social improvement over a given period of time, that is,
over one generation. If these sociological indicators are
taken into consideration, the majority of our respondents
have improved their socioeconomic conditions over and above
those of their parents. In an effort to determine their
feelings on this issue, we asked our respondents the following question: "Given your origins and your personal
circumstances, do you think that you have done well in
this life?" As anticipated, the majority (80.2%) gave a
positive response. Only 16.5 percent felt that they had
not done well in their lives. Given our field observations
we can certainly agree that the majority have experienced
a significant degree of social mobility, that is, when compared with their parents.[5]

Of those who felt that they had done well in their
lives, two out of five (39.3%) expressed this opinion because they had a "good job." The second largest group
(27.9%) felt good about themselves because they had been
able to provide better opportunities for their children.
Some (11.5%) felt good about themselves because they had
a "nice family" and others (13.1%) attributed their success
to "home ownership," while a few (8.2%) said that they
had been able to provide "better living conditions" for
their families. The fact that the majority (80.2%) felt
good about themselves is probably a reflection of the poverty that they experienced as children. Therefore, they
realize that conditions are much improved, not only for
themselves but, in a more important sense, for their
children.

Another consideration is the strong propensity to
compare their present socioeconomic situation, in this country, with the socioeconomic conditions of their parents and
siblings who are still living in Mexico. Therefore, while
it may well appear, from an ethnocentric perspective, that
they are not very well situated economically, consideration
must be given to their own perception and interpretation
of their current situation. Therefore, if they perceive

their situation as much improved, then from their perspective this is the "real" situation regardless of the external or objective conditions that they observe from day to day. Indeed, the fact that they immigrated to the greater Southwest is a precursor of social improvement as most felt successful because they had a "good job." In a similar vein, many felt successful because they are now in a position whereby they can provide "better opportunities" for their children. It is also important to note that the majority of responses relate to the social improvement of their families, that is, "a good job," "better opportunities for their children," and "having a nice family," while the material considerations, such as "home ownership" and "better living conditions," rank among the lowest in importance.

When asked if they expected to improve their situation in the future, two out of three (62.6%) were sanguine about the future. However, one in four (25.3%) felt that they would not be able to improve their situation in the future. Apparently, they felt that they had reached the apex of their potential for social improvement and were rather pessimistic about any possibility for further social advancement. The remainder (12.1%) were not sure about their futures and did not know whether they would be able to improve their lot to any significant degree.

The optimists felt that they would improve their conditions in the near future by means of "job advancement" or "job improvement." In most cases this simply meant that they expected to find a better job within the agricultural industry. Some felt they would locate a non-agricultural job while others (10.5%) looked forward to the day when their children would "support themselves." A handful placed their faith in education and said that they would "learn English" (8.8%) and just "improve" their level of education in general (7.0%). The remainder offered a mélange of reasons why they felt they would improve their current situation, for example, they stated that they "expected to secure a salary increase," "expected to purchase a home in the near future," "expected to acquire new job skills," "expected their poor health to improve," "expected their wife to start working," and so on.

When asked what sort of characteristics or attributes they considered important in measuring success, there was unanimous agreement that a "good education" (79.1%) was essential. The second-most important characteristic of the successful person was a "good job" (13.2%). These two responses were followed by a potpourri of answers, such as "having a nice family," "having a good trade," "the ability to speak English," "having good luck," and so on.

While the majority felt that education was a key to success (79.1%), only 7.7 percent felt that people were successful because of their education. In fact, when pressed on this issue, half (56.0%) felt that people were only successful because they were either lucky or they inherited their positions. For example, the following responses were attributed to either luck or inheritance: "some people are just lucky" (39.6%), "some people are born into the money" (9.9%), and "some people just inherit their positions" (6.6%). However, a significant proportion (38.5%) attributed the success of certain individuals to personal efforts and abilities, such as "hard work" (17.6%), "language ability" (13.2%), and "a good education" (17.7%). But the fact that half were of the opinion that success was strongly dependent on having good luck or inheritance indicates that many felt that success is simply a matter of fate and consequently, some people are fortunate enough to be successful and others are not.

In order to obtain a different perspective on their views of success each respondent was asked what his or her advice would be to a young person who wanted to be successful. As anticipated, the value of an education ranked very high as three out of four (75.8%) said that they would advise a young person to "get a good education." Therefore, in measuring success (79.1%) and in giving advice to a young person (75.8%), the majority of our respondents felt that a good education is a most important consideration. However, in viewing successful people they felt that only 7.7 percent were in successful positions because of their educational achievements. Hence when viewing success as a value or as a goal orientation the majority feel that education is a very good thing; but in giving credit to those who are already successful, education is only given slight consideration. In addition to obtaining a good education, our respondents also advised young people to "get a good job," "obtain a good skill," "work hard at whatever you do," "be good to people," "learn to speak English," and so on.

Following this evaluation of success, we asked each respondent what, in their opinion, were the major obstacles to self-improvement. Given their personal situations, almost one out of three (29.7%) viewed their difficulties with

the English language as their most serious obstacle to success. One in five (22.0%) felt that the basic "lack of job
opportunities" was a major obstacle to success. Others
pointed to a basic "lack of education and training"
(16.5%), "lack of a good salary" (16.5%), while some felt
they "were too old" (6.6%), and the remainder gave an olio
of answers to this question. Overall, their perception of
major obstacles to success can be viewed as a personal
lack of preparation for movement into a more successful
position; for example, note their statements concerning
their "language difficulties" and their "lack of education
and training."

On a more general level our respondents were asked
if they thought it was possible for the average working
person to get ahead. We discovered that almost two thirds
(62.6%) felt that it was possible, and that they could do
well if they worked hard and applied themselves. However, the others were of the opinion that it was not possible for the working person to ever get ahead. This
finding is particularly significant as it does provide a
key indication of the general mobility orientation of our
respondents and their opinions concerning the possibility
for social improvement. However, this does not necessarily
mean that they are either optimistic or pessimistic about
their own personal situation, but the comparison does appear to be rather close. Indeed, when asked directly if
they felt that they would be able to improve their own
personal situations in the future, two out of three (63.6%)
felt that they would be able to do so. This response dem-
onstrates complete congruence with the two out of three
who were of the opinion that it was possible for the average working person to get ahead. In sum, it appears
that their general mobility orientation is very positive and
is an indication that most will continue to demonstrate social progress in the future.

In a similar manner, each respondent was asked
what he or she considered to be the most serious difficulties confronting Mexican people who attempted to better
themselves. One out of four felt that there was a "lack of
job opportunities" for Mexican people in general and an
equal number referred to their "difficulty with the language," that is, their inability to communicate in English.
Others felt that their wages were not commensurate with
the required tasks (13.2%), lack of education or training
among Mexican people (12.1%), the low income of Mexican

people in general (9.9%), lack of ambition among certain individuals (7.7%), and multifarious other answers.

As we might suspect, Mexican agricultural workers are very much aware of the shortage of job opportunities within the industry; this results in a concern over their general inability to communicate in English well enough to secure a nonagricultural job. Therefore, given the shortage of jobs within the agricultural industry, they realize that they must find employment in another segment of the economy, but then discover that they are limited, and otherwise handicapped in their job search efforts by their inability to communicate in English, a requirement in most nonagricultural jobs. As a result, many find themselves in the classic double-bind of not being in a position where they can alter their current situation.

In an effort to approach this problem from yet another perspective we asked each respondent why he or she felt that there was so much poverty among Mexican people. As expected, most responses were phrased in economic terms and were directed to the problem of "low salaries" (24.2%) and a "lack of jobs" (23.1%). Once again, these responses verify our earlier findings that the major problems confronting Mexican agricultural workers are of a strictly economic nature. The general feeling is that they are not paid a decent or justifiable wage for their labor, and to make matters worse they cannot always find work when they want to work. Their ideal situation would be to secure a steady source of employment that would also pay a justifiable wage for their labor.

However, when asked the following question: "Do you believe that conditions will improve for Mexican Americans in the future?" three out of four (74.7%) were optimistic about the future and only one in five (18.7%) were clearly pessimistic. Therefore, regardless of the current social and economic conditions found among Mexican agricultural workers, the majority remained optimistic about the future.

ATTITUDES CONCERNING SOCIAL MOBILITY AMONG MEXICAN-AMERICAN AGRICULTURAL WORKERS

A substantial portion of our formal interview schedule sought information concerning the attitude of respondents regarding their potential for upward social mobility.

Primarily, we were interested in learning more about their views of (1) the existing "opportunity structure," (2) their acceptance of their present socioeconomic situation, and (3) their views concerning the corruption of the opportunity structure. In addition, a number of statements dealt with their feelings concerning the meaning of success and the available routes to success.

Given the fact that the majority of our respondents were immigrants from Mexico, and migrated with the intention of improving their social and economic conditions, we put the following statement to them: "There are many opportunities for people to better themselves in this country." There was unanimous agreement with this statement, as only one out of eight disagreed (12.1%). Therefore, our original hypothesis regarding the "openness" of the opportunity structure, as viewed by our respondents, is confirmed by these results. In sum, the majority of Mexican agricultural workers view the opportunity structure in a very positive light and feel that their present situation will improve in the near future.

While it is abundantly clear that the majority of our respondents agreed that opportunities do exist for those who want to better themselves, we also wanted to obtain their opinions regarding the opportunities that exist for young people in this country, and formulated the following statement: "The problem with young people today is that they have everything given to them." Eight out of ten (81.3%) agreed with this statement and therefore felt that the opportunity structure is very open to young people; if anything, it is the case that they have it too easy. They probably feel that they had to work much harder to obtain the things that they have, as compared to the many opportunities that are available to young people today. However, one out of eight (12.1%) did disagree with this statement.

In view of their optimistic attitude regarding the opportunity structure, we also wanted to learn more about their feelings concerning the idea of "deferred gratification" and their plans for the future. Hence, the following statement was read to each respondent, "It is better to have fun now than to try and have fun later." Half (50.5%) agreed with this statement and therefore have not fully accepted the idea of deferred gratification. When asked why they felt this way, most said that they would prefer to enjoy themselves while they were still young, instead of waiting until they were old, when they could not really enjoy themselves. This attitude corresponds with their view that old age is very restrictive and therefore would not allow them to enjoy themselves. However, one out of three (33%) disagreed with this statement and therefore felt that people should put off certain pleasures and make sacrifices in order to enjoy the fruits of their hard labor in the future. On the other hand, 16.5 percent were undecided on this issue.

However, the majority of our respondents (71.4%) agree with the idea that people should accept their position in life and accept things just as they are, and simply try to make the best of their current situation (see Table 3, A). This consensus of opinion reflects what might best be referred to as a "don't rock the boat" philosophy in which the feeling is often expressed that even though things are not so good, things could get worse if anyone attempts to make any changes. This point of view also reflects fatalistic acceptance of things as they are at the present time. Obviously, this attitude would stifle any social or economic change and therefore serve to eliminate any possibility for improvement in their current social and economic situation.

But in fact, this fatalistic attitude is not uncommon among those who must survive on a day-to-day basis as the bottom of the socioeconomic heap. In a more general sense, they see themselves as manual laborers who work with their hands and therefore cannot conceive of themselves in any other occupational role. This appears to be a very reasonable interpretation. In general, they are willing to accept things as they are, as their only hope is to make things a little better for themselves and their families within the limitations of their current strengths and abilities.

Fortunately, one out of four are not in agreement with this statement and therefore do not accept its fatalistic message (Table 3, A). Obviously, they have developed a "mobility orientation" and are not willing to accept things as they are at the present time. Most have high hopes of making constructive changes in their current situation and therefore have a very optimistic outlook for the future. Since most of the younger workers have not become completely entrenched in their occupational positions as agricultural workers, we would suspect that a majority of these optimistic responses were obtained from

TABLE 3 Statements Concerning the Acceptance of Present Position
and Fatalism

	Agree		Disagree		Undecided	
	%	#	%	#	%	#
A. People should not try to change their position in life but should accept things as they are.	71.4	(65)	25.3	(23)	3.3	(3)
B. Everyone has a certain position in life and a certain destiny, there- fore people should just be satisfied with what they have.	68.1	(62)	31.9	(29)	--	
C. People who are poor now and have a hard life will get their reward after death.	24.2	(22)	51.6	(47)	24.2	(22)
D. It is only right that in every society there are a few individuals who are successful and have everything and the majority of the people have very little.	3.3	(3)	92.3	(84)	4.4	(4)
E. The average working person cannot expect to get ahead the way things are now.	63.7	(58)	31.9	(29)	4.4	(4)
F. The rich get richer and the poor get poorer.	83.5	(76)	9.9	(9)	6.6	(6)
G. There are really only two classes of people in society, the rich and the poor.	73.6	(67)	26.4	(24)	--	

Source: Compiled by the author.

this younger group. In addition, it is generally true that the younger segments of any population are always more willing to accept change and adapt to new conditions; therefore, we would naturally expect that the younger members of our sample would also be more averse to accept things as they are.

Our second statement also focuses on the general acceptance of their present position and reveals a fatalistic attitude (Table 3, B). Once again, seven out of ten (68.1%) respondents agree with this statement and believe that every person has a certain destiny in life and a certain role to play, therefore they should be satisfied with what they have. Agreement with this statement lends support to the view that the social system is not only rigid but also preordained, that is, in the sense that fate determines the position that each person occupies and the role that each individual must play within that system. The acceptance of this idea means that very little change can occur, as attitudes of this ilk serve to anneal the position of each individual within the social system. Therefore, "satisfaction with what they have" only indicates an acceptance of existing conditions and does not mean that they have experienced a true sense of contentment with themselves.

However, one out of three (31.9%) of our respondents did not agree with the statement that "Everyone has a certain position in life and a certain destiny" (Table 3, B), but rather were of the opinion that people should try to improve their current conditions and better themselves in any way they possibly can. Obviously, these individuals are not satisfied with what they have and therefore are of the opinion that all individuals must work to improve themselves and thereby provide a better future, not only for themselves but also for their children.

Every society maintains a system by which it supports and justifies the basic social inequalities that are congenital to any system of social stratification. One of the most effective ideological techniques adopted by various societies, and particularly traditional societies, is the view that is most often promulgated in terms of a religious doctrine, that is, "there is life after death." The basic belief is that life on earth is but a sojourn and the unfortunate who have a harsh and difficult life in this world will gain their true reward in the next world, that is, if they prove themselves worthy of this ultimate reward by their good behavior in this world. Consequently, we would expect that those with a strong religious indoctrination would cheerfully accept their position in this world, particularly if they find themselves at, or near the bottom of the social hierarchy.

However, when put through the test, half (51.6%) of our respondents were not in agreement with the statement that "people who are poor now and have a hard life will get their reward after death." (See Table 3, C.) This simply means one of two things, either that they do not have a very strong religious orientation or they simply do not believe in life after death. Consequently, they must deal with their current social and economic conditions and do not have the psychic consolation of viewing this life and their conditions in it as an ephemeral state of affairs. This means that they must accept their situation for what it is, or they must make an extra effort to improve their current situation. On the other hand, one out of four (24.2%) agreed with the statement and therefore were of the opinion that the poor would receive their reward after death. The difficulty of expressing an opinion on this matter is revealed by the fact that one-fourth of our respondents (24.2%) were not able to formulate an opinion on this issue. In fact, many of those who did respond found it difficult to respond to this statement.

At first glance it appeared that our respondents were content to accept their low-status positions within society and seemed resigned to their positions, but this does not necessarily mean that they feel good about the situation. This became apparent when they were asked to voice their opinions on whether it was right that there should be a handful of individuals in every society who have everything and the remaining population should have very little (Table 3, D). In response, nine out of ten (92.3%) did not agree with this statement. When the objective situation is viewed in this manner most felt that any social system that provided a majority of its benefits to a chosen few was not a "just" system in view of the fact that so many have so little.

However, if our respondents were of the opinion that American society was a completely just system, in the sense that opportunities for advancement and the distribution of social and economic benefits were completely equal, we would expect a majority to express this attitude when confronted with a statement such as, "The average working person cannot expect to get ahead the way things are now (Table 3, E). But in fact, two out of three (65.7%) agreed with this statement. Many expressed the opinion that they could not really expect to improve their current conditions so long as they had to rely on "wage labor," as they realized that their ability to earn a wage only provided them with a "subsistence level" of existence. Therefore, most viewed their work as simply a means of surviving from one day to the next and many were of the opinion that they would never be in a position to improve themselves economically. However, on a more optimistic note, one-third (31.9%) disagreed with this statement (Table 3, E) and therefore felt that it was possible for the average worker to get ahead. The general feeling was that if an individual applied himself to a particular task he or she would most certainly be successful in the end. The consensus was that through hard work and diligence anyone could overcome various obstacles and be successful in whatever endeavor he or she decided to pursue.

When the inherent inequality of the system of social stratification is presented in a blatant fashion, as in the statement, "The rich get richer and the poor get poorer," four out of five (83.5%) of our respondents were in agreement (Table 3, F). Once again, the consensus indicated that most felt that the system was designed in favor of the wealthy and to the great disadvantage of the working person and the poor. However, the observation could be made that these results simply reflected the general socioeconomic conditions, that is, it is the case that the rich do get richer and the poor do get poorer.

Similarly, three out of four (75.6%) of our respondents agreed with the statement that "There are really only two classes of people in society, the rich and the poor." (See Table 3, G.) When presented in this fashion a majority were of the opinion that there was a sharp division between the nabobs of society and the destitute. However, the remainder did not agree with this statement.

In addition to our interests in their opinions regarding the basic inequalities of society, we were also interested in learning more about their attitudes regarding their own social and economic improvements, specifically their feelings concerning upward social mobility. Therefore, our immediate objective was to learn more about their feelings concerning the success model of American society. This model included such characteristics as the

sacrifices that must be made to be successful, the characteristics of the successful person, the basic definition of
success, the value of material objects and success, the
social consequences of success, and their views concerning
the probable success of the total ethnic group.

Strong support for the virtues of hard work and
dedication to the task were revealed in their unanimous
agreement (92.3%) with the statement that "It does not
matter what sort of job you have, but what really counts
is that you always do a good job." (See Table 4, A.)
Therefore, in their opinion the most important thing about
any job was that a person apply himself and perform his
assigned task diligently. Furthermore, their unanimous
opinion on this issue lent strong support to the idea that
each person had a role to play in society and therefore
should do his best to fill that position.

Our second statement concerning the virtues of hard
work (Table 4, B) revealed that the most prevalent attitude
was that if an individual expected to be successful then
he must be willing to apply himself and work hard at his
assigned tasks, as four out of five (82.4%) were in agreement with this point of view. But if we viewed the possibilities of success in terms of the virtues of hard work
combined with a basic lack of education, then a change in
attitude was observed. Nonetheless, six out of ten (57.1%)
still agreed that "even those individuals with little education can do well if only they work hard at whatever job
they have to perform." (See Table 4, C.) However, four
out of ten (39.6%) were not in agreement. Therefore, they
were of the opinion that given a basic lack of education,
the possibilities of ever being successful, even in the
light of hard work, were rather limited. Most likely this
attitude resulted from their own personal experience in the
agricultural labor force, where most had a limited education and the majority were assiduous workers, but were
rarely successful.

The final statement (in this series), dealing with
the virtues of hard work, revealed that a majority viewed
the "opportunity structure" as basically corrupt (Table 4,
D). When we read the following statement: "If you want
to get all the promotions it does not really matter how
much you know but rather who you know," three out of
four of our respondents (75.8%) were in agreement. In a
sense these results seemed to contradict some of the previous opinions expressed concerning the nature of the

TABLE 4   Statements Concerning the Need for Hard Work in Order
for a Person to Be Successful

	Agree		Disagree		Undecided	
	%	#	%	#	%	#
A. It does not matter what sort of job you have but what really counts is that you always do a good job.	92.3	(84)	7.7	(7)	--	
B. If an individual applies himself and works hard, then he will certainly be successful.	82.4	(75)	11.0	(10)	6.6	(6)
C. Even those individuals with a little education can do well if only they work hard at whatever job they have to perform.	57.1	(52)	39.6	(36)	3.3	(3)
D. If you want to get all of the promotions it does not really matter how much you know but rather who you know.	75.8	(69)	16.5	(15)	7.7	(7)

Source: Compiled by the author.

opportunity structure and the value of hard work.   However, this probably indicates that they viewed the overall
opportunity structure as basically "just" but that certain
individuals, if given the opportunity, would utilize sur-
reptitious methods to obtain their goals.   But this could
also represent an effort to placate their own personal lack
of success, sort of a sour grapes interpretation of those

who are successful. However, one out of six (16.5%) were of the opinion that hard work, diligence, job skills, and technical knowledge were very important when an individual was under consideration for a promotion. From their perspective, personal ties were not necessarily important or essential for job advancement.

In sum, the majority view held that while the opportunity structure was open and accessible to those who chose to take advantage of any available opportunities, diligence and dedication to assigned tasks were of utmost importance. Overall, the majority adopted and applied one of the principal values of the Protestant work ethic, that is, the inherent value of hard work and diligence.

These results indicate that the guiding force to ultimate success, according to our respondents, is diligence and hard work. The general attitude seems to be that if an individual is dedicated to his or her work and always strives to do a good job, then that person will be successful. The question then occurs, "What are some of the most important characteristics of the successful person?" In an effort to obtain more information regarding this question, it was decided to obtain their attitudes concerning the value of education and the role of "luck" or "fate" in the life of the successful person.

Our respondents expressed unanimous agreement (96.7%) with the statement that "The only way to get ahead is to get a good education." (See Table 5, A.) Therefore, they had a very high regard for the value of an education. These findings were congruent with our previous cultural observation that an educated person always receives universal admiration and superlative plaudits from the members of the Mexican-American community. In addition, they viewed education as one of the most dependable methods by which an individual could emerge from a life of impecuniousness. In their view education was something that a person could always use, and furthermore it would always make life a little easier to endure. Several commented that education was an achievement that no one could ever take away from the individual; consequently, educaton was viewed as an inalienable characteristic and was considered a lifelong possession.

The value of an academic education was given priority when our respondents were offered a choice between having a college degree, or having the opportunity to master a skill. Seven out of ten (71.4%) felt that it was

better to attend college and obtain a degree than to spend
the same amount of time learning a good skill (Table 5, B).
Our original hypothesis held that in view of their own
backgrounds as manual laborers, the majority would hold
that learning a good skill would be more important than
simply obtaining a college education. However, our results do not support our original assumption. Nonetheless,
our results do coincide with the findings obtained in regard
to the overall value of an education (Table 5, A). However, it is noteworthy that one out of four (23.1%) of our
respondents were in agreement with this statement (Table
5, B). In a sense, one fourth of our respondents took a
very practical view of the situation and felt that being a
skilled craftsman is much more desirable than being a
college graduate. By the same token, it could be that most
took an idealistic view of the situation and were simply
reflecting the cultural ideal of the value of an education.

TABLE 5 Statements Concerning the Value of Education and the
Role of "Luck" in the Life of the Successful Person

	Agree		Disagree		Undecided	
	%	#	%	#	%	#
A. The only way to get ahead is to get a good education.	96.7	(88)	3.3	(3)	--	
B. It is better to learn a good skill than to go to col- lege and get a degree.	23.1	(21)	71.4	(65)	5.5	(5)
C. To be successful you just have to be in the right place, at the right time.	76.9	(70)	19.8	(18)	3.3	(3)
D. In order to really make it big in this world you just have to be real lucky.	70.3	(64)	26.4	(24)	3.3	(3)

Source: Compiled by the author.

Nonetheless, education does rank high as a significant value to our respondents, that is, not just as a cultural goal but also as a viable means of upward social mobility. Therefore, most felt that a "good education" would open up a new world of opportunities for self-improvement, and in the end would provide a sure means for upward social mobility. Hence, they recognized the value of an education as a means of improving their current situation and providing more opportunities in the future for their children.

In conjunction with the value of a good education, we also wanted to know how our respondents felt about the role of "good fortune" or "good luck" in their eventual success or failure. When presented with the following statement: "To be successful you have to be at the right place, at the right time," three out of four (76.9%) of our respondents agreed (Table 5, C). The implication, obviously, is that regardless of education or skill level, "luck" or "good fortune" was still important to those who hoped to be successful. These results also indicated that "being at the right place at the right time" was more important than preparation or qualification for a particular position. Perhaps they were saying that fate or the good luck of the successful person were more important in accounting for their success than academic preparation or the possession of certain skills. Therefore, following this line of reasoning, successful people were only successful because they "just happen to be at the right place at the right time," that is, they are just plain lucky.

In contrast, one out of five of our respondents (19.8%) disagreed with this point of view and did not feel that "being at the right place at the right time" was all that important for success. In their opinion, just being lucky was not enough but rather viewed academic preparation and occupational skills as far more important. Many expressed the opinion that if one was academically and occupationally prepared, then various employment and promotional opportunities would automatically present themselves. In their view, it was essential that the individual be prepared and not place any undue reliance on the role of luck or fate in the determination of their success.

Our second statement, in this regard, was much more direct: "In order to really make it big in this world you just have to be real lucky." As predicted, we found a significant level of concordance with this statement,

as seven out of ten (70.3%) of our respondents were in
agreement (Table 5, D). These results corresponded with
our previous findings and substantiated our observation
that much credence is given to the role and effectiveness
of "luck" in the ultimate success of the individual. From
their perspective, the rays of good fortune could only
shine on a chosen few, and it was these blessed ones who
were successful and did well in life. However, one out of
four (26.4%) did not attribute any significance to the role
of good fortune or good luck in the eventual success of
any one individual. Rather they were of the opinion that
hard work and preparation were much more important for
eventual success, as opposed to a blind dependence on fate.

In the final analysis, the majority of our respondents (73.6%, i.e., the average of 76.9% and 70.3%) were
of the opinion that luck and fate were important considerations in the ultimate success of the individual (Table 5,
C & D). Consequently, only certain individuals were
"destined" to be successful, while most would remain at
the bottom of the social and economic hierarchy. This
pervasive attitude served a dual purpose, that is, it could
account for the apparent success of only a handful of individuals within the Mexican-American community, and
simultaneously it could also account for the general lack
of success found among Mexican agricultural workers, in
other words, only certain lucky individuals were successful.

In the development of the attitude survey, we designed a number of statements to allow for some insight
into their attitude concerning the meaning and the measure
of success. Specifically, our principal objective was to
learn more about their perception of the value of money
and material objects as they related to the measurement
and determination of success in American society. In this
manner a sound assessment was made of the importance of
money and material objects in relation to their evaluation
of the successful person, that is, from the cross-cultural
perspective.

Their response to our first statement revealed that
the attitudes of the members of the community toward an
individual were far more important than the amount of
money that a person earned (see Table 6). This statement
drew a sharp distinction between the value of money and
the importance of the social standing and reputation of the
individual in the community. Therefore, nine out of ten
(92.3%) of our respondents felt that a favorable public

TABLE 6   Statements Concerning the Value of Money and Material
Objects as a Measure of Success

	Agree		Disagree		Undecided	
	%	#	%	#	%	#
A. It is not how much money you make that matters but rather what people in the community think of you.	92.3	(84)	4.4	(4)	3.3	(3)
B. Earning a lot of money is the most important thing.	39.6	(36)	57.1	(52)	3.3	(3)
C. People who do well are the ones who save every penny they make.	84.6	(77)	14.3	(13)	1.1	(1)
D. It is far better for a man to have a nice family and good friends than to have all kinds of material things.	90.1	(82)	7.7	(7)	2.2	(2)
E. Success cannot be measured by how many cars you have or the kind of house you live in, but rather it is a matter of what kind of person you are.	96.7	(88)	3.3	(3)	--	

Source: Compiled by the author.

opinion was much more important than the amount of money
that an individual earned. Our findings coincided with,
and indeed confirmed, the observations made by other researchers who had held that within the Mexican cultural
tradition it was more important for an individual to gain
the respect of his neighbors than to have an abundance of
money and material goods. These views are most frequently
associated with traditional societies, in which the family
and the community are of utmost importance, and in which
the acquisition and possession of material goods is a
secondary consideration. However, another interpretation
of their overwhelming reaction to this statement could
simply be a "rationalization" of their present situation,
that is, they do not have much money or possess an abundance of material goods, but they do have strong family
and community ties. Therefore, they would tend to inter-
pret their current situation as an "ideal situation."

If we accept this consensus, then we would expect
that only a few would agree with the statement that "earning a lot of money is the most important thing." (See
Table 6, B.) However, two out of five (39.6%) of our respondents agreed with this statement. These results seem
to contradict their reaction to our first statement, in which
we found unanimous agreement, that the values of the
family and the community were far more important than
economic or material considerations (Table 6, A). This
could simply mean that although some respondents felt
that the values of the family and the community were important, when setting priorities in their own lives they
felt that money was of utmost importance. Nonetheless,
over half (57.1%) were consistent in their beliefs and disagreed with the idea that "money is the most important
thing."

The predominant view among our respondents was
that the rich and the successful were rather miserly in
their ways, as four out of five (84.6%) agreed with the
statement that "People that do well are the ones who save
every penny they make." (See Table 6, C.) They viewed
successful individuals as a "money grabbing" minority,
whose sole purpose in life was to accumulate more capital.
For example, a number of respondents made comments about
certain co-workers who appeared to be destitute while they
were living and working in this country but were known to
be rather wealthy landowners in Mexico. Therefore, their
perception of the wealthy in this country might in fact

have been based upon their personal experiences with certain successful individuals from their own ranks, who proved to be pennypinching misers.[6]

Upon further examination, the predominant opinion among our respondents was that it was far more important for a person to cultivate meaningful relationships with family and friends than to have a plethora of material goods. This point was made abundantly clear in view of their consentaneous approval (90.1%) of the statement that "it is far better for a man to have a nice family and good friends than to have all kinds of material things." (See Table 6, D.)

Lending strong support to our previous findings was their consentience with the statement that "Success cannot be measured by how many cars you have or the kind of house you live in, but rather success is a matter of what kind of person you are." (See Table 6, E.) Their predominant opinion held that the development of a well-rounded personality was more important in life than the acquisition of material goods (96.7%). The question that presents itself is, why would our respondents have supported the ideal of a well-rounded personality as opposed to the practical acquisition of material goods, particularly in view of the fact that these material goods would certainly make life more comfortable and serve as easily recognized status symbols? Perhaps this was a reaction, and indeed an acquiescence, to their own situation and they had correctly concluded that they would probably have very little or no opportunity of ever being a success in the material sense. Consequently, they adapted to this improbability by placing their major emphasis on the personal attributes that were within their power to develop, for example, their personality, family relations, and personal interactions.

It seems that this attitudinal adaptation is just a convenient psychological mechanism that allowed them to confront the reality of their situation, in other words, they realized that material success was out of their grasp and therefore modified their definition of success to conform with their potential for success in the establishment of interpersonal relationships. Our observations and interpretations were sustained by the consistency of opinions expressed in statements A, D, and E of Table 6. In each case we observed almost unanimous agreement with the point of view that a person, the personality, and family and friends were far more important in the ultimate evaluation of the successful person, than the possession of material goods.

Since most respondents measured success in terms of social characteristics, and not in terms of material possessions, we wanted to find out how they felt about those individuals who were successful. Therefore, a number of interrelated statements were designed to obtain their feelings concerning those individuals who were successful within the Mexican-American community (see Table 7).

TABLE 7 Statements Concerning the Effects of Success on Individuals in the Mexican-American Community

	Agree		Disagree		Undecided	
	%	#	%	#	%	#
A. People who are successful usually let it go to their heads and try to act like they are really important.	83.5	(76)	4.4	(4)	12.1	(11)
B. People who start out small and then make it big only think of themselves and forget about their family and friends.	74.7	(68)	15.4	(14)	9.9	(9)
C. Successful Chicanos like to think they are like the Anglos and they forget where they came from and ignore the problems of their people.	87.9	(80)	7.7	(7)	4.4	(4)
D. People cannot be successful unless they step on a few toes first.	56.0	(51)	37.4	(34)	6.6	(6)

Source: Compiled by the author.

The results of our attitude survey revealed that four out of five (83.5%) of our respondents felt that "people who are successful usually let it go to their heads." (See Table 7, A.) The overall impression was that they were somewhat resentful of those individuals who were successful, and particularly if they flaunted the fact. This strong reaction was also associated with the prevalence of "envidia" (envy) within the Mexican-American community, whereby people were sometimes envious of those who were successful. Under such circumstances some individuals assumed a fault-finding attitude toward successful individuals, particularly if they had disassociated themselves from the community.

Our second statement dealt with the effects of success on individuals who started out at the bottom and managed to improve themselves and were recognized as a success in the Mexican-American community. The prevalent attitude held that these individuals tended to forget their family and friends when they finally made it to the top. Not surprisingly, three out of four of our respondents (74.7%) agreed with this point of view (Table 7, B). In these situations the successful individual would snub and otherwise ignore old friends, and even avoid certain relatives. From their perspective they were simply beginning to move in different social circles and had taken up new and different interests, which might not have been congruent with the activities and interests of the majority of the members in their community. Their feeling was that they were simply adapting to a new lifestyle and therefore must, of necessity, associate with people who shared their new interests and activities. However, from the perspective of the average person in the Mexican-American community, they were simply behaving in a very supercilious fashion and therefore were often given a bad name in the community as one who "thinks he is too good for us."

The gist of our third statement (Table 7, C) was closely associated with our previous point and this consonance accounted for the high degree of consensus among our respondents on both of these issues. The statement that "successful Chicanos like to think that they are like the Anglos and forget where they came from and ignore the problems of their people" was similar to our previous statement, but with the critical difference that this statement took the central point of the first statement one step further—Is it really the case that successful Chicanos

behave like Anglos and forget where they came from and
ignore the problems of their people? When presented with
the choice, nearly nine out of ten of our respondents
(87.9%) agreed with this statement. When viewed from the
perspective of the core society it did appear that some
successful Mexican Americans had completely assimilated
and therefore no longer demonstrated an interest in the
problems of their people. Therefore, the majority of our
respondents would have preferred to see successful Mexican
Americans remain in their communities and work for the
social and economic improvement of all Mexican Americans
and not abandon their responsibilities to their brothers.[7]

However, the unanimity of opinion dissolved when
given the statement that "People cannot be successful un-
less they step on a few toes first." (See Table 7, D.)
Just over half of our respondents (50.0%) agreed with this
statement. This would imply that they viewed the wealthy
as the exploiters of the destitute and the disadvantaged.
In their view there were limited resources in the world and
the the wealthy had taken control of these. As a result
the wealthy had placed the majority of the population at a
gross disadvantage in their efforts at self-improvement.[8]
However, just over one-third of our respondents (37.4%)
disagreed with this statement.

In sum, the majority opinion held that Mexican
Americans who were successful were self-centered, arrogant,
abandoned their families and friends, behaved like Anglos,
were not concerned with community problems, and half of
them had taken advantage of other people in order to insure
their success.

When viewed from the perspective of our respondents,
it appeared that the successful Mexican American did not
possess the most desirable characteristics. However,
these attitudes focused on that group of individuals who
were successful, and who had abandoned the cultural
values and goals of the community. In this regard we
formulated a number of statements that were designed to
tap our respondents' opinions regarding the probable or
eventual success of the ethnic group in an Anglo-dominated
society (see Table 8). Our objective was to gain a better
understanding of their feelings in regard to the probable
success of Mexican Americans in general and the manner in
which this success would affect the social relations between Mexican Americans and Anglo Americans.

TABLE 8 Statements Regarding the Probable or Eventual Success of Mexican Americans

	Agree		Disagree		Undecided	
	%	#	%	#	%	#
A. Anglos cannot stand to see a Mexican do well at anything.	68.1	(62)	15.4	(14)	16.5	(15)
B. The only way to get ahead is to beat the Anglo at his own game.	50.5	(40)	47.3	(43)	2.2	(2)
C. If you are going to be successful you have to act and think like an Anglo.	23.1	(21)	74.7	(68)	2.2	(2)
D. Mexicans are just like any other immigrant group and in a few generations they will be better off all around.	83.5	(76)	11.0	(10)	5.5	(5)
E. People are always envious of those individuals who are successful.	86.8	(79)	11.0	(10)	2.2	(2)

Source: Compiled by the author.

Our results revealed that two-thirds of our respondents (68.1%) believed that Anglo Americans "cannot stand to see a Mexican do well at anything." (See Table 8, A.) This high level of agreement led us to believe that the feeling among our respondents was that Anglo Americans had made and were continuing to make a conscious effort to keep Mexican Americans in their place. Obviously, a strong "we-they" relationship existed between the majority group and the minority group. This view held that in order for Mexican Americans to get ahead it was necessary to overcome the resistance to social improvement posed by Anglo-Americans. Further examination revealed that our respondents believed that they must combat the effects of prejudice and discrimination in order to be successful. However, one out of seven (15.4%) were in disagreement and therefore did not feel that racial animosity played a very significant role in their efforts at social improvement.

Our respondents were evenly divided on the issue of whether it was true that "The only way to get ahead is to beat the Anglo at his own game." (See Table 8, B.) Half (50.5%) were of the opinion that it was necessary to be as good as an Anglo in order to be a success in American society. Apparently, they viewed the road to success as a conflict between Mexican Americans and Anglo Americans for the few available positions within the labor and economic markets. However, half (47.3%) were of the opinion that "beating the Anglo at his own game" was not the only way to get ahead. They felt that the most important consideration in being successful was to work hard at your job, and success would come along as a result of this natural process. Others were of the opinion that the struggle for success could not be viewed as a game, and that Anglo Americans did not have any significant impact on whether Mexican Americans were successful or not. They were expressing a rather individualistic point of view inasmuch as they viewed preparation, hard work, and diligence as the most important considerations in the eventual success or failure of the individual.

The following statement was designed to elicit the attitudes of our respondents regarding the system of social mobility as applied to the Anglo world, as compared to its effects on the system of social stratification in the Mexican-American community: "If you are going to be successful you have to act and think like an Anglo." (See Table 8, C.) Our respondents voiced a high degree of disapproval with this statement, as three out of four (74.7%) disagreed. On the contrary, they felt that a person could retain all of his or her cultural values and still be a success in the Anglo world. This attitude coincided with the view that success or failure depended on the preparation and hard work of the individual, and was not necessarily guaranteed by the adoption of a new cultural system.[9] However, it is also significant that only one in four (23.1%) agreed

with this statement. These respondents took the "assimila-
tionists" view and felt that it was important for Mexican
Americans to change their ways and adopt the cultural
values and goals of Anglo-American society.

From the broader perspective, the majority of our
respondents (83.5%) were very optimistic about the eventual
social and economic improvement of Mexican Americans in
general (Table 8, D). Most agreed with the statement that
"Mexicans are just like any other immigrant group" and
therefore should realize substantial improvement in a few
years. This optimistic view was given strong support by
some of our other findings. However, one out of ten
(11.9%) were of the opinion that Mexican Americans were
not like other immigrants and therefore, they would not
realize as high a degree of social improvement. Nonetheless, the majority felt that, when compared to other immigrant groups in this society, Mexican Americans would do
well for themselves in the long run.

Our final statement in this series attempted to tap
our respondents' feelings regarding the relationship between those individuals who were successful and a common
cultural reaction to successful individuals, that is, envidia
(Table 8, E). The majority opinion (86.8%) held that
"people are always envious of those individuals who are
successful." As was observed in our earlier discussion,
it is sometimes the case that successful individuals in the
Mexican-American community attract a certain amount of
envidia primarily as a result of their adaptation of new
ways of doing things and new lifestyles.

Thus far, our discussion has focused on the various
characteristics of the successful person, and community
opinions concerning success in general. However, in this
concluding discussion we shall concentrate on the attitudes
of our respondents regarding the apparent lack of social
and economic advancement among Mexican Americans, that
is, how do they account for, or otherwise explain, this
basic lack of success?

Sometimes ethnic group members blame the members
of the majority group for their problems. In an effort to
determine if this was the case among our respondents we
read the following statement: "Mexican people like to
blame all of their troubles on the Anglos." Given the long
history of prejudice and discrimination in this country, we
anticipated that there would be a good deal of antagonism
addressed toward Anglos, in general, since they represented

the dominant, and often the repressive force in society. However, our findings did not support this assumption, as our respondents demonstrated a strong sense of disagreement with this statement, since three out of four (76.9%) objected to its tenor (see Table 9, A).

TABLE 9 Statements Regarding the Apparent Lack of Success Among Mexican Americans

	Agree		Disagree		Undecided	
	%	#	%	#	%	#
A. Mexican people like to blame all of their troubles on the Anglos.	16.5	(15)	76.9	(70)	6.6	(6)
B. The problem with many Mexican people is that they want everything given to them and do not want to work hard to better themselves.	26.4	(24)	68.1	(62)	5.5	(5)
C. The reason why so many Chicanos are poor is that they try to live by the old traditional ways.	44.0	(40)	49.5	(45)	6.6	(6)

Source: Compiled by the author.

During the course of our interviews, we read the following statement to our respondents: "The problem with many Mexican people is that they want everything given to them and do not want to work hard to better themselves" and discovered that two out of three (68.1%) disagreed with this statement (Table 9, B). Therefore, they were of the opinion that the lack of diligence or assiduousness in their work was not a problem among Mexican Americans. The adamant rejection of this statement was in direct agreement with our earlier finding that the majority of our respondents regarded the lack of jobs and low rate of pay as the most serious problems confronting Mexican Americans today. Indeed, most voiced strong opinions concerning the need for hard work and diligence in whatever task they were assigned. In fact, most considered themselves hard workers and many took pride in their occupational skills and abilities. However, a notable proportion of our respondents (26.4%) did agree with this statement. This was probably the response of the more successful members of our sample, who would probably have agreed with the statement. This would appear to be the case since they had advanced themselves and therefore felt that many of those who were not successful had simply not worked hard enough, or had not applied themselves.

A view often held by the more successful members of the Mexican-American community states that the problem with so many Mexican Americans "is that they try to live by the old traditional ways." This reaction often stems from the fact that the more urbane members of the community are frequently critical of those who do not appear to be making progress. In this context it is often said that these phlegmatic members of the community cannot expect to improve their social and economic conditions because they are trying to live by the old traditional ways, that is, they are trying to maintain the ways of bucolic Mexico. Our results revealed that half of our respondents (49.5%) disagreed with the statement, while nearly half (44.0%) were in agreement.[10] It is probably the case that the more cosmopolitan members of our sample were the ones who agreed with this statement, while those who disagreed were most likely of the opinion that the old traditional ways were not a problem in and of themselves, but rather the basic lack of jobs and decent salaries were pinpointed as the source of the pervasive pattern of poverty among Mexican Americans today.

NOTES

1. See: Fernando Peñalosa, "Class Consciousness and Social Mobility in a Mexican-American Community," Ph.D. dissertation, University of California, 1963, p. 172.

2. Ibid., p. 209.

3. Ibid., p. 197.

4. Ibid.

5. This subjective analysis of social mobility is very useful in the sense that it takes into consideration the feelings of each individual and his or her personal evaluation of the current situation as compared to that in which he or she was reared.

6. These pejorative views of the wealthy and those who are otherwise well off are representative of the views that are frequently held by members of the lower class in Mexico. In many cases the wealthy are viewed as the exploiters of the poor, while the politicians are always assumed to be corrupt and "on the take."

7. These opinions coincide with the views of Karl Marx that the capitalists will always draw away or drain off the potential leaders of any oppressed community of people, usually by offering them some innocuous position within the economic structure.

8. For a complete theoretical explanation of this view, see George Foster, "Peasant Society and the Image of Limited Good," in Peasant Society: A Reader, ed. Jack M. Potter, M. Diaz, and G. Foster (Boston: Little, Brown & Co., 1967).

9. However, there is also the distinct possibility that our respondents were simply reacting to the national-istic implications in this statement and the protection of their cultural traditions.

10. In his analysis, Peñalosa has elaborated on this point and has commented that the "continuing adherence to Mexican cultural values and a failure to acculturate to the majority culture are factors retarding upward social mobility for the Mexican-American population." Peñalosa, "Class Consciousness and Social Mobility," pp. 42-43.

INDEX

ABOUT THE AUTHOR

JUAN L. GONZALES JR. is Assistant Professor of Sociology and Director of La Raza Studies at California State University, Hayward. Dr. Gonzales has written a number of articles in the areas of undocumented Mexican immigration and the Mexican-American family. At the present time Professor Gonzales is preparing a book length manuscript on the origins of the Sikh community in California.

Dr. Gonzales holds a B.A. from California State University, Fullerton, an M.A. from California State University, Long Beach, and a Ph.D. from the University of California, Berkeley. Dr. Gonzales is also a former fellow of the American Sociological Association.